Pursued by a Bear

The Art of William McClure Brown

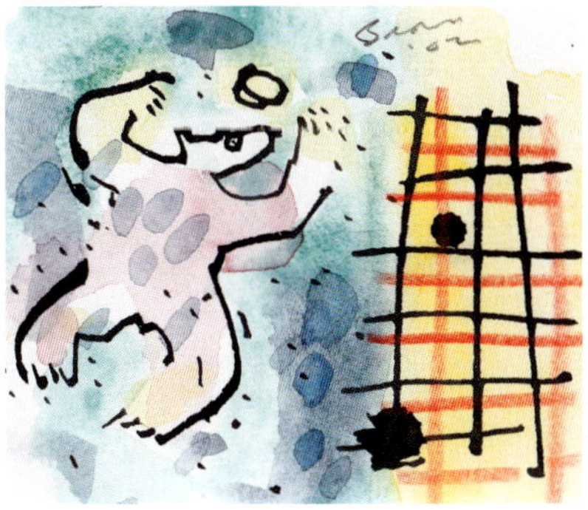

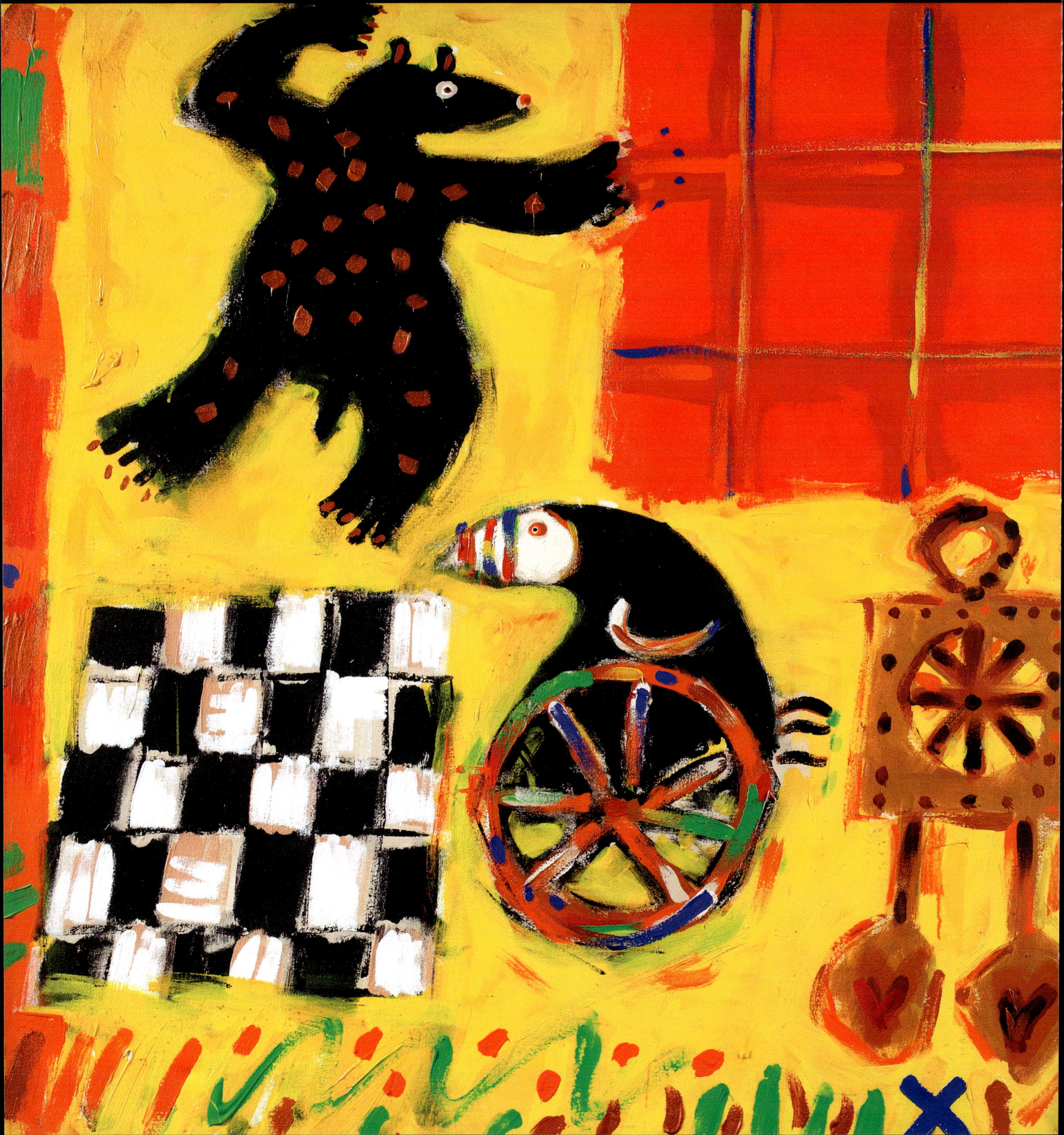

Dreaming Awake 1 (Yellow), 2001, oil on canvas, 120 x 180 cm

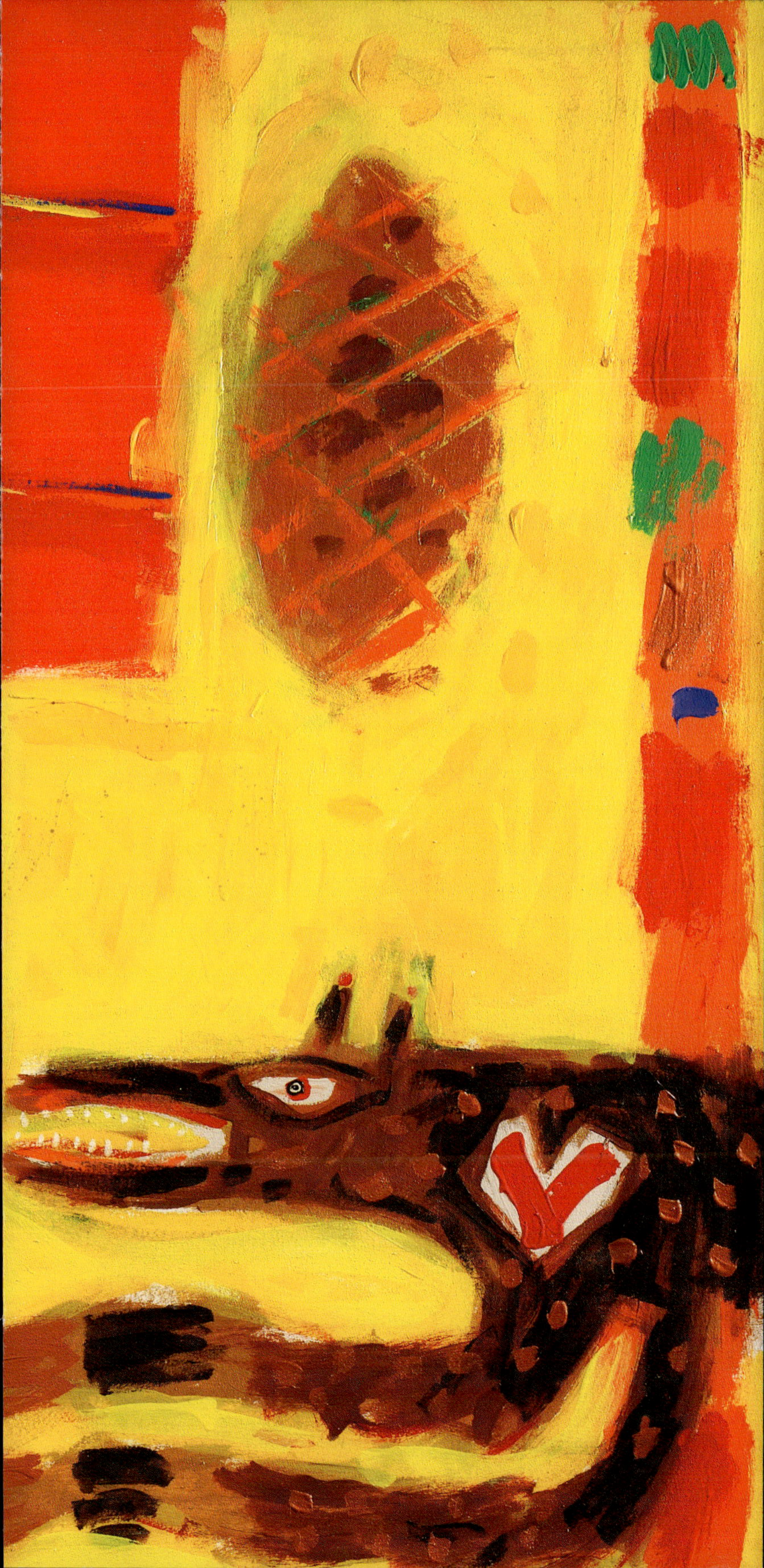

PURSUED BY A BEAR

THE ART OF WILLIAM McCLURE BROWN

PETER WAKELIN

Half-title image:
Dancing Bear,
2002, ink and
watercolour,
7 x 10 cm

Below:
Loup Garou, 1998,
oil on canvas,
90 x 154 cm

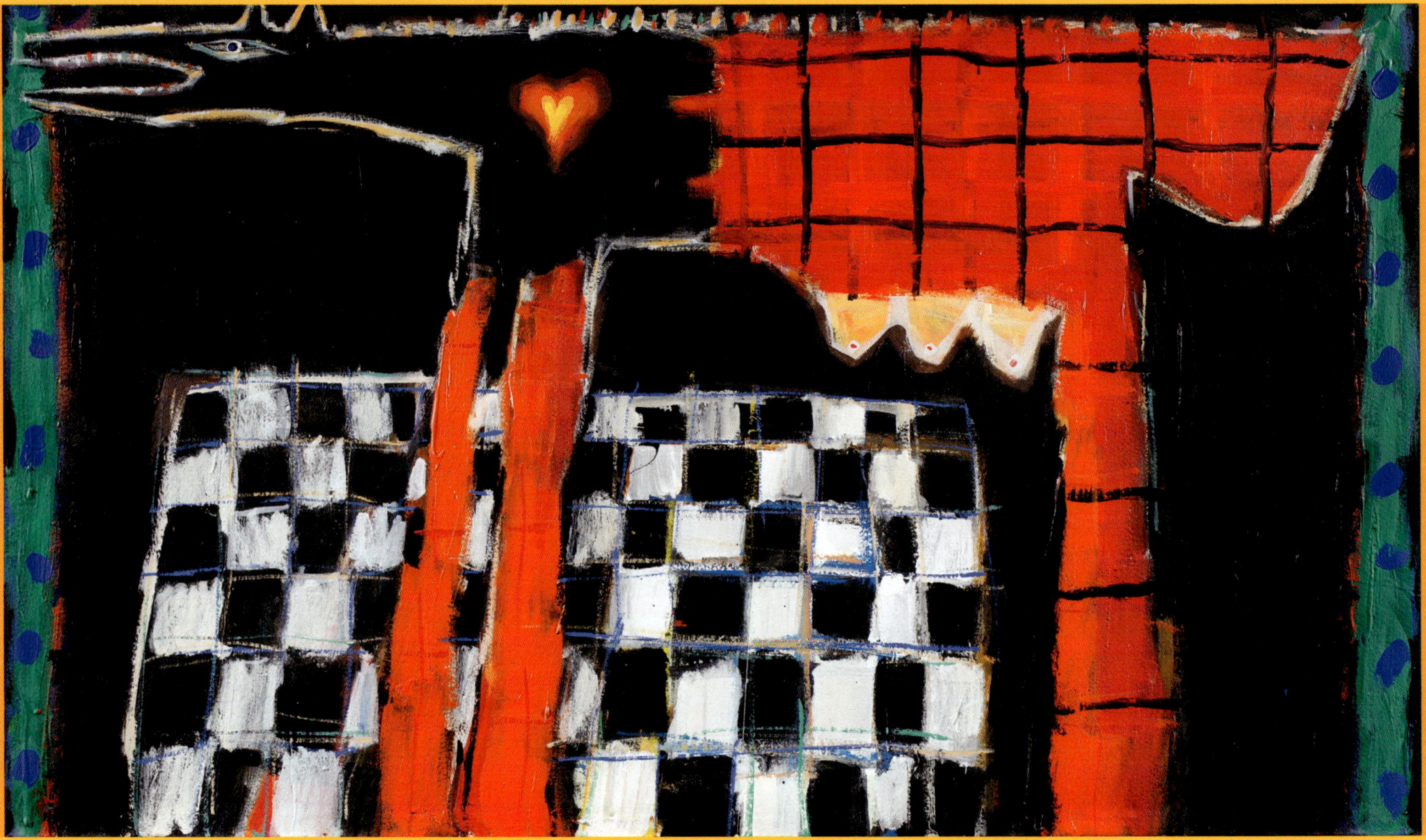

ISBN: 978-1-914595-99-8
Text © Peter Wakelin 2026
All works by William Brown
© Estate of the artist
Poem on page 11 © David Woolley
Principal photography
by Vince Bevan

Designed by Olwen Fowler
Printed by Gomer

The publisher acknowledges
the support of the Books
Council of Wales

Parthian
The Old Surgery
Napier Street
Cardigan SA43 1ED
www.parthianbooks.com

PARTHIAN

This book has been generously supported by the family of Carys McClure Brown through a bequest in her estate and through their commitment and enthusiasm for the art of William McClure Brown.

The publishers would like to thank Sue Alder, Huw Griffiths and Tim Alder for their support and the time given, and Peter Wakelin for his illuminating, engaged and perceptive narrative.

Contents

Tanker / Mirage,
1993, oil on canvas,
122 x 152 cm

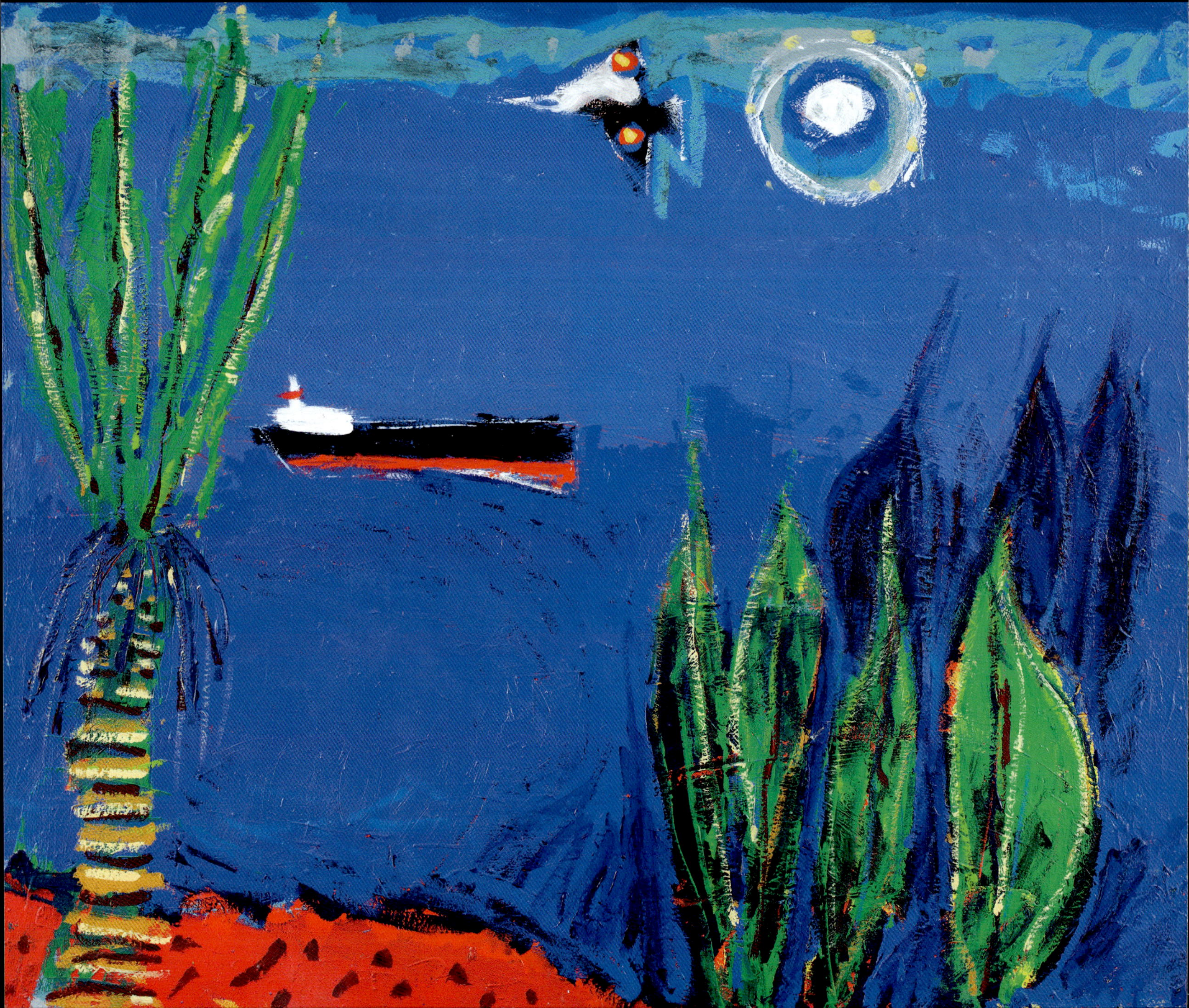

Preface

I met William Brown's art before I met William Brown. One lunchtime over thirty years ago I wandered into a group exhibition in Cardiff's Old Library after a work-congested morning and lingered in front of a large canvas of a ship seen from a desert shore and a fighter jet racing through the sky. I remember saying to a colleague that I sensed a shift towards another state of mind – perhaps resting my left brain and switching to the right – prompted by a painting so pure and direct that its effect was felt, not thought.

I soon learned of William as impresario of the inspired multi-artist exhibition *6" x 6"*. His projects appeared frequently in my roundups of exhibitions in Wales for *Art Review*. Our first long talk was at his magnificent solo show at the Glynn Vivian Art Gallery in Swansea in 1996, where he cut a slightly isolated figure, hovering in the middle of the gallery: tall and broad, tweed-jacketed, hidden by a dense, dark beard and thick hair, a defensive glass of wine in his hand. I found his expansive, many-headed conversation difficult to follow but he was an unforgettable and animated presence. Later, he and the artist Keith Bayliss invited my partner Clive Hicks-Jenkins to take part in the exhibition, *Dreaming Awake*, which toured the Czech Republic. After that William often rang or wrote and there were other occasions to meet – in a crowd of Czech Surrealists, in his exhibition at Newport Museum and Art Gallery, which I reviewed, or at the private views of mutual friends.

When I selected artists' shows at Café Brava in Cardiff for a few years around the millennium, William readily accepted my offer to take part. That he was delighted for people to glance at his pictures over their soup or to obscure them while they disentangled quarrelling children exemplified William's unstuffy attitude to the purposes of art, which he believed should be shared in daily life, not set apart or venerated. Not all artists I approached were so willing to show at a café – one agreed and then withdrew when his then wife told him it was beneath his dignity.

I was invited to write this book by William's widow, Carys McClure Brown. Carys brought her insights as a primary school headteacher to the project. She said what she wanted and how she could help and then left me to get on with my homework. Right at the start, she wrote to me: 'William did have an extraordinary life and some parts of it won't be easy to unravel but I can assure you, you won't find it dull!' I'm sad that Carys died in 2021, long before my essay was handed in.

As Carys predicted, writing about William has not been straightforward. Some aspects of his life remain enigmas; some stories about him cannot be true, including some he told himself. Whether to obfuscate or entertain, he had a talent for 'creative recounting' that is as tantalising as it is frustrating for a biographer. (If I have been punctilious with endnotes it is because I had to track my evidence.) William held back a great deal in his lifetime. As one close friend of William's, Keith Bayliss, tells me, 'he was purposefully, annoyingly, frustratingly unfathomable' and yet 'he might be amused that someone was trying to make sense of it all'.

This book is a critical biography, primarily about the art, and there is much about William's personal history that none of us can ever know. I'm comforted by a remark by Raymond Williams: 'Only the line of a life, hardly anything of its area, can be articulated, and reduced to grammar.'[1] The paintings expand on that to make the richer picture.

After Carys, her son Huw Griffiths, daughter Sue Alder and son-in-law Tim Alder have been a fine support team, supplying archives, information and images and as committed as Carys was to seeing the project through. Carys and I had sought help from her friend Tim Lewis to catalogue the art works that she held at home, and he ably took on that colossal task, without which my own job would have been far harder. Pauline Griffiths and Lucienne Evans of the Art Shop in Abergavenny, who looked after William's work for Carys and now do so for her estate, have helped generously. Vince Bevan took photographs specially for the book. Further images were scanned by Michael Jones of the National Library of Wales.

I thank David Woolley for permission to include his poetic tribute to William here. When I chose 'pursued by a bear' for my title, I was thinking of Shakespeare and I was unaware David had used that famous line already as the title of his anthology, which bore a Brown brown bear on the cover.

It has been my pleasure to work with the team at Parthian on a third book. Unbeknownst to me, Richard Davies had long admired William's work and when I mentioned the project to him his enthusiasm was instantaneous. I was grateful to be supported by Carly Holmes as editor. Knowing Olwen Fowler's enthusiasm for William's work and her craftsmanship for image quality and layout has been the ultimate reassurance.

Staff in public collections have been kind when answering my enquiries: Ellie Dawkins of the Glynn Vivian Art Gallery, Terah Walkup of The Box, Plymouth, Andrew Renton of Amgueddfa Cymru, Katie King of Manx National Heritage, Louise Jones-Williams and Savanna Dumelow of Llantarnam Grange, Nick Moreau of Region of Peel Archives in Ontario, Oliver Blackmore of Newport Museum and Art Gallery and Maya Wassell-Smith of Royal Museums Greenwich. My thanks to many others who have contributed advice, images or information, sometimes during interviews, including Keith Bayliss, Sharon Berg, Alison Bevan, Joady Brennan, Carys Brown, Claire Curneen, Lara Davies, Lucienne Evans, Robert Harding, Kathleen and Boston Hommel, Bernard Mitchell, David Moore, Jill Morgan, Margaret Rees, David Solomon, Ceri Thomas and Pete Williams. I must single out David Greenslade, whose friendship and collaboration ran deep with William as a creative cousin and a literary, and literal, fellow traveller. David has been a guardian of William's memory, gleaning information from many sources, and has been generous, insightful and patient. Many others whom I might have interviewed I quote instead from their recollections of William in the book *William Brown in Wales*, which David and Carys collated in 2018.

I am fortunate to have critical friends who have read the text for me. Thank you to Sue Alder, Keith Bayliss, Alison Bevan, Richard Edwards, David Greenslade, Huw Griffiths and Clive Hicks-Jenkins. Others thanked above read sections.

Time and again during the gestation of this project I have been struck by people's reactions when I told them what I was doing. Many had never heard of William Brown, which I hope this book will remedy. But almost all who had known William or his work reacted with conspicuous delight – even long after his death – as they recalled their pleasure in his effusive and perplexing personality and his bold, beautiful paintings.

Peter Wakelin

Abergavenny, summer 2026

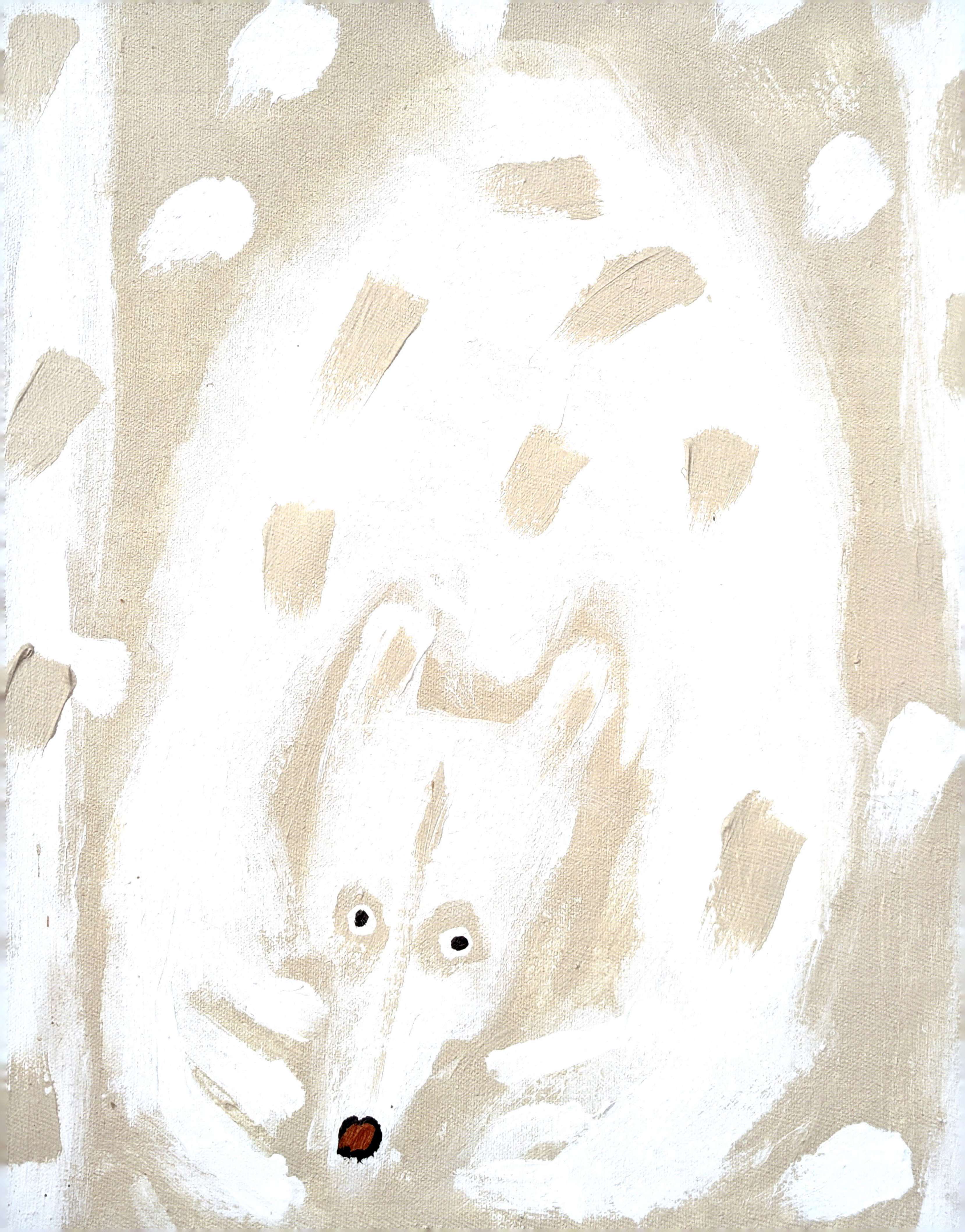

For William Brown

David Woolley

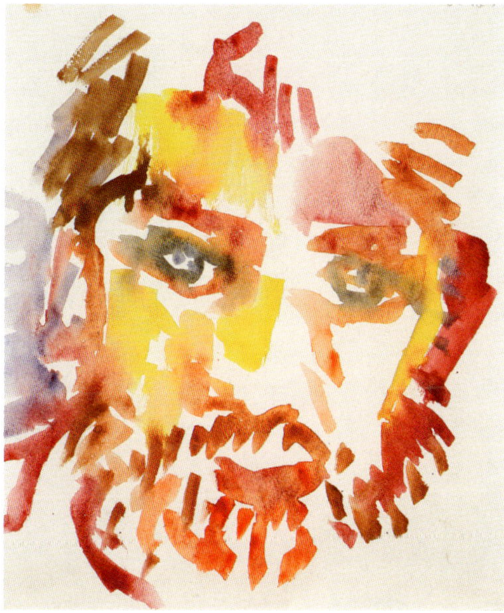

Untitled, 1989,
watercolour on paper,
40 x 35 cm

Untitled (polar bear)
undated, c. 1995
acrylic on canvas
43 x 34 cm

You never know
when the plane's
going to strike the tower
the shit
hit the fan
the scorpion sting, so
it's best to plough on
pick up the paint
drink deep, jack
daw up all the little
bits and pieces of this
absurd mess, make some
language out of it – a bit
of anglo-saxon, celt, queb-
ecois, scoop up all the
world's strange creatures,
tales from the far edge
of places. Distil them
with a measure
of humanity, dis-
regard for the bureau-
critic crap, the ivory tower.
Hard work is a virtue
you upheld, and lived
enough for two
lifetimes, yet still we're
all amazed that you're not there.
Drink up and get on with it
you'd have said:
exit William Brown
pursued by a bear ...

It's probably true that painters should
not talk about what / why they do it at all.

Artist mythmaker

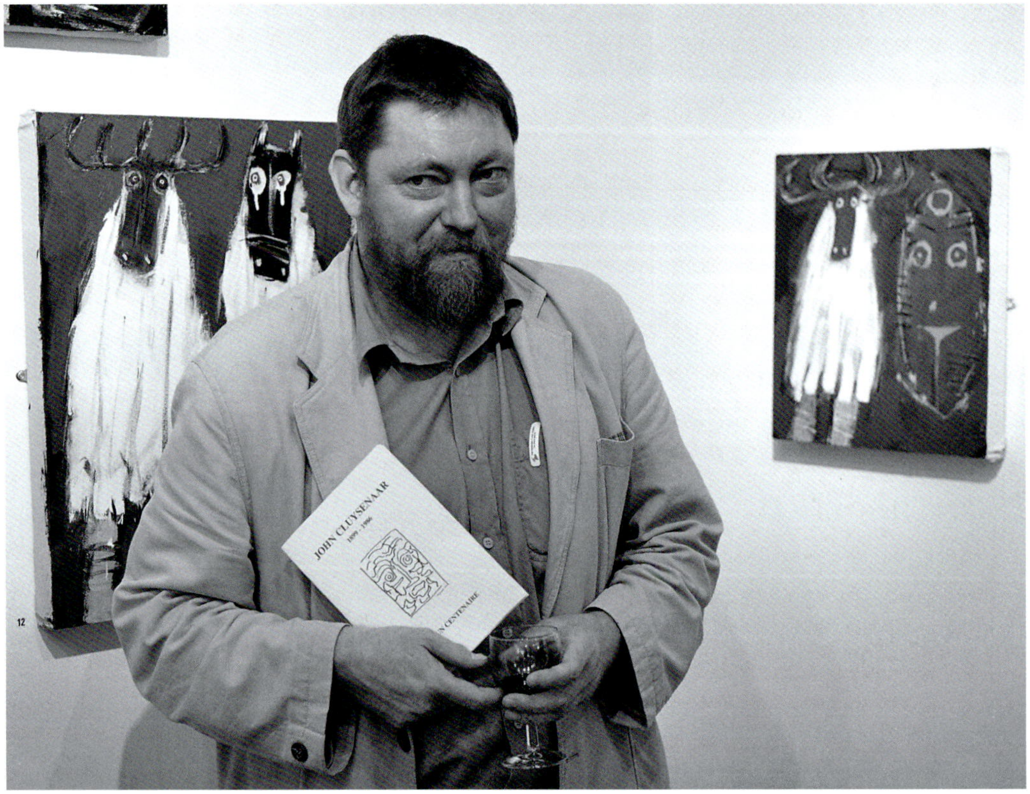

William at Oriel Canfas, Cardiff, 1999. Photo: Bernard Mitchell

William Brown was pursued by bears. They animated his imagination from the time he first saw them as a child in Canada to the end of his life. He observed them whenever he had opportunities to revisit their wild country and he painted them unstintingly: brown bears, polar bears, black bears; bears in a procession among pines, playing in the snow, striding beneath stars. More unexpectedly, he pictured them hiding under kitchen tables, arguing or 'agreeing to differ' (as his titles sometimes let us know). In his big, bold pictures, bears might dance, sport tartan, see visions of the constellation that bore their name or reveal their beating hearts.

William identified with bears and with the French-Canadian werewolf, the *loup-garou*, which he called 'a reminder of the animal in the human, powerful, cunning and unsophisticated.'[2] In his physical presence, once his bean-pole youth was passed, he had a bear-like stature – broad, tall, big-boned and hirsute. There was an ursine growl to his Canadian-Scots voice

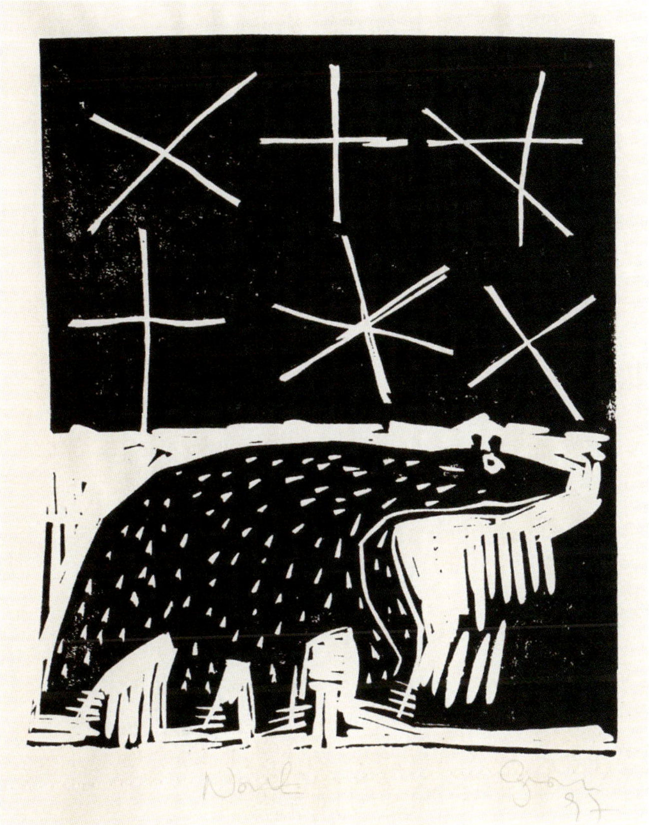

North, 1997,
linocut, 30 x 22 cm

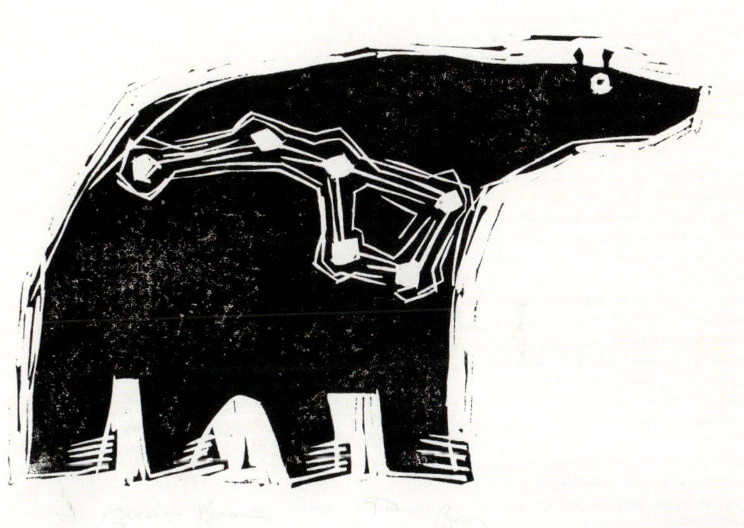

Great Bear, 1997,
linocut, 15 x 20 cm

softened by the hint of a stammer and rushes of words that sometimes seemed to start before the last had finished. He was as capable as a bear of camouflage and laying low, and as impressive when he was roused.

Just as bears characteristically are curious and omnivorous, William scented out ideas and experiences to nourish his art: cultures and places, collaborations and friendships, words, stories, myths and encounters. He called himself a narrative painter because stories were so essential to the workings of his mind. He said in a television interview:

> I suppose as a child I was brought up not just with books and stories but also visiting theatres and carnivals. The stories are very simple and the language is usually quite simple too. I bring my little cast of people, historical figures, imaginary figures [...] Sometimes I don't honestly know where things are coming from. I'm not stupid about it. I've an idea of control, of manipulating the characters but often arrival in a new place occasions arrival of characters.[3]

Next page:
Untitled (bear diptych), 1996, oil on canvas, 157 x 270 cm

At the heart of this was William's lifelong pleasure in 'mythopoeia', the generation of myths. He might begin each painting or unfolding series sparked by a known myth or tradition, but then the alchemy began as he translated it into something new, invariably more personal and far more playful. He gathered legends and traditions from every quarter. Hence the Welsh

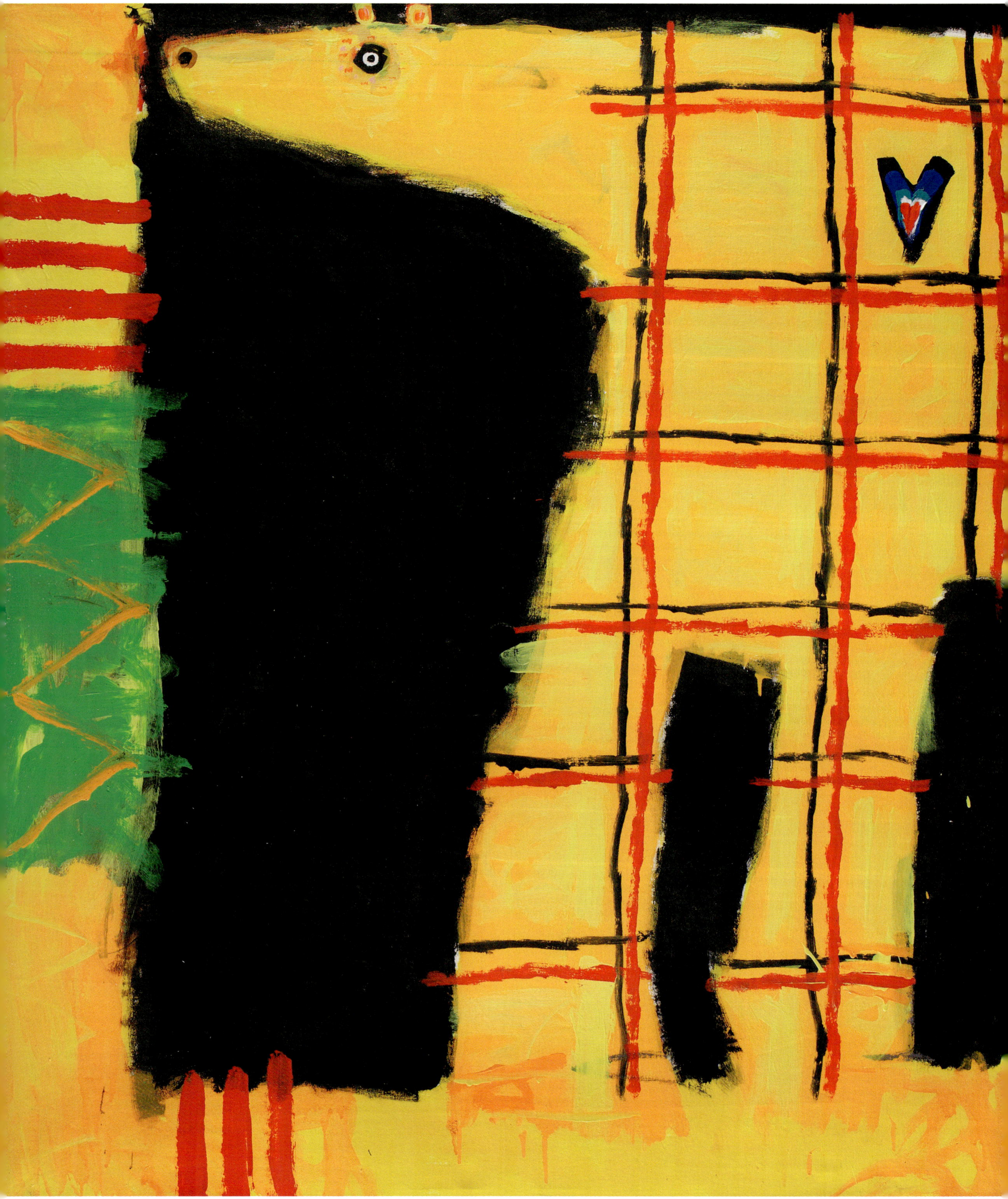

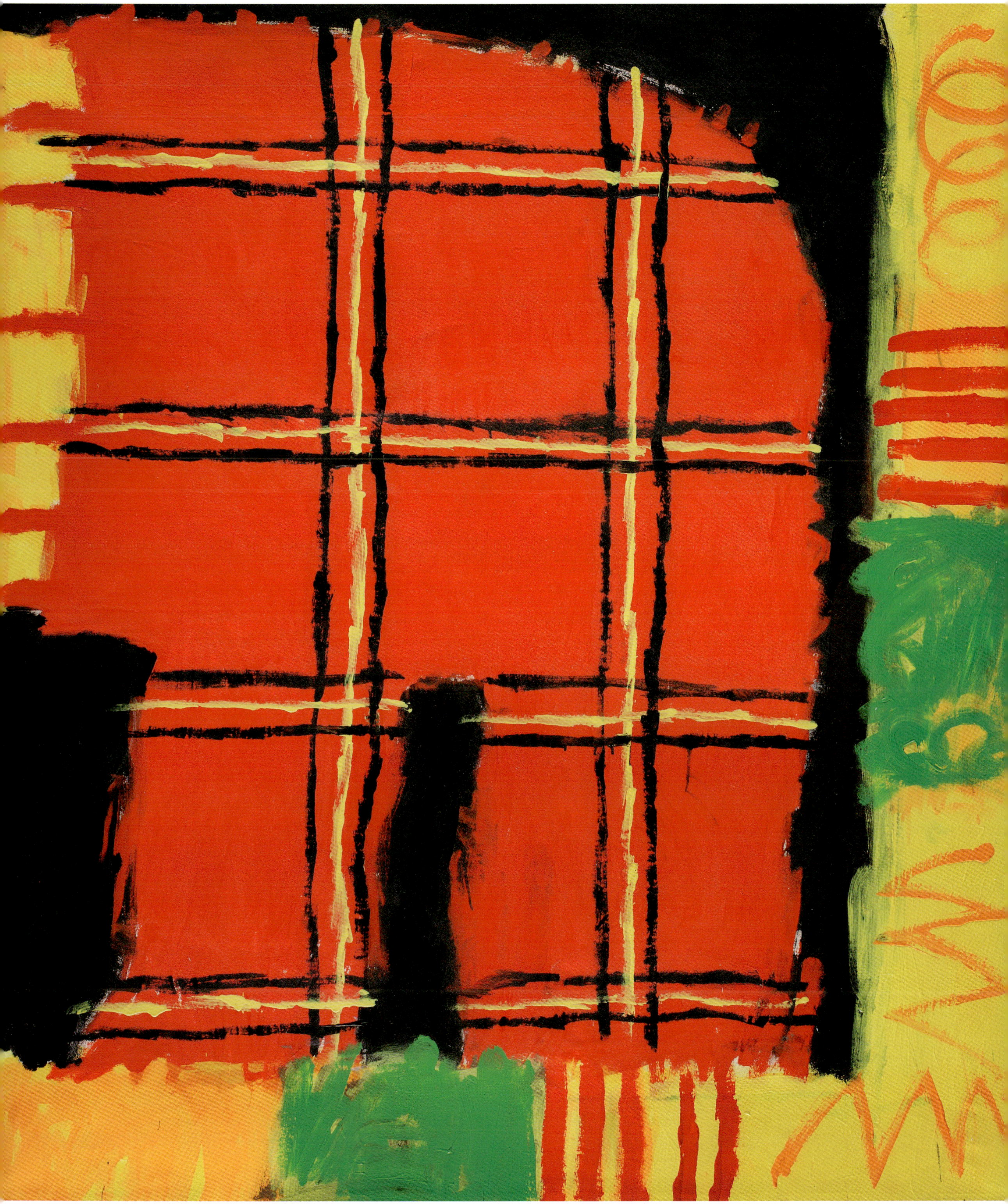

mid-winter folk-tradition of the Mari Lwyd, a beribboned horse's skull puppeteered by a sheeted operator and accompanied by mummers, became instead a creature with human feet and horse's head – a centaur upside down – striding lost and lonely through the night. When he read *The Little Prince*, it was the mythic potential in the life of the author, Antoine de Saint Exupéry, that caught his eye: 'airman / postman, night flights and air-drops, crashed in the desert among the Tuareg, disappeared in 1944 and his aircraft dredged up by fishermen off Marseilles'.[4]

Even William's artistic training was a myth of his creation. His entry in the *Dictionary of Artists in Wales*, submitted by 'the artist', said he studied at the École des beaux-arts de Montréal 1981–3, but he never attended college and in 1981–3 he was in Somerset. *The Dictionary of Artists in Britain since 1945* suggested he trained as a sculptor but his knowledge of bronze casting seems to have come from melting lead to cast small sculptures in his teens. There is no reason to believe that he assisted at a foundry in Pittsburgh nor that, as he told one journalist, he had attended Ontario College of Art. Was he being playful when he commented to the interviewer, 'I owe them nothing'?[5] Hopping continents as he did, he could risk what seem to be invented credits from the other side of the Atlantic – a first exhibition at Toronto when he was eighteen, a sculpture fellowship at Clarion State College, Pennsylvania, at nineteen. He dropped these from his cv by the late 1980s.[6] Such misrepresentations by other artists might be fraudulence, yet in William they spoke of mischievous delight in invention. He never wished to shatter anyone's illusions. Did he need to convince himself that his years of preparation as a self-taught artist were equal to the education of academies? Ironically, those artists who have passed through foundation, degree and post-graduate courses at successive colleges often say they learned little from their tutors, but grew thanks to time, facilities and fellow students.

Perhaps it was further myth-making when William protested at the evils of self-promotion that might take him away from his art. In truth, he was a brilliant and prodigious organiser of exhibitions that kept his output in the public eye. In the 1990s alone he had twenty-one solo exhibitions. As to publicity, the cuttings about his projects, from Canada, France, Germany, Italy and Britain, prove his effectiveness at spreading news and cultivating reporters, reviewers and eloquent friends. Only in the photographs at private views does his discomfort show: in jacket and tie, standing with head bowed and one wrist clasped by the other hand like a bystander at a funeral.

Once he had sketched and noted realities, he recast them. After drawing the broad landscape of the Pas-de-Calais he made it mythic with a church falling from the sky [page 103]. When he saw the replica of John Cabot's caravel, *The Matthew*, he made it an archetype in the stories of Canada's explorers [90 left]. The critic John Furse wrote: 'The iconography is complex – the method relatively simple – layers of meaning enticed to revelation through layers of paint.'[7]

A freewheeling association of ideas was one of William's gifts. His mind travelled naturally down many paths, consciously, unconsciously or synaesthetically conjoining subjects

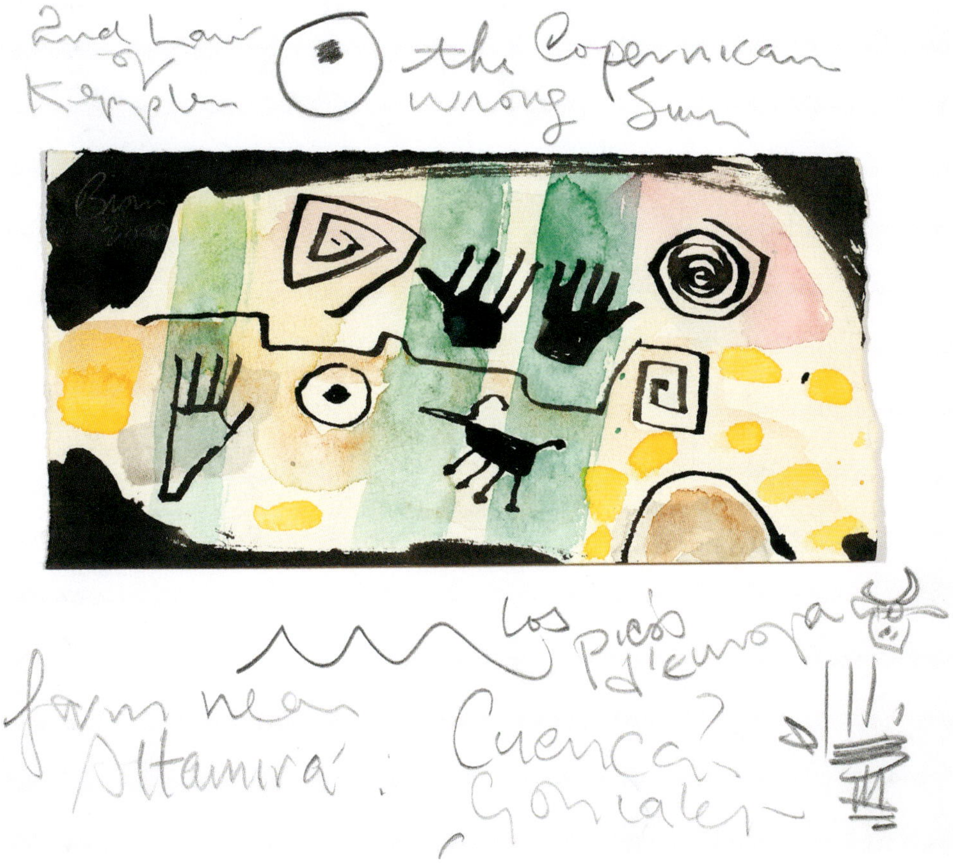

Farm near Altamira, 2000, watercolour and pencil, 24 x 24 cm

to surprise his viewers, and perhaps himself. Around a drawing inspired by the prehistoric art of the Altamira cave he wrote: '2nd Law of Keppler; the Copernican Wrong Sun farm near Altamira, Los picos d'Europa, Cuenca? Concales.' The references take untangling. Elsewhere he had Scott's Antarctic expedition welcomed by Canadian walrus, in Welsh [26]. The artist Iwan Bala recalled: 'His thoughts came in a torrent and it was a challenge keeping up as he constantly leapt from one topic to the next.'[8]

Restless travel was a main source of imagery and ideas, narratives and conversations. He went frequently to North Africa, returned to Canada, explored around his homes and met artists and writers across Europe. His images encompassed the vastness of the Canadian Shield and the textured landscapes and retold tales of Europe and North Africa. The artist Robert Harding recalls that, when journeying together across Belgium, William recognised placenames from the Battle of the Bulge and demanded detours 'to follow General Patton and photograph a few tanks'.[9] War was one among many disasters, impending or actual, that he absorbed for future use, together with storms, lost ships, fighter-jets, lumbering oil tankers, the Twin Towers and powerful beasts.

He noted a quotation from Jean-Siméon Chardin: 'Strive to paint the most ordinary thing in the most ordinary manner and the extraordinary will appear.'[10] He raved about how Chardin's painterliness could capture the elusive radiance of a child or a board of fruit. In William's hands,

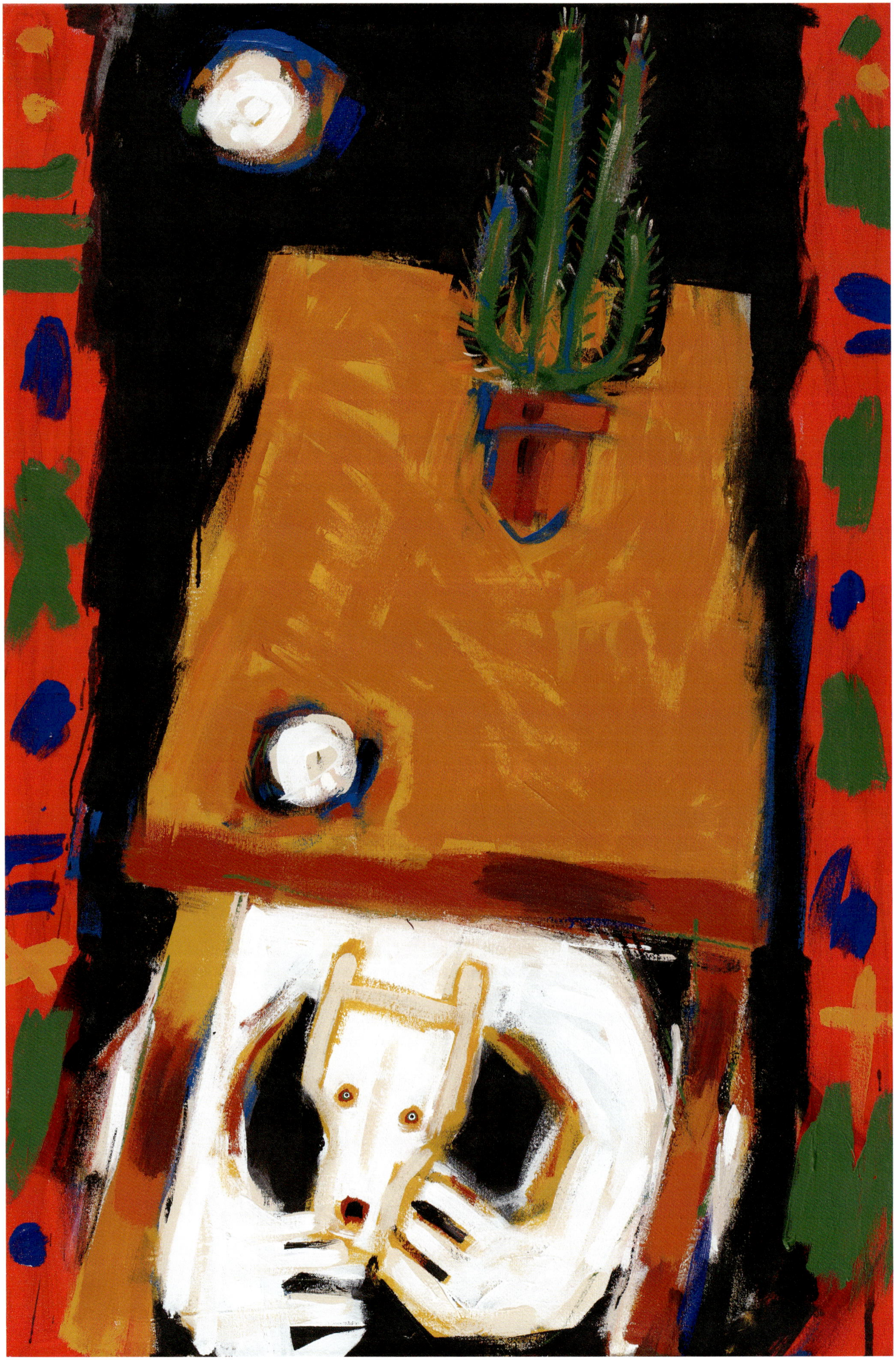

though, the extraordinary elements were unmissable – an ordinary table hid a bear; ordinary houses lay below the impossible arc of a night-time rainbow.

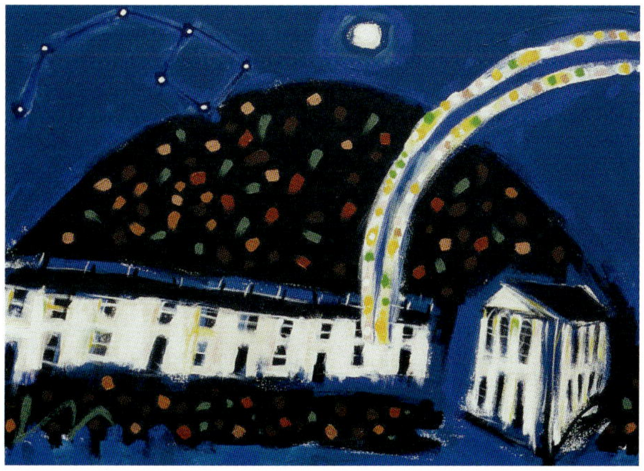

Untitled (night rainbow), undated, *c.* 2001, acrylic on canvas, 53 x 77 cm

Poets, with their open channel to metaphor and allusion, were favourite company. He befriended Anne Cluysenaar, Tony Curtis, Peter Finch, David Greenslade, Colin Jones, Peter Meilleur (aka Childe Roland), Goff Morgan, Malcolm Parr, Lucien Suel and David Woolley among others, and he worked in depth with several of them on books, performances and exhibitions. He returned frequently to the company of dead poets, too, including Baudelaire, Rimbaud and W. H. Davies.

He delighted in diverse languages. English, French and Welsh were those he used most often, but words in other tongues rolled round his mind – Arabic, Czech, Latin, Gaelic, Cree, Inuktitut and more. In Canada he had learned French, conversational Portuguese from his friend Manuel and, more unusually, Russian and Mandarin from customers in the bar where he worked. In his forties, he learned Welsh from Colin Jones and Anthony Evans (though he claimed it was from children's television and the animation about a duck, *Wil Cwac Cwac*). He read Rimbaud in the original; and yet when he spoke to French-speaking collaborators such as Peter Meilleur and Lucien Seul or to people he met on travels he was dismayed that they struggled with his Québécois accent. (On their journey to Belgium, Robert Harding resorted to his schoolboy French to get them by.)[11] Perhaps this problem merely reflected the occasional difficulties of understanding him in English.

Opposite: *Iolo Polo*, undated, acrylic on canvas, 117 x 76 cm

When he drove from Bilbao to Santiago de Compostela with Malcolm Parr in 1998, William was gratified to journey through '3 languages: Basque-Castilian-Galician.'[12] In picture titles, he preferred the romance of *Vol de Nuit* to 'night flight', which despite its attractive rhyme evoked 'red-eye' more than the spirit of adventure; prints of a cottage at night were titled variously or all at once *La Maison Noire*, *Tŷ Du*, *Tigh'na-Bruaigh* (after a village in Argyll and Bute). He rolled out compulsively the words still life, *nature morte*, *natura morta*, *stilleben*. The playfulness extended to his own name – sometimes Guillaume Lebrun and often Whim (spelled Wm) – and to punning exhibition titles like 'The Moose Man Cometh' or 'Someday my Prints'. He would riff on names, as when calling a tented stall where he and David Greenslade sold books 'the Yurt of Hurt, the Teepee of Temerity, the Wigwam of Wishes, the Stall of All, the Marquee de Sade.'[13]

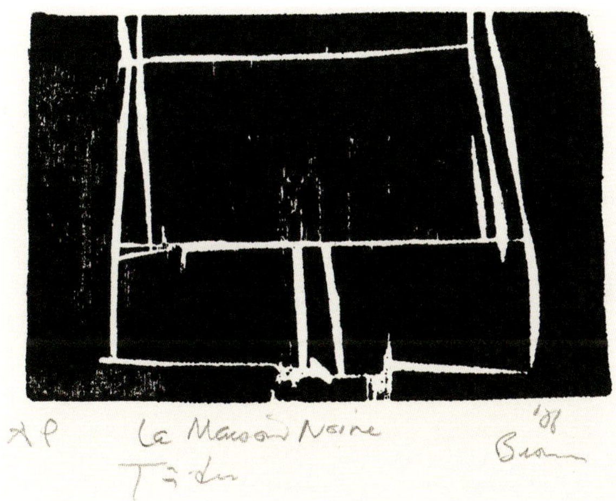

La Maison Noire / Tŷ du, 2006, woodcut, 20 x 18 cm

He produced a snowstorm of paper correspondence with friends and colleagues, refusing to join the coming email generation and instead writing by hand (often barely legibly) and incorporating symbols and scribbles, rubber stamps and postcards, doodles, flyers and newspaper cuttings. Letters typically conducted business in a line or two before a sequence of one-liners and *bons mots*. When he was in a dialogue with someone, for example planning an exhibition, he sent letters every day. He kept up a continuous correspondence with those who were important to him – his sister and his parents, friends he made on his travels and collaborators past and present. Perhaps his most unusual correspondent was the famous drug smuggler Howard Marks – 'Mr Nice' – in Terre Haute penitentiary, Indiana, who had been at the same school as Carys and taught by her father. William's envelopes were unmistakable, peppered with notes, stickers and miniature prints, and often addressed as postal puzzles – such as one to 'Belle Vue Croissante, Cwm Taf, Caerdydd', rather than Bellevue Crescent with its English address and postcode.[14] How many might still be in the lost letters section of a sorting office somewhere? This was 'mail art' even though not for exhibition, and correspondents cherished it.

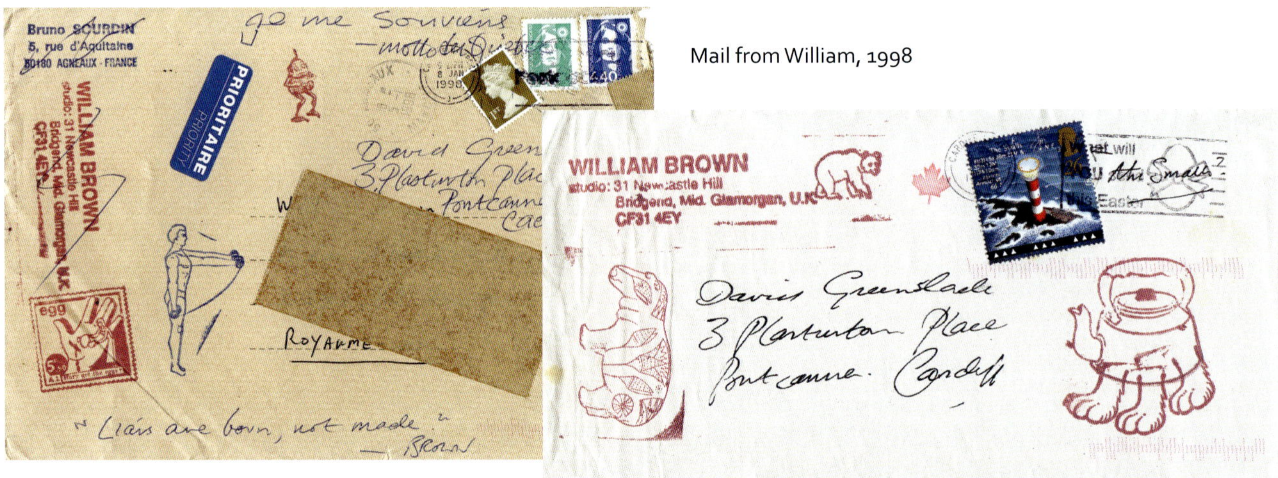

Mail from William, 1998

In William's paintings and prints, by contrast with his intricate letters, boldness was everything. Strong colours and powerful forms were the central qualities in his art. In his later work he used paint straight from bottle, tub or tube and laid solid grounds of a single colour with large, flat brushes on which other colours were applied in bold shapes, lines or daubs that could shimmer with an optical colour-mixing effect. Paints were seldom mixed physically, even wet-on-wet, apart from a tint such as the rose where white dragged over red or, in watercolour, where one tone showed through another. He said: 'I like colour. I'm conscious of that in language and in pictures. Not mixing the colours also enables you to work in an impasto manner, that is to say you're overpainting and building up a surface.' Much enjoyment lay in the observation of the changes as he worked: 'I don't want to mystify painting, but it's the most rewarding of things. It has a life.' He knew when a painting was resolved, and never over-worked it.[15]

Charcoal in large drawings and black ink in woodcuts and linocuts made forms prominent through strong negative spaces, fluid lines, bold patterns and elemental motifs. 'Squiggles for waves, zigzags for pine trees', noted the critic Laura Gascoigne, were 'instantly readable by a child, but the meanings remain tantalizingly elusive.' That mysteries remained appealed to William, and he would not reveal whether certain motifs might secretly represent an essence of people or places; it was for the onlooker to decide. He said, 'Pictures work because they remind the viewer of something. All art is about recognition – memory is the defining human trait.'[16]

He sought spontaneity through rapid movements. A little painting of the owl and the pussycat is so swiftly achieved that the owl in flight is no more than a round face and a blur of feathers [22]. He welcomed accident and randomness, validating it with Zen philosophy. Big brushes or large chisels were joined by less readily controlled tools at times: Colin Jones saw William drawing with a blunt stick dipped in ink. He made swift marks on ink-coated glass for monoprints with pieces of plastic, ends of brushes, rags and fingernails. His quickness of mind was brilliant at times, as when he devised a logo for the animation company Cinetig, which specialised in making films with schoolchildren. The design came instantly – a handful of lines that summed up childhood drawings, fun and movement, children playing, two eyes and a cine

Untitled (bread, canoe, seal and girl), undated, woodcut, 40 x 50 cm

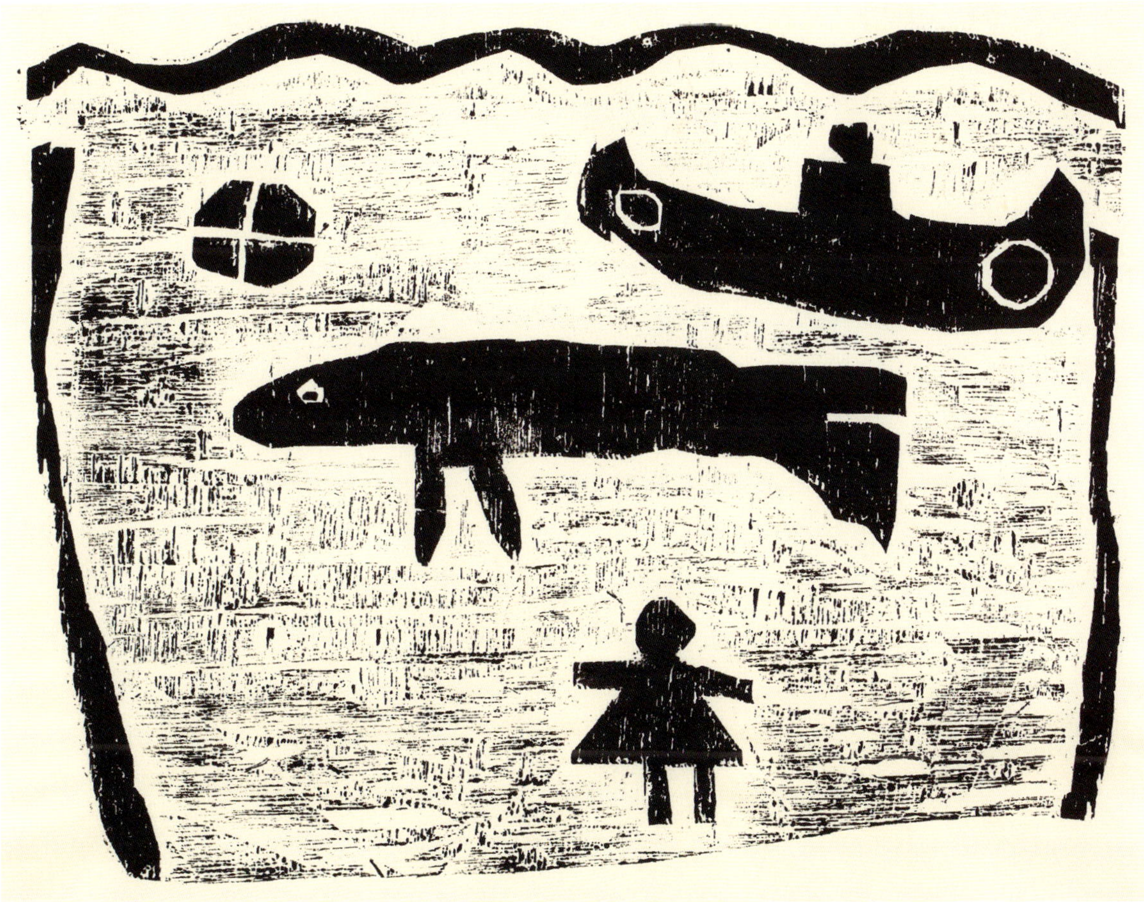

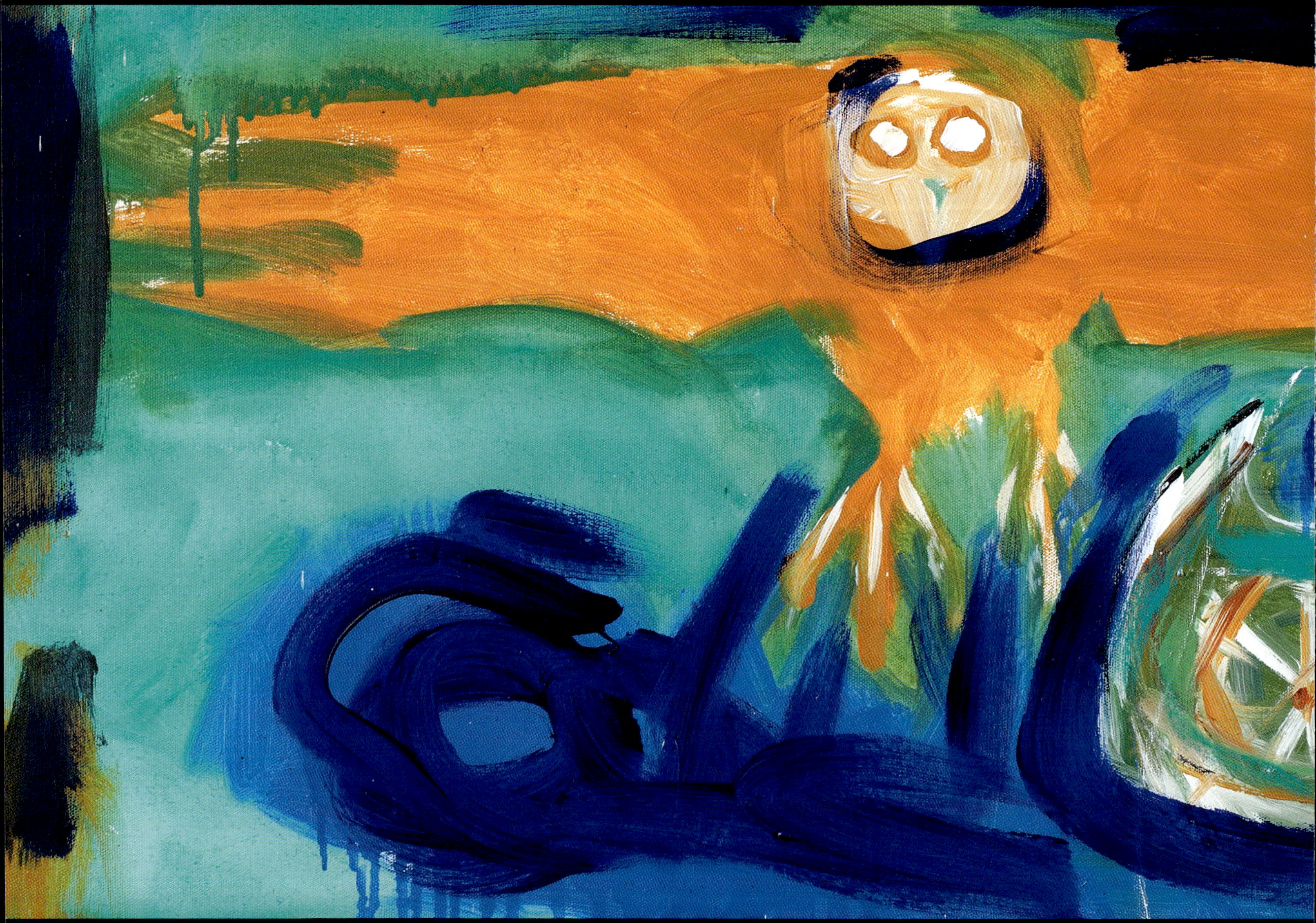

Untitled (Owl and
Pussycat), 2008,
Oil on canvas,
40 x 120 cm

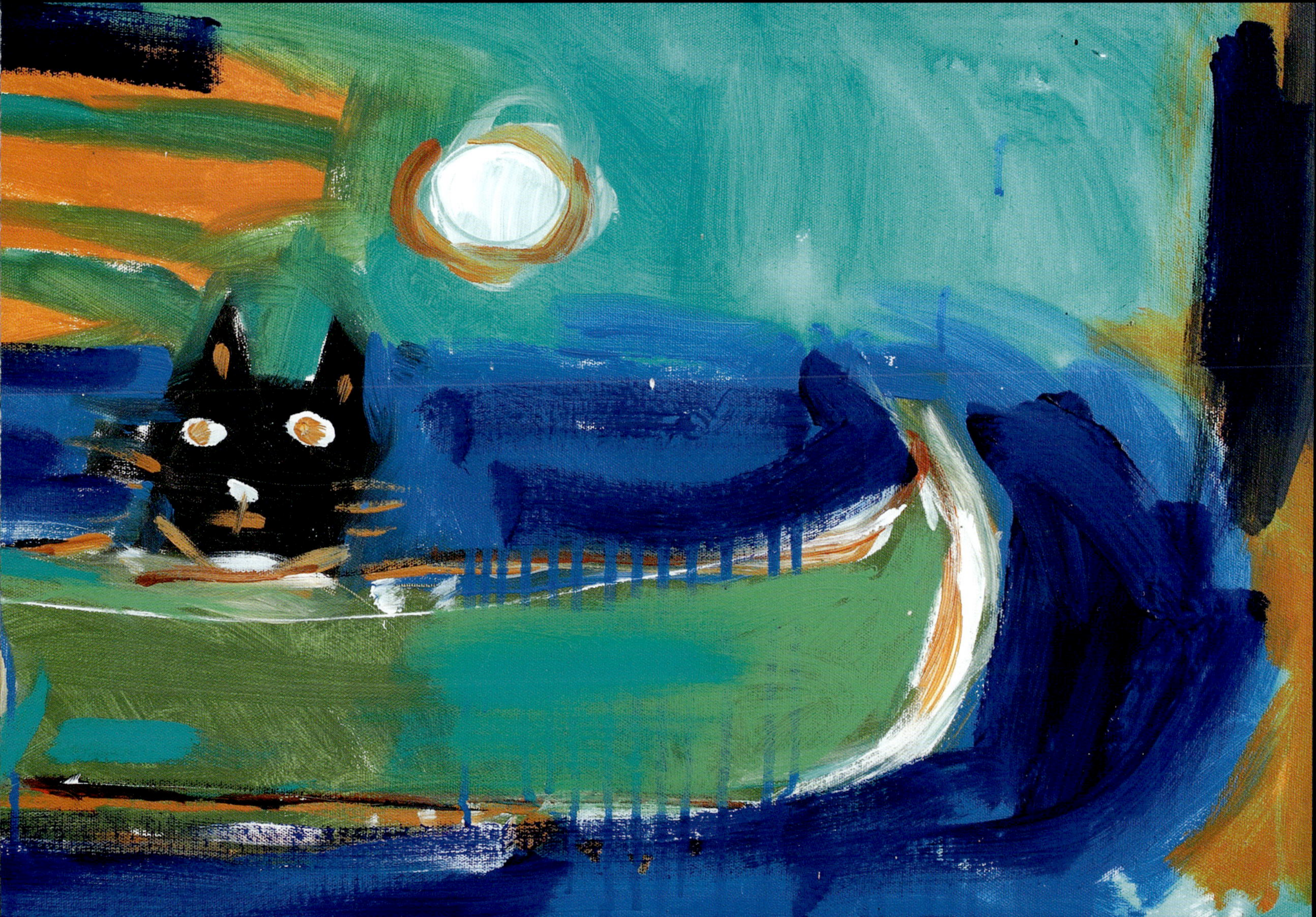

camera on legs. He produced an equally apt graphic image to express Brecon Jazz in 1995: two hands and a bongo drum that appeared on programmes, mugs and T-shirts. (Commissioned by Branwen Dawson, he only appreciated as the festival was beginning that he could exhibit work and rushed off to paint pictures of Brecon, which were exhibited still wet.)[17]

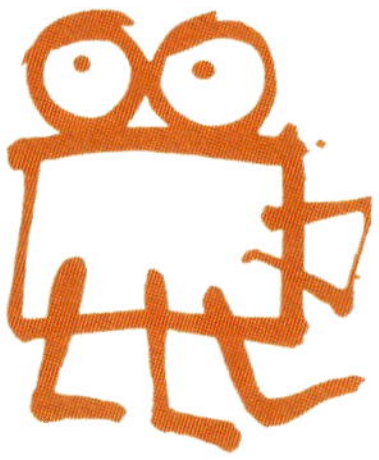

Cinetig logo

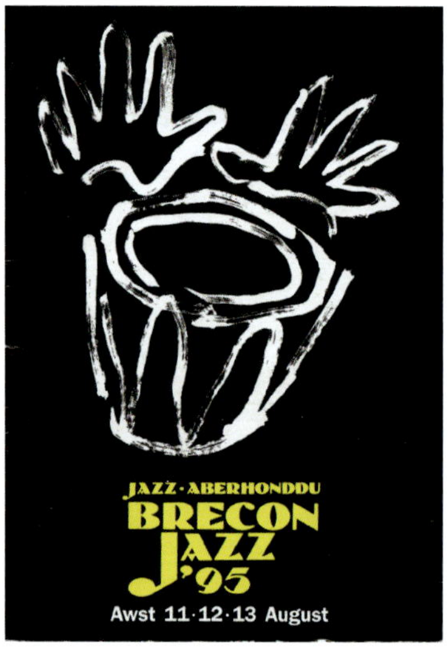

Brecon Jazz promotional image, 1995

He returned repeatedly to subjects and motifs, with the result that pictures sometimes take an effort of comparison to tell one from another. Was he satisfying an obsession with particular motifs or searching for the exact expression of his idea? The repetition was never a production-line with sales in mind but a desire for getting out his toys again, arranging them in different combinations, telling himself different variations on the same story. It was all one with his capacity for play and his enjoyment of child-like imagination. This was echoed in his repetition of speech. Phrases burrowed into his consciousness for days at a time – 'There's no stopping us now', 'They just don't geddit do they?' or Tommy Cooper's catchphrase, 'Just like that!'[18] His visual motifs, though, could mean different things on each outing. White circles could be the moon, the sun, an owl's eyes, snowballs, snowflakes or the snow of a malfunctioning television.

In spite of this humour and spontaneity, though, many of his paintings showed a commitment to commentary. *Arts Review* noted in 1986: 'Confident and knowing with an eye to Matisse and perhaps Nolde, he has the intelligence and astuteness to adapt his precursors' ploys to the needs of his personal imagery. Once slatted shutters opened onto calm seas and bobbing boats at Collioure, but now the room-with-a-view frames the spiteful delta-winged-jet [44] and laden oil-tanker, both weighted with economic necessity and moral responsibility.'[19]

Carys said painting was William's whole life; 'like a stomach-ache,' he told her, which he soothed by spending every hour he could in the studio. When he was younger he set himself the target of making a hundred drawings a day. Later, the drawings went uncounted but were still continuous. Perhaps it was an obsessive compulsion masked as a work ethic. He often said he drew like some people would knit. Drawing kept his hands busy and built a barricade against social awkwardness. Always on edge at his exhibition openings, he would withdraw into sketching people, sometimes tearing pages from his notebooks to give away. He said it was his thinking process: 'I can sit at a table and do 200. I've a 10% success rate with drawings – editing is the most important. Stream of consciousness is all very well, but the critical faculty is central. It's knowing when to stop: knowing *which* one.'[20]

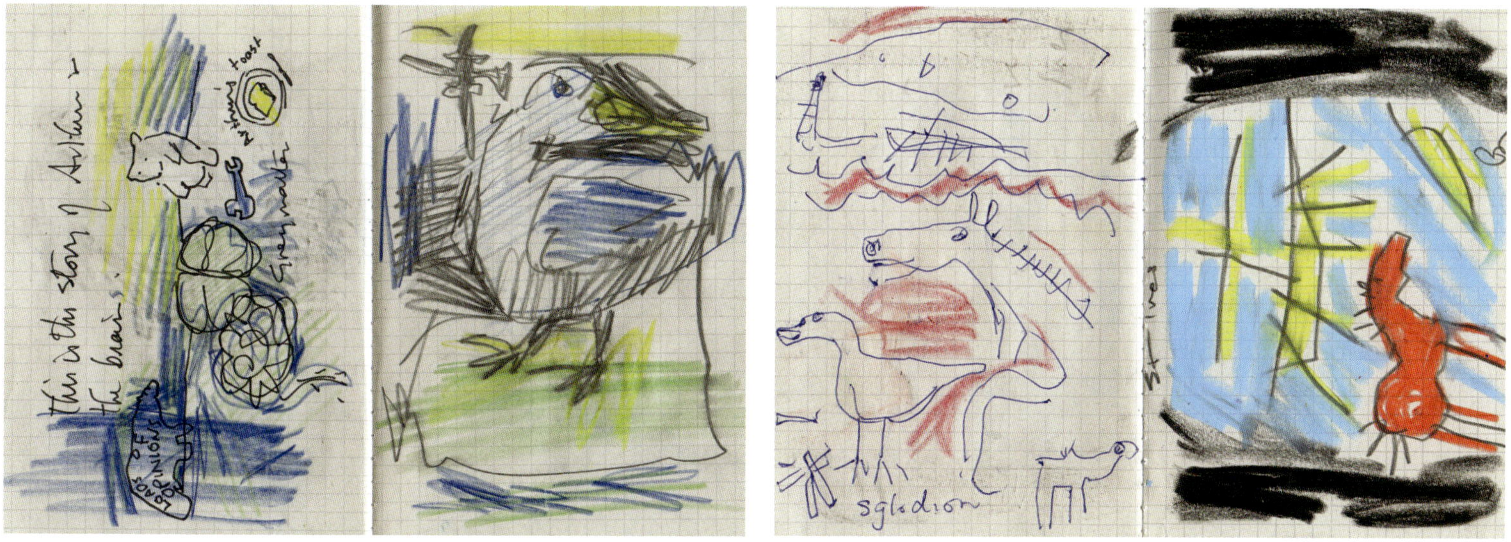

Sketchbook, 1993, mixed media, 15 x 21 cm

While William was a painter resolutely himself and largely untrained, he was absorbed by the lives and thoughts of earlier artists, and his discoveries about them reinforced his instinctive choices. From his teens onwards he consumed artists' biographies, perhaps looking for clues to guide his path. He was fascinated by van Gogh's troubled progress towards genius and the faithful support of his brother, Theo. He wrote once that German Expressionist printmaking before the First World War remained for him 'fresh and current'. He talked about Chaïm Soutine and James Ensor, and the carnivals Ensor created have echoes in William's series *The Dark Fairground* [130].[21] He admired particularly artists who saw the essences of animals, and consequently he bought the work of Inuit sculptors in Canada and a watercolour of waddling ducks by Ben Hartley, humorously titled *Quack, Quack, Quick*.

One of the first artists he knew personally was the Polish Holocaust survivor Gershon Iskowitz, who had become a leading abstract painter in Canada. William made some paintings in the 1980s that tried out similar motifs to Iskowitz's. His love of narrative meant that abstraction would never be for him but he continued to use dot patterns like those of Iskowitz, roughly daubed, to leaven surfaces.

The artists whose work was most closely parallel to William's were those who, like him, were not products of the academies. Foremost among these artists sympathetic to his own vision were the children he led through school workshops in printmaking and the anonymous artists of prehistory – the maker of the Venus of Willendorf, the carvers of rock-art spirals and the painters who conjured animals on the walls of caves. These artists above all, whose sophistication could so easily be underestimated, helped him unlearn some skills and embrace his instinctual gift. Iwan Bala wrote: 'Bold colours, clear, powerful iconographics, and a unique body of work replete with narratives. There was no mistaking a William Brown painting when you came across it – there was a directness and a lack of guile that a child would recognise at once – but his work was also extremely resourceful in its "simplicity".'[22]

I could begin by stating that
I was raised … by bears or wolves.

O Canada!
1953–1977

One of William Brown's statements as an artist, written a year before he died, opened with a phrase about his origins that says much about his love of storytelling but little about the facts of his early life: 'I could begin by stating that I was raised (very Kipling) by bears or wolves but that wouldn't be the whole truth.' He told the whole truth rarely; and never if it got in the way of a story he found amusing, but as the statement continued it revealed something crucial: 'In fact, I was born of Scots parents in Toronto, 50-odd years ago. Story telling – and listening both were inculcated early and I seized on stories / myths / legends / folk customs.'[23]

Croeso Captain Scott (diptych), undated, *c.* 1996, oil on canvas, 152 x 228 cm

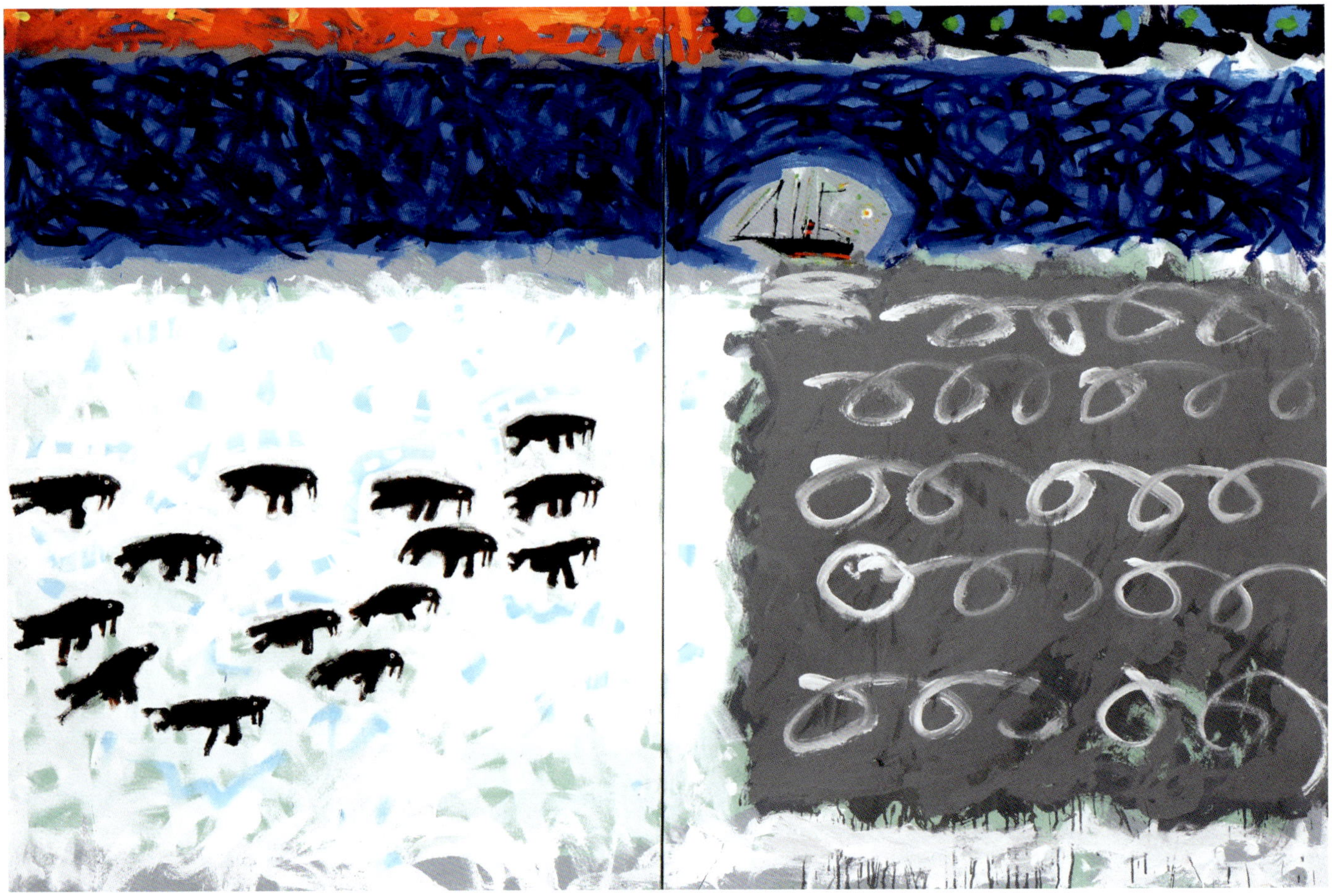

His parents were indeed Scots, and William spoke with a Scots burr running through his Canadian accent. They had emigrated from Glasgow with their daughter Kathleen. His father Alex came in 1951 to find accommodation and his mother Cathy and Kathleen in 1952. As to the stories, one that William sometimes told was that his Scottish great-grandfather McClure had come to Canada – an attractive creation myth that harked back to an age of exploration, highland clearances, far-flung trading posts and frontiersmen; but unfounded.

William offered two more true essentials in another interview: 'I was born on the shores of a great grey lake ... I cannot recall a time when I did not make pictures.'[24] He did start life on the edge of a great lake – a Great Lake – when he was born at St Joseph's Hospital on the Lake Ontario shorefront in Toronto on 11 December 1953; and his obsession with drawing began in infancy.

Cathy was a stay-at-home mum between part-time positions at Toronto City Hall, Canada Post and a grocery store. She was quiet and contained, but warm in her relationships, the model of a Scottish ma. Alex had served as a tool and die maker in the Royal Air Force during the War and worked in the aircraft industry in Canada for over thirty years. He straddled stereotypes as both a tough working-class Glaswegian and a man of cultural curiosity who visited the library every week to discover books and music that he didn't know.[25] Will and his father enjoyed a close bond in boyhood, though it would evaporate as he reached his teens.

The family lived in Bramalea, a new planned town of parks and leafy if monotonous drives; their street, Belmont Drive, was a curving road of single-storey houses set back from open lawns a short walk from schools and shops. The town was mostly 'blue-collar', populated by reasonably well-off working families. It was a satellite to Brampton, which was still small but grew prodigiously to become one of the largest cities in Canada, almost indistinguishable from the Toronto conurbation.

Will (as he was known at home) was a small child when he began to look at art. He was five when, he recalled, he visited a museum in Toronto and saw 'a roomful of pictures of a dumpy little man with an assortment of hats on. This was (I realised much later) the internationally touring exhibition of Rembrandt's Self Portraits and it subtly impressed on me that all paintings do not have to be beautiful – at least not conventionally so.'[26]

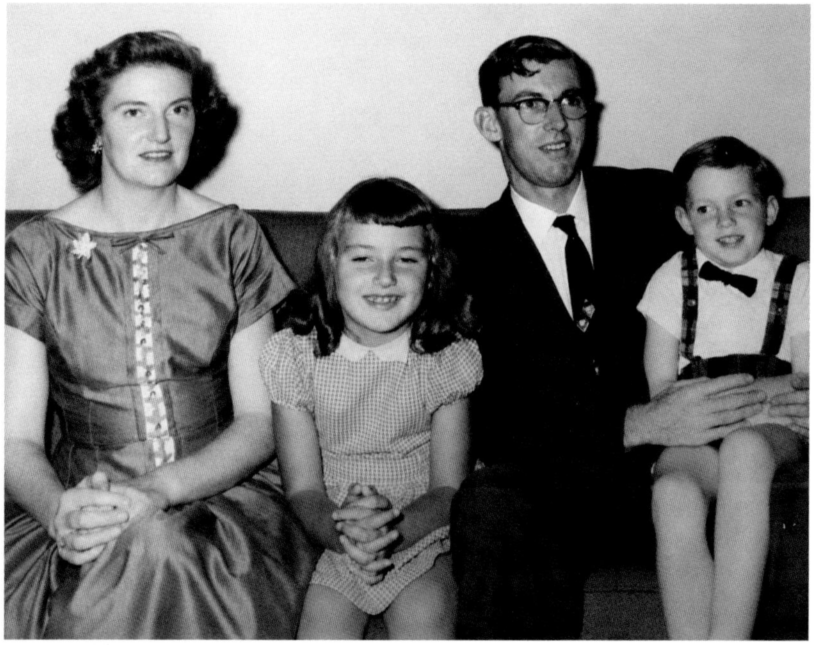

The Brown family in 1957: Cathy, Kathleen, Alex and Will

The wildness of the North captured Will's imagination when the family took camping trips up the Trans-Canada Highway to Parry Sound and Pointe au Baril on the east of Lake Huron. When he was eight they drove along the north of Lake Superior to Thunder Bay, a thousand miles into the woods, into bear country. His sister Kathleen recalls him sketching everywhere he went. While he recuperated from operations on his feet to compensate for exceptionally low arches, reading and drawing became his substitute world.

His rebelliousness began early, when teachers and his parents tried to break Will of his left-handedness (they called him 'corrie-fisted' in Scots), and he fought back. He was exceptionally bright and voracious in his reading and it was decided he should skip two years in primary school. But on the transition to the newly built Bramalea Secondary he almost immediately began to tune out; an encouraging art teacher and extracurricular activities such as painting backdrops for theatre productions failed to make up for all the rest. His relationship with his parents and his sister soured as his attendance plummeted. A teenage anarchist, he grew dismissive of the goal of 'settling down' and found his father strict, intolerant and easily enraged. When he announced that he planned to be an artist his father said a man without calloused hands was not a man. William ran away from home repeatedly and abandoned school at fifteen without graduating. Yet decades later he would write that more significant than any formal education had been 'the instilling on my father's part of an artisanal approach in my work.' This informed his choice of deep, unframed canvases. 'Coming from Clydebank shipbuilders, boilermakers and my father a toolmaker,' he said, 'I like the idea of the thing being proud from the wall. That's why I have these heavy stretchers and I guess the surface of the pictures again is a projection into the room, the space. And actually it's very satisfying because I'm building things.'[27]

By now a tall, gangly boy with red hair over his shoulders, Will at sixteen shared a flat in Queen Street in Brampton with his best friend from school, Philip York, and the slightly older Brian Purdy. They were joined soon afterwards by Brian's younger sister Sharon Berg, when she too ran away from home. Will, seventeen, and Sharon, sixteen, became a couple.

This period was the nearest William came to the art-school experience at which he sometimes hinted. Sharon describes a pact 'to talk philosophy, share our news and opinions about the [Vietnam] war, share the biographical details of various painters and opinions about who was really accomplishing something.' She had done a high-school programme in life drawing, pottery and design and owned a complete set of the Time-Life Library of Art, which they read together. Philip was focused on becoming a professional artist and Brian would go on to be a poet like his father, Al Purdy, whose fame was growing. Phil and Will could be rackety together, drinking hard liquor at times and committing petty crime, but they talked about light and colour, materials and composition, and the four housemates spurred each other creatively. When Will was struggling with figure drawing, Sharon passed on what she knew and modelled for him: 'Hours upon hours, until the tingling in my legs or arms died away into numbness [...] He quickly developed the goal of executing 100 drawings a day.'[28]

Will used any materials he could get, including newspapers, noticeboards and stolen art pads. Emulating Picasso, he wrote the date boldly on the face of each drawing.

Money was tight but Sharon received welfare cheques because she was pregnant. Birth-control support was hard to access – the contraceptive pill had been decriminalised as recently as 1969. Sharon was seventeen when they had the child, in May 1973. The boy was kept secret from Will's parents and successfully put up for adoption. Small-town Brampton was hostile to teenage runaways and instituted a 10pm curfew for under-eighteens, which the police interpreted as reason to come to their flat if lights were showing in the early hours. Sharon recalls they were singled out as subversives because of Will's long hair and the nude drawings on the walls, which the officers would 'gawp at'. Will and Sharon headed to downtown Toronto and Philip set off to study art in Pittsburgh.[29]

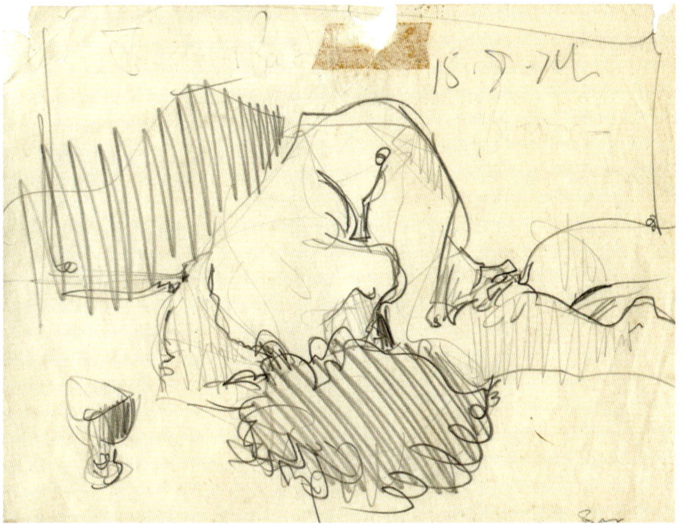

15.1.74 (life drawing),
1974, pencil,
21 x 28 cm

Among the scarce survivors of William's explosion of artwork is a painting of Sharon behind a vase of flowers. It reveals how much he had learned by seventeen in his painterly

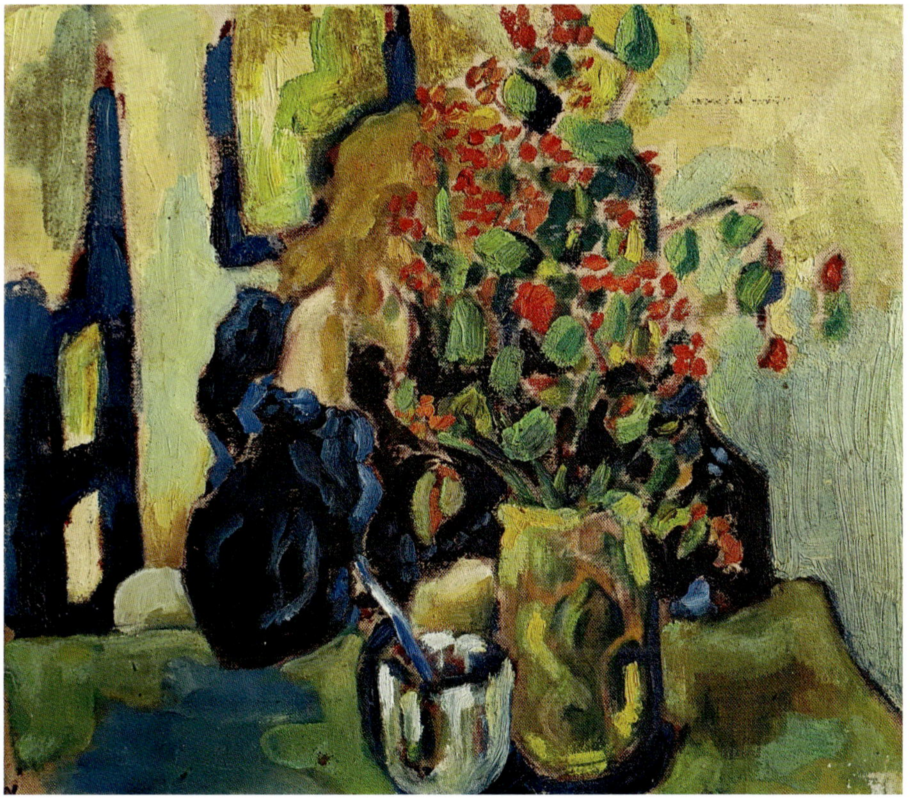

Sharon Behind Vase,
undated *c.*1970,
oil on canvas,
30 x 30 cm

expression of form and sophisticated use of complementary colours – oranges with blues, yellows with purples and reds with greens – and his willingness to approach his subject obliquely, creating not a portrait, still life or interior but a mash-up of the three. Sharon recalls paintings critical of war, carcasses of ships, sailing boats and nudes on the beach. A few photographs of drawings and a painting from around 1974 suggest that William was reaching for the bolder artistic language he would use long afterwards. He made three-dimensional assemblages, lead statuettes, woodcuts, lino prints and loosely observational pen-and-ink drawings. He developed linear emblematic imagery of moons and stars, bare light bulbs and clock-faces that link recognisably to his mature style.

He was going to exhibitions whenever he could, in the Peel Art Gallery in Brampton as well as museums and galleries in Toronto. One event with meaning for him was at Ontario

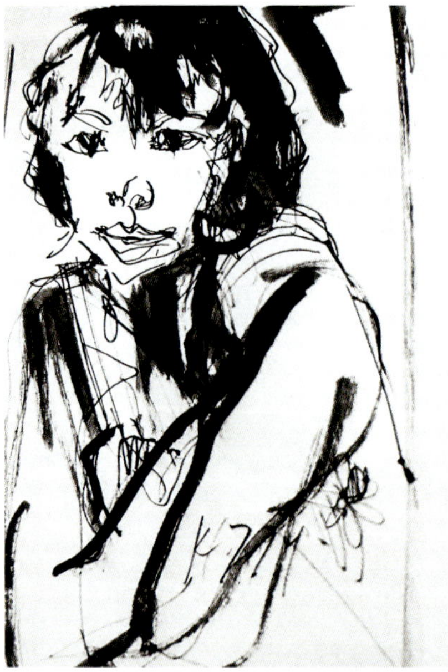

14.7.74 (Sharon), 1974, ink, dimensions unknown

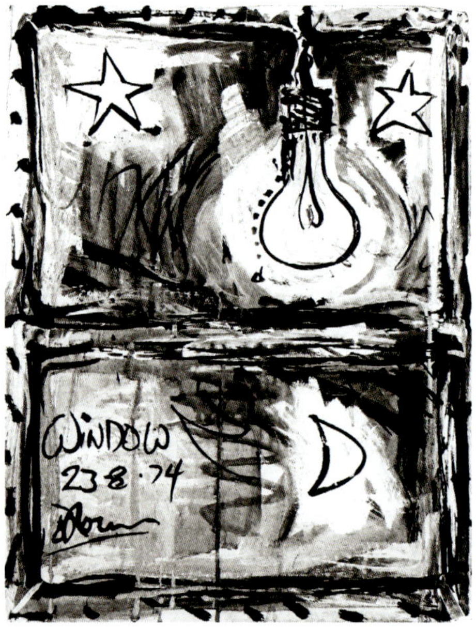

Right:
Window 23.8.74, 1974, ink and watercolour, (black and white photograph), dimensions unknown

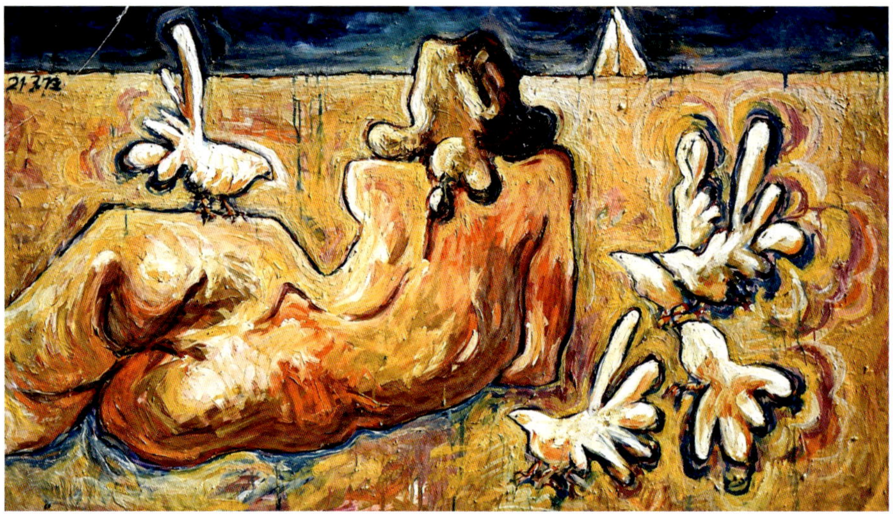

21.3.73 (nude on a beach), 1973, oil on board, dimensions unknown

Science Center in summer 1974. *In Praise of Hands: Contemporary Crafts of the World* showed 1,000 craft objects from 79 countries. It celebrated expression as well as function, as the titles of the themes suggested: 'Apparel and adornment', 'The home: utility and embellishment', 'Play, ritual and celebration' and 'The maker's statement'. The exhibition and accompanying book amplified William's passion for rituals and symbols and his commitment to play as complement to study.[30]

Toronto was more expensive than Brampton but Sharon and Will took jobs. He worked moving beer crates – finally getting those calloused hands and proudly building some muscle, noting the milestone when he reached 135 pounds (still under 10 stone despite his 6 feet 2 inches). He waited tables at Grossman's Tavern on Spadina Avenue, a hangout for artists and writers with live music, readings and performances. The poet Joe Rosenblatt recalled 'a grungy drinking hole', which he guessed appealed to Will, though free meals for staff were even more attractive.[31] Spadina was a traditionally Jewish area of tailors' workshops, delis, cafés, theatres and bookstores on the edge of the university district and a cosmopolitan environment for refugees. William worked some hours at Gwartzman's art supplies store, just up Spadina Avenue, which gave him opportunities to befriend artists and sometimes visit their studios.

In autumn 1975, Sharon was four months pregnant with another child, conceived despite more knowledge and an IUD, when William left her. He returned to the flat to eat and paint while she was at work but refused to speak to her until she confronted him at Grossman's. He took away the work he had done while they were together and destroyed it. Sharon had their daughter Ila on her own. Years later, Sharon learned William tried to find them on a visit to Toronto but Philip, to protect her, told him no one knew where they had gone. Later again, in 2005, William and Ila would correspond and talk of a trip to Wales, but they would never meet.[32]

After a long drinking session with his schoolfriend Richard Nelson, William crashed on his living-room floor. Richard's housemate Joady Brennan recalls her first impression: 'reed-thin, golden and glowing', reminding her of the translucent self-portrait of the teenage Samuel Palmer that she had seen in the Ashmolean Museum at Oxford. William asked her to marry him that morning; she declined, but he moved in.

Joady was two years older than William. After school in Oxford she had come to Canada to visit her parents, who had moved there in pursuit of business projects. She stayed on in Toronto to study literature at York University. William didn't tell Joady about his children with Sharon. When she learned about them much later, William responded that it was Sharon's business and nothing to do with him. Thinking back to William in his early twenties Joady says he seemed flummoxed by fatherhood:

> William was in many ways quite unproblematic – very shy, very bright, no underlying pathologies or tendencies – but extraordinary in that he had a path, a job, a task, however we'd like to put it, to which he managed to cleave, unlike most of the rest of us. Nothing mystical, certainly, but an exceptional sense of knowing what he was for, what he could do.[33]

William's shyness certainly went deep. Joady, who later trained in psychotherapy, thinks that when he drank it was a way to cope with this and an entwined lack of confidence, echoing 'a certain archetypal kind of fiercely intelligent Scottish working-class lad who has to take a drink before they get up on a platform.' In his twenties, she says he had 'a physical and emotional loathing of (weighted/purposeful) social interactions' such as talking up his work, schmoozing on the gallery scene or 'making a show of himself', because 'time spent on hawking your work is time not spent on the work itself'; though he could do all when fortified. When he was working or with his closest friends, Joady recalls that he often went without alcohol for weeks on end.[34]

He drew and painted unremittingly in the shared house in Major Street, two blocks west of Spadina, using a corner of Joady's bedroom and a cellar for bigger work. He kept up his target of a hundred drawings and five paintings a day, most of which he would destroy. He surrounded himself with work in progress, pictures drying on the floor, one on top of another. By now his parents were happy to visit and more supportive of his career.

He met artists through Grossman's and Gwartzman's who helped and encouraged him. The installation artist, painter and experimental filmmaker Michael Snow was one. The deepest relationship was with Gershon Iskowitz, who studied in Warsaw in the 1930s, survived the Kielce ghetto and the Auschwitz and Buchenwald concentration camps and studied art again in Munich after the War. William described him as 'a supportive friend to me as a very young artist.' Iskowitz reached Toronto in 1948, became well known after he turned to abstraction and represented Canada at the Venice Biennale in 1972. He kept a studio at 435 Spadina Avenue, across the road from Gwartzman's. When he came to the house to eat with William and Joady, she recalls that he brought a bottle of vodka frozen in a block of ice and ate everything on his plate, bones and all. (William was an excellent and enthusiastic cook but this was surely a shadow of the camps.) He told Joady he admired William's devotion to his art: 'the real thing'. William wrote: 'He and I shared a passion for both painting and liberty [...] After the war he had for a time worked with Oskar Kockoczka who had encouraged him to draw and

Below: Untitled, 1979, medium and dimensions unknown

Right: Untitled, 1979, medium and dimensions unknown

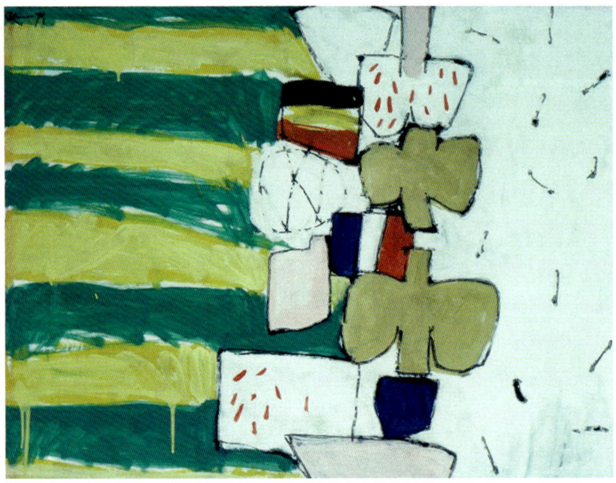

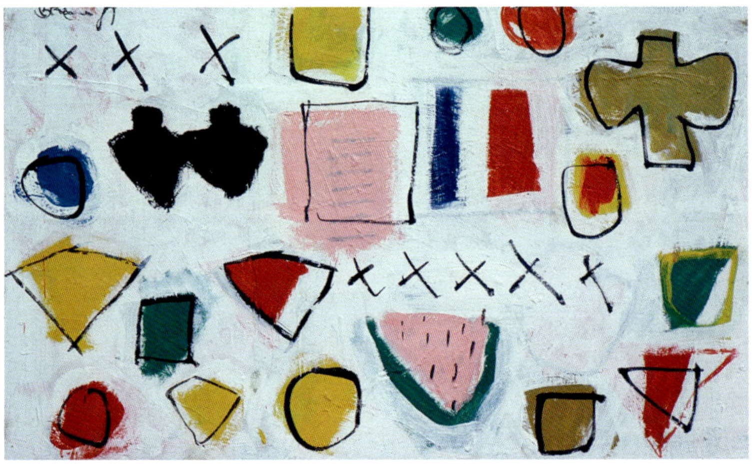

retrieve stories and memories from his own childhood (not simply the horror) and try to unlock such material from others. An enduring lesson for me.'[35]

Iskowitz took William on a research trip to the far north, flying over uncountable lakes and hundreds of miles of forest and tundra. It was after this visit that William began not only sketching bears but making them the subjects of his paintings.[36] Through the late 1970s he seems to have been painting bold compositions of abstract shapes of stripes, dots, crosses and rough triangles and circles that may have had their starting points in symbolism of birds, buildings or other objects – neither the paintings nor their titles are preserved, only some photographs. While this abstraction was to be left behind, lasting influences from Iskowitz can be detected in William's flat areas of colour enlivened by dots and his re-engagement with the vast north of his own country as an enduring subject.

Joady and William married at City Hall in Toronto in 1976 with only Joady's brother present – their friend Jeff Aaron, who had brought them, missed the ceremony as they didn't wait for him to return from parking the car.[37] They took a transatlantic trip to visit Joady's parents, who had moved to Somerset. In the blasting heat of the drought-ridden summer of '76 they wandered the country. William was absorbed immediately by the intimacy of the landscape and the richness of history evident in monuments all around. With the excitement of new subjects came the appetite for a new start in the old country. They decided to go back to Toronto only to pack up their Canadian lives.

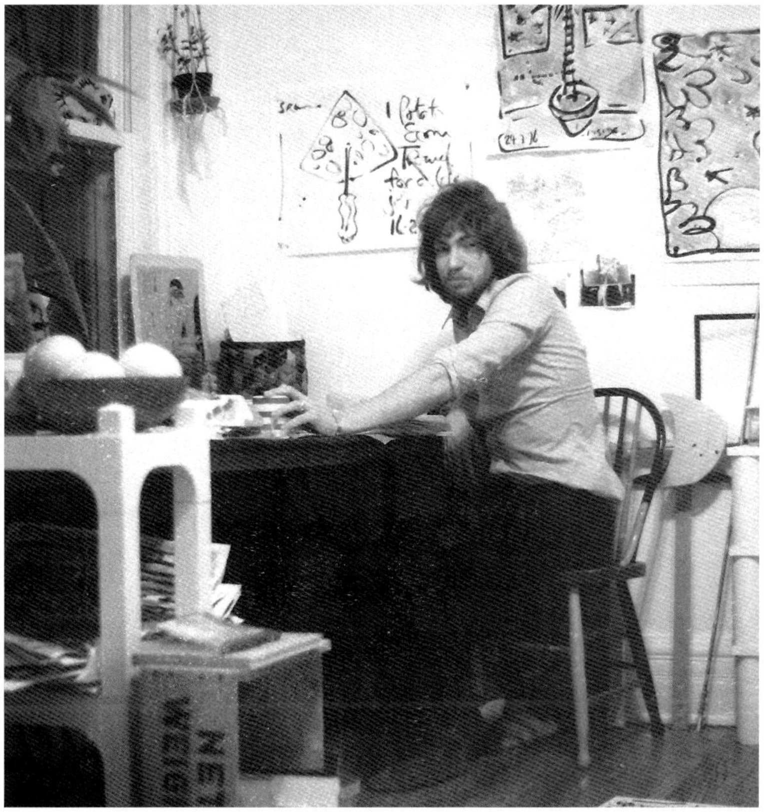

William working in a corner of the bedroom in Major Street, Toronto, 1976. Photo: Joady Brennan

I steal ideas, usually from children,
because they're smaller.

The old country
Somerset, London and Devon 1977–1990

In 1977, William and Joady sailed east with a multitude of trunks (painted yellow with pink polkadots) on a Polish liner, the *Stefan Batory*.[38] They arrived in Somerset and spent a few days with her parents in their villa on the edge of Taunton, Roughmoor House, before finding a cottage a few miles away at the village of Ash Priors. Finally, they moved to another cottage at nearby Buddle Oak, set in arable fields near Halse. At the age of twenty-four, William grew into his maturity an ocean's distance from his past. He fell into rural life: they had hens, a house rabbit called Bap and a collie called China. They saw a lot of Joady's mother ('Moot') and her two Irish wolfhounds, which would lean on William until he fell over – perhaps a glimmer of the *loup-garou* wolfman that would preoccupy him later. Neither Joady nor William drove at the time so they used bicycles and buses or had lifts with friends.

Opposite:
Untitled (church and cross), undated, *c.* 1981, mixed media on board, 75 x 60 cm

William's work occupied half the living space of the cottage. He often sat on the floor to paint panels against the wall. He continued the abstract work through the late 1970s but it seems to have come to an end as the history and environment of south-west England impinged. A painting dated 1978 appears to reference Beaker pottery, whitewashed buildings and a church. The last known abstracts are dated 1979, while some Somerset landscapes are dated 1980.

A visitor recalled: 'every surface held some drawing, painting or maquette that engaged the eye and intrigued the intellect.' William built a miniature furnace in the garden for melting

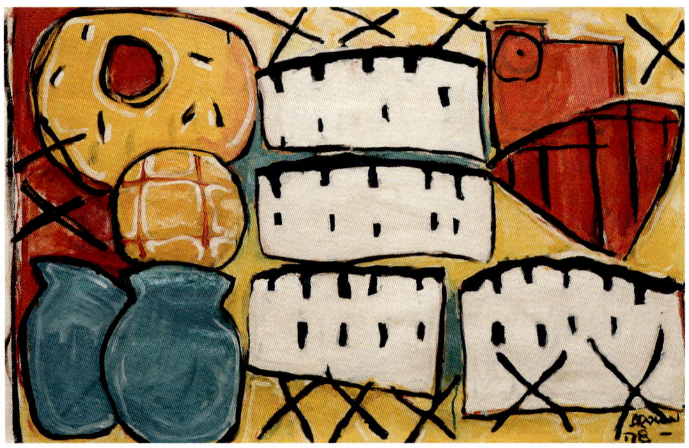

Untitled (houses, church, pots and bread), 1978, oil, dimensions unknown

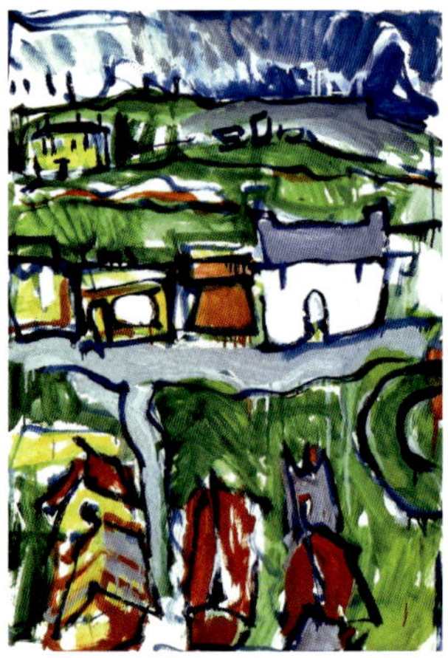

Right:
Norton Fitzwarren, 1980, oil, dimensions unknown

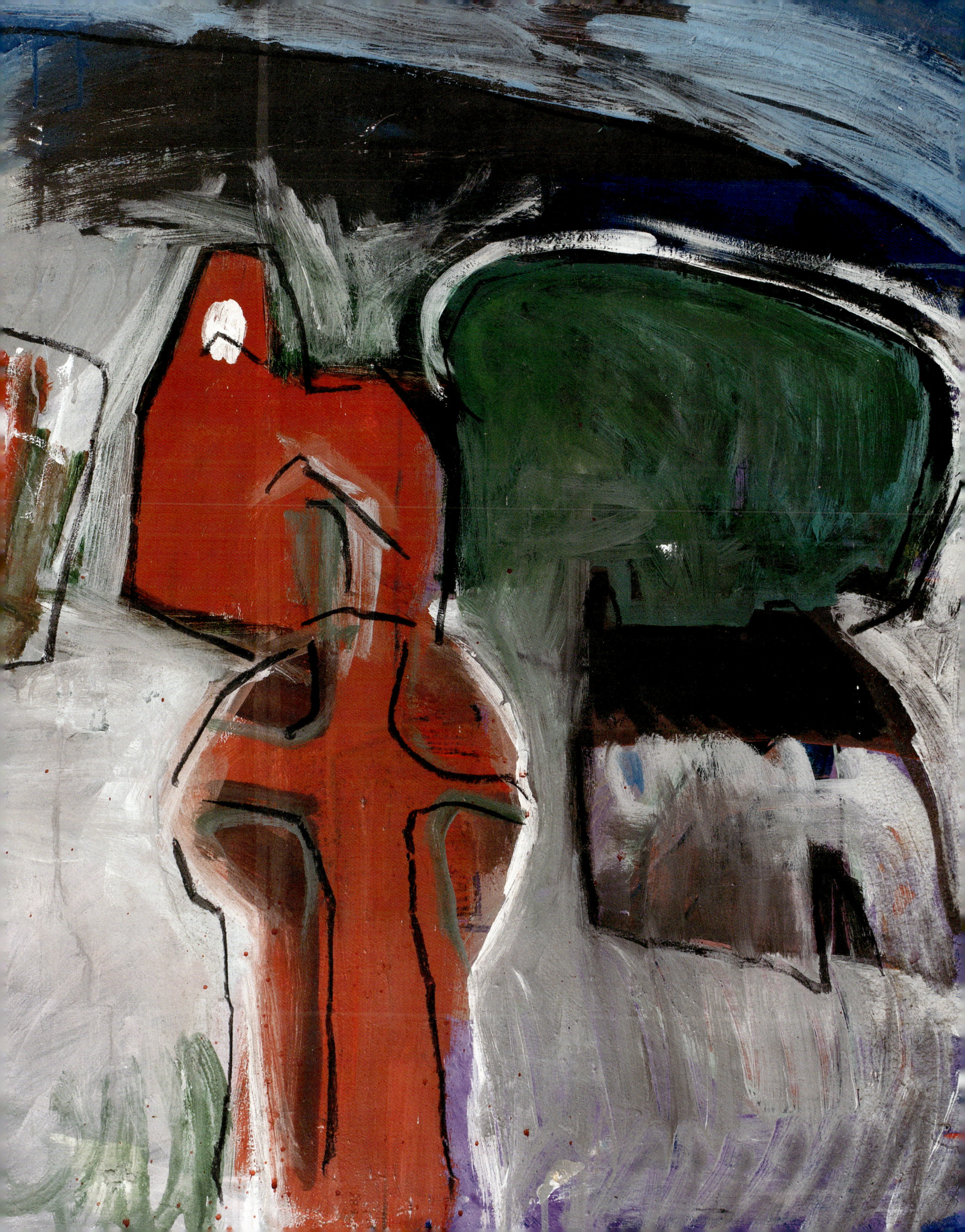

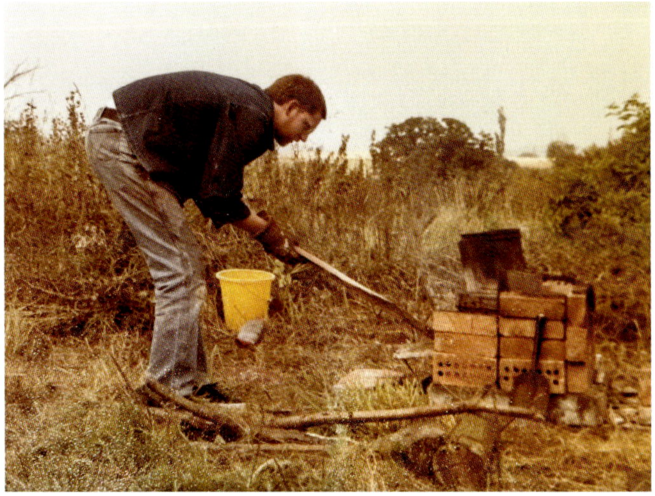

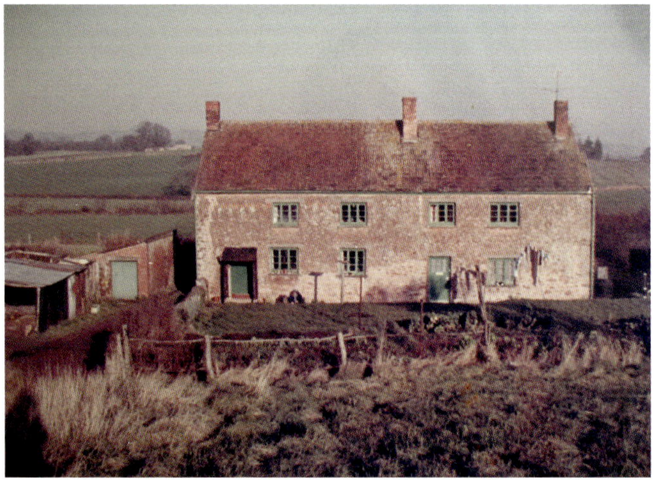

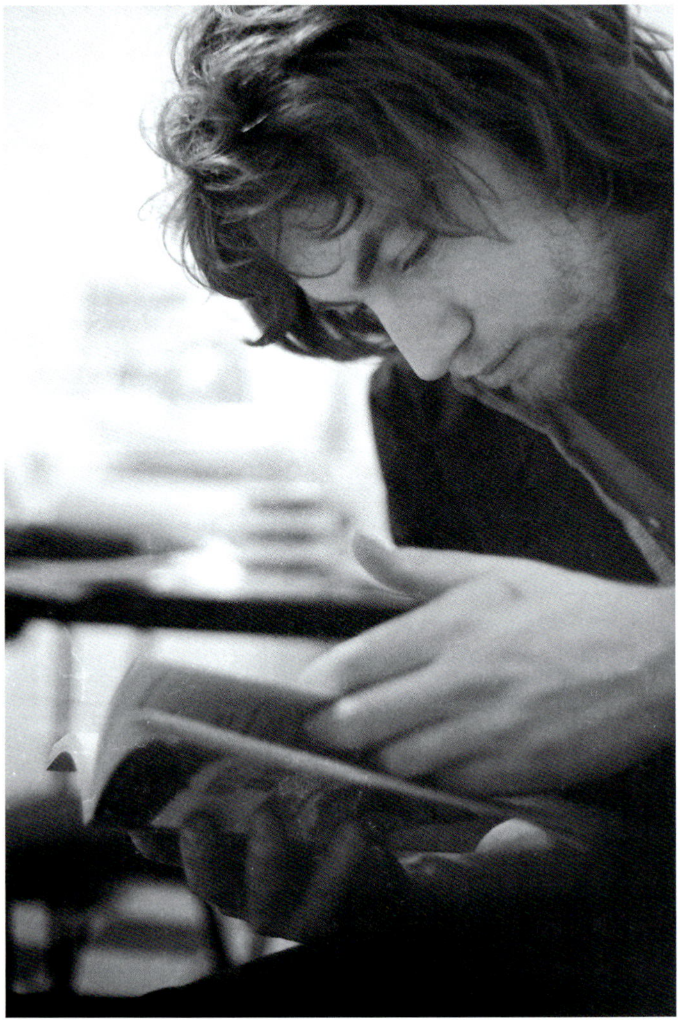

Top:
William at his furnace for casting, Buddle Oak. Photo: Joady Brennan

The cottages at Buddle Oak. Photo: Joady Brennan

William at Buddle Oak. Photo: Joady Brennan

lead pipes or aluminium cans to cast sculptures by the lost-wax process, as he had done with Phil York in Toronto. He worked outdoors on droll sculptures of animals, often using waste timber, polystyrene, and plaster poured into rubber gloves as moulds.[39] Sometimes he affixed models to paintings or placed sculptures in front of them to create the effect of a diorama [40]. He made an installation of several dogs constructed like crude benches.

Since money was tight, he took 'day jobs', first at a factory and later as a technician for three-dimensional work in the Foundation Course at Somerset College of Arts and Technology in Taunton, which gave him access to free resources and, importantly, to printing equipment. He had shown no interest in attending art school himself, but the association amused him and he was pleased to add it to his resumé. He found a larger workspace at the abandoned Tone textile mills near Wellington. As he had done in Toronto, he read extensively about art – never

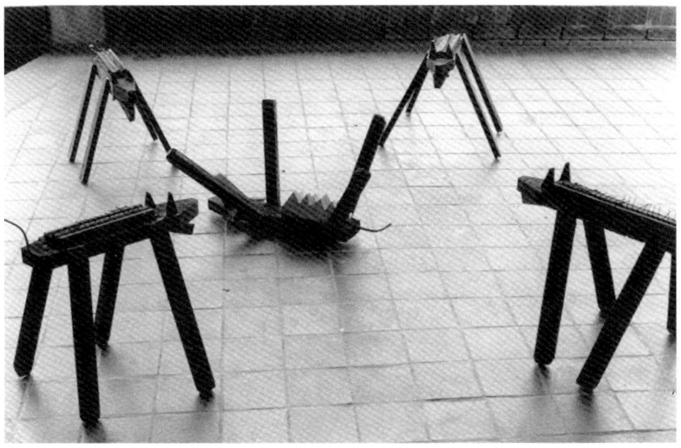

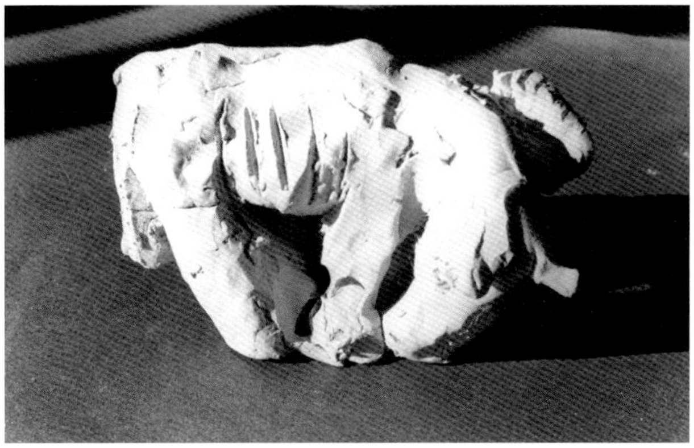

Left:
Down among the Dingoes (North Africa), 1984, timber and metal, assembled approximately 50 x 250 x 250 cm

Right:
Untitled (Dartmoor pony), c. 1983, ceramic, approximately 20 x 30 x 20 cm

theory but artist's lives – and focused relentlessly on art as his purpose and vocation. Joady recalls playing the 'burning house' game about what they imagined rescuing from a fire. Joady would save the crying baby; William would make off with the Vermeer.

William explored prehistory in his new surroundings – hillforts and standing stones – and they took some longer tours to explore antiquities in Ireland and the Penwith peninsula of Cornwall. William gloried in Somerset pubs where you could still play skittles and shove ha'penny in a lively community. He was popular and made friends through the art college, among them two brothers who were involved in arts education in the south-west, Malcolm and Garry Plastow, and the artist Peter Bartlett. Another new friend was Michael Clarke, with whom William went 'spelunking': exploring caves and tunnels. Michael and his elder brother, the writer Arthur C. Clarke, had grown up at Ballifants, Ash Priors, a ten-minute cycle ride from Buddle Oak.

The sociable, hard-drinking and prolific artist Mick Owens had studied at the Royal College of Art and taught at several art schools, including Taunton's.[40] Mick made bold, intuitive prints with a personal repertoire of symbols inspired by words or phrases. His example and technical support pushed on William's shift from sculpture towards printmaking as the companion to his painting, and his friendship catalysed William's fascination with North Africa. They began taking trips to Tunisia and Algeria together, often travelling recklessly: on one occasion they were shot at by police, on another Mick contracted intestinal parasites by drinking infected milk.

North Africa prompted rapid developments in William's work as he found new motifs that demanded expression, often in compositions of anachronistic or contrasting elements – animal and monumental, ancient and searingly modern. Over a period of a few years he found his lasting iconography in both painting and printmaking, a language capable of embracing complex themes with directness and apparent simplicity. He was drawn particularly as a motif to the Mirage fighter-bomber – a beast that spat cannon fire, rockets, missiles and bombs, used by the French and popular with other regional powers. He invariably showed a Mirage banking on its side to reveal its delta-winged, triangular silhouette and French air-force markings like a pair of eyes. An early example showed a wingtip almost touch the brown soil of Carthage, beside a snake, an ancient column and a crescent moon [38].

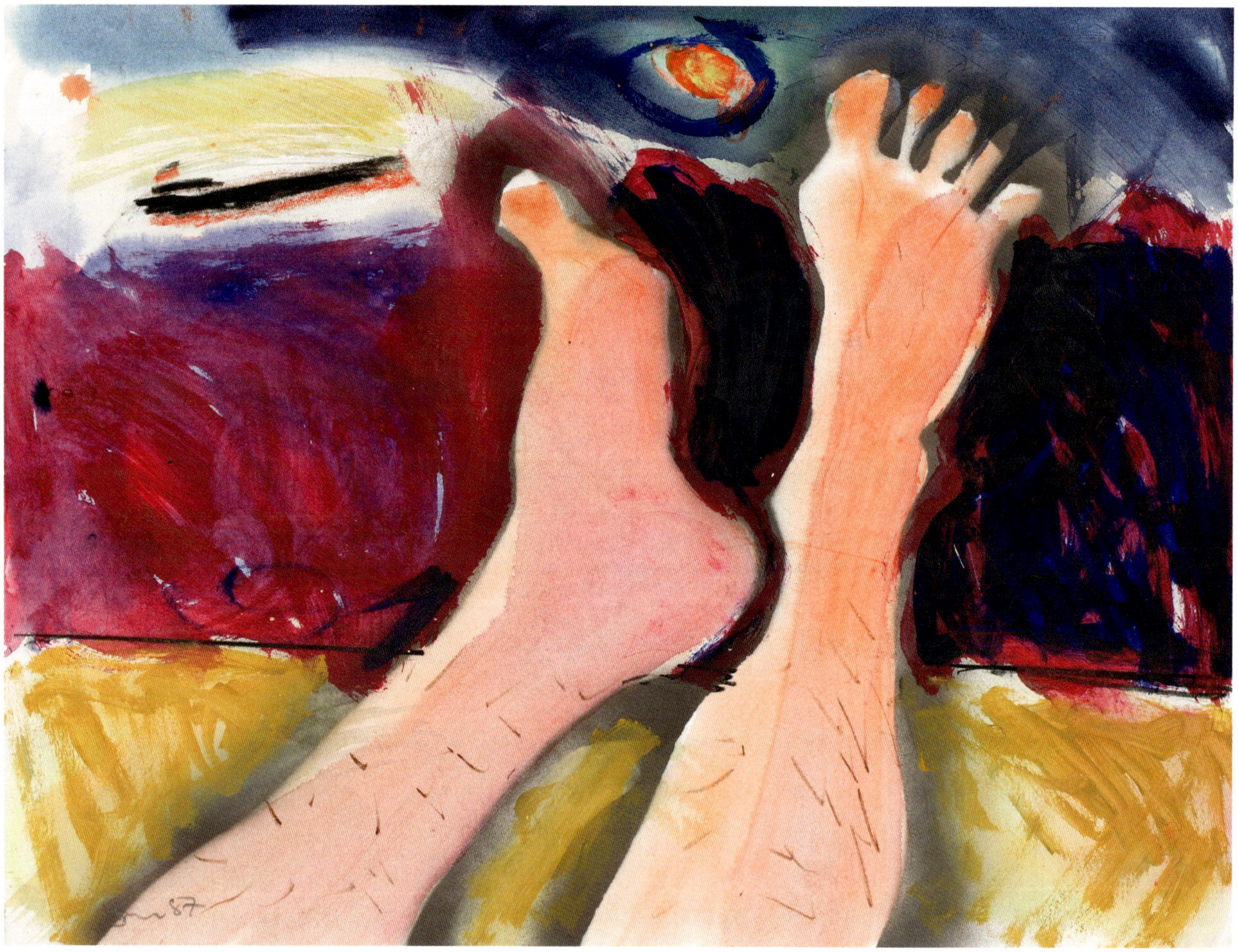

Untitled (North Africa), 1987, mixed media on paper, 50 x 60 cm

William joined the Masons in the mid-1980s, following in the footsteps of his father and encouraged by the Plastow brothers. If, as Tolstoy diagnosed in *War and Peace*, freemasons are divided according to their motivations – mysticism, guidance, ceremony and personal advancement – the greatest attraction for William was ritual and symbolism. He corresponded with the library and museum at Freemason's Hall, joined a lodge devoted to masonic research and took a correspondence course with the International School of the Golden Rosycross in Haarlem.[41] The chequerboard black and white of Masonic floors often appeared in paintings. He joined further lodges in the south-west (and later that of his future father-in-law at Llangeinor in south Wales).

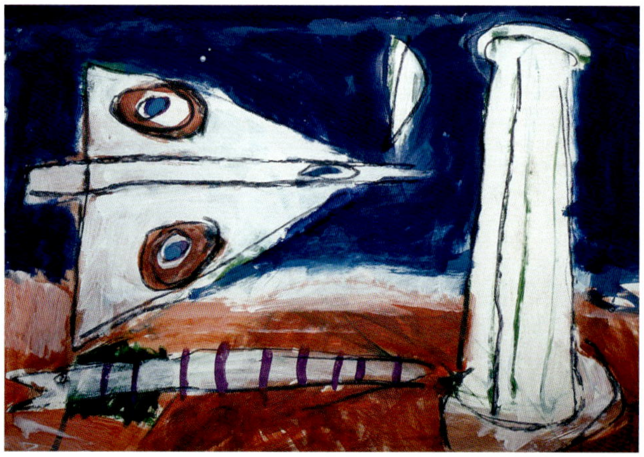

At Carthage I, 1985, mixed media on paper, 30 x 45 cm

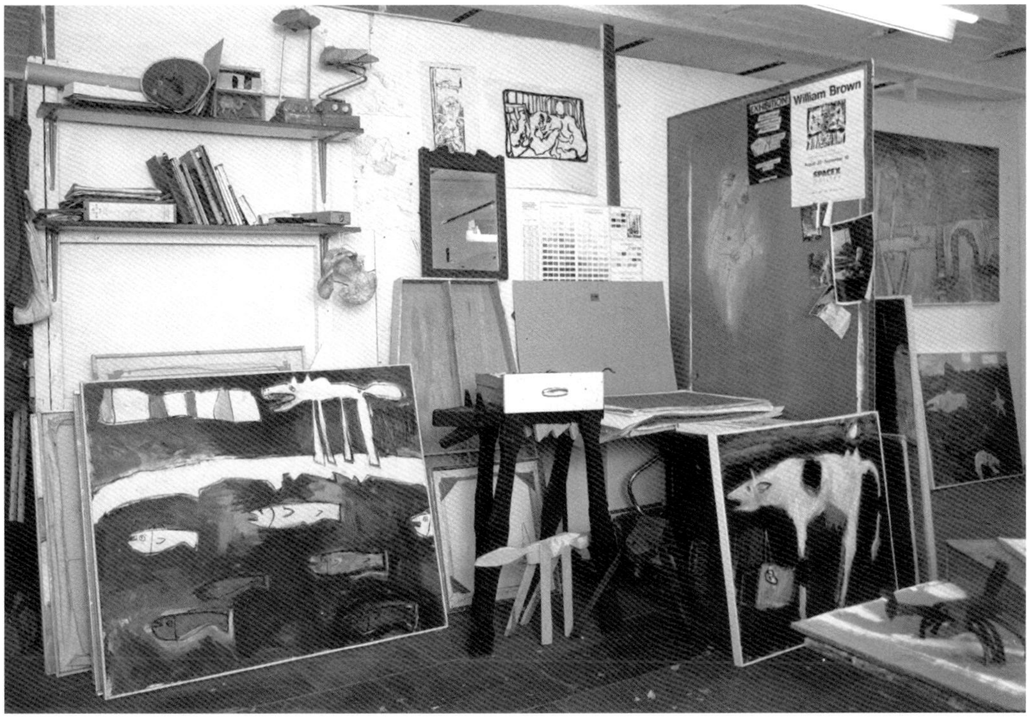

William's studio at Tone Mills, around 1985

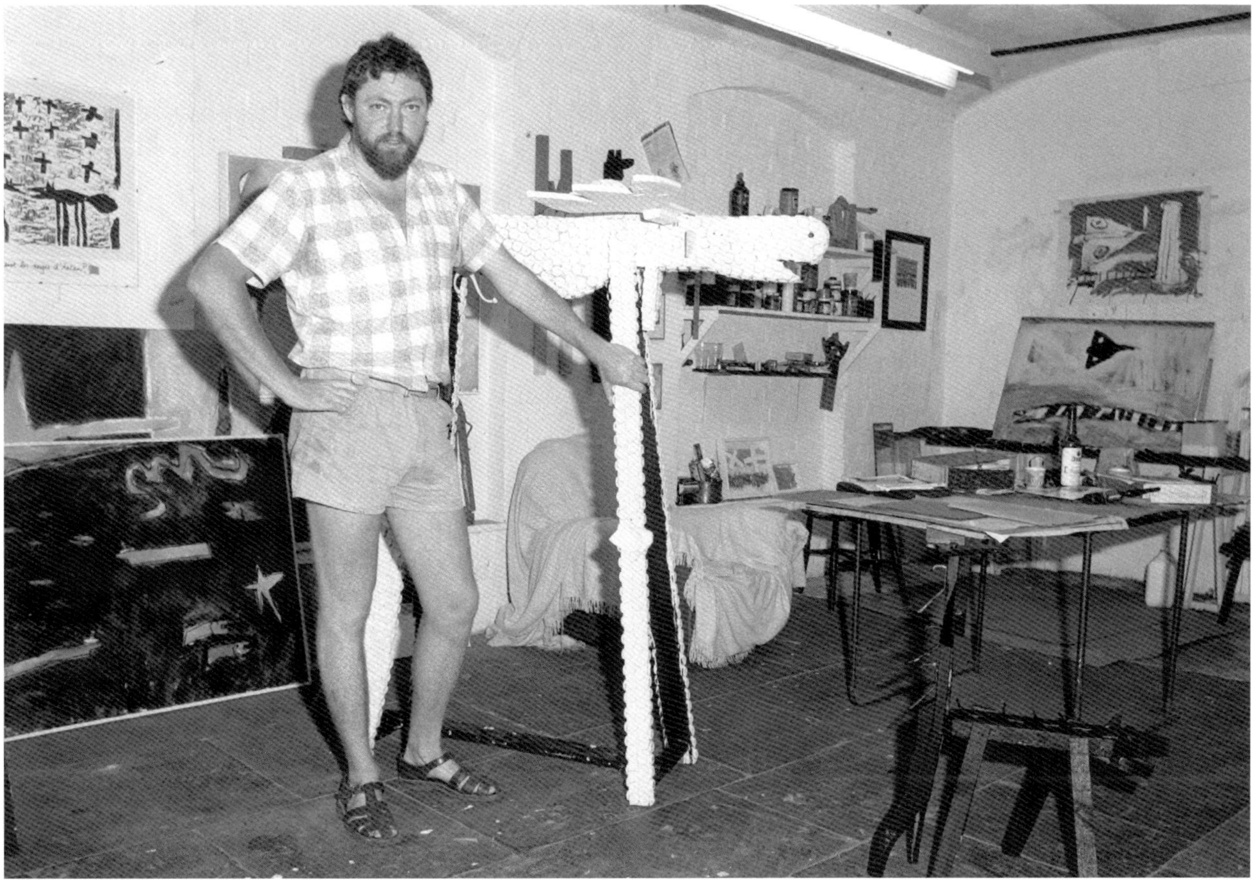

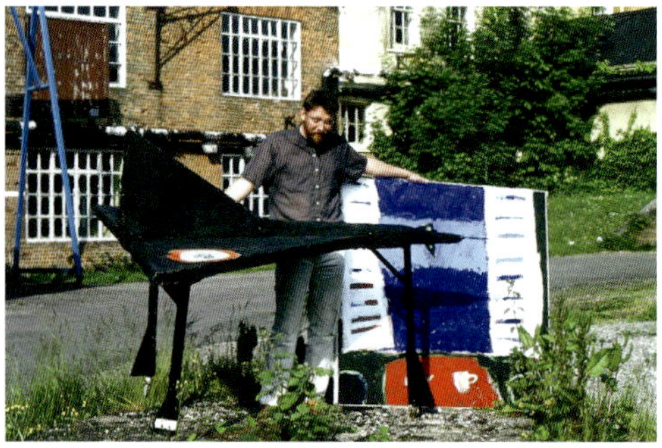

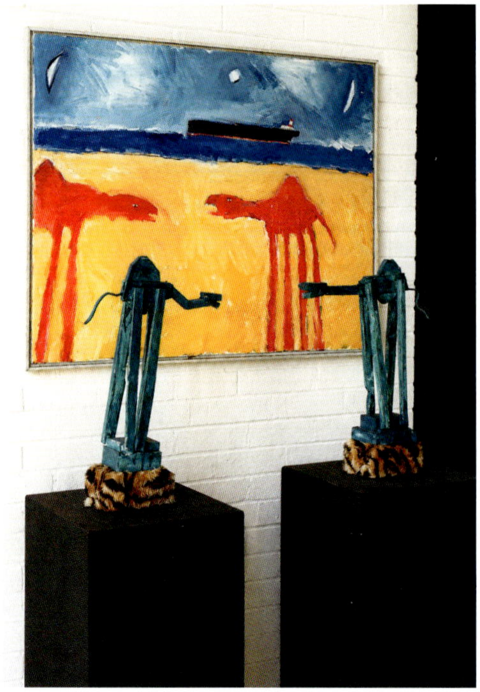

Quarrelling Camels, 1986, Installation, oil on canvas with fake fur and painted timber, approximately 200 x 140 x 50 cm

Top:
William outside Tone Mills in around 1984 with model of Mirage in front of painting

William began his commitment for the rest of his life to organising group exhibitions with fellow artists. Among the first were the Plastows and Peter Bartlett. An exhibition titled 'West Country Artists' took thirteen participants to Edinburgh College of Art for the Festival in 1981. A review in the *Glasgow Herald* noted: 'Some are less lively than others and a couple decidedly below par.'[42] William's work went unmentioned. By this time he was combining many of the motifs he would continue to use – wolves, moose, fishes, fighter jets, tankers, moon and stars. As in Canada, he used bold linear shapes but he was layering and mixing colours to a more painterly and less vivid effect than he would do a few years later.

Joady was now training as an art therapist in St Albans and William was leaving for a year in Morocco. They were focused on distinct lives and agreed on a separation in 1982. The stresses on the relationship increased when Joady's father died and her mother needed a lot of her attention. William was ill on his return from North Africa, bloated and suffering some kind of delirium. Joady had intended to come back to Halse but she moved instead to Taunton and took a job in a psychiatric hospital. They divorced in 1983, more through circumstance than breakdown, and they remained friends for the rest of William's life. Joady hadn't realised how ill he was: he had surgery for bowel cancer the next year at the Freemasons' Hospital in London; he announced that he was cured and never mentioned it again.

An unstable period followed for William. He slept on friends' sofas, then moved into his studio at the abandoned woollen mills. He made extra money as an occasional pub bouncer. When Tony Foster of the South-West Arts Council met William it proved lifechanging. Tony was working on the Artists in Schools programme for Devon with Bob Clement, the innovative art advisor to the county's schools. Bob was in the midst of writing *The Art Teacher's Handbook* (1986) and was passionate that children should have tools to express themselves.[43] He and Tony sought out William in the former textile factory:

> We wandered together through the empty and derelict spaces of the old mill, littered with bits and bobs of old machinery, spools and bobbins [...] We finally turned a corner and found ourselves in a floor to ceiling paradise of drawings, paintings and woodcuts celebrating the flora, fauna of the wild life of Canada! There were polar bears raiding rubbish dumps, moose in transit and wolves cogitating, all in bleak and frozen landscapes and deep and dark forests. We were greeted enthusiastically by William who instantly produced a bottle of sherry and three glasses so that we could have a 'proper' private view of his work. It was immediately obvious that William,

ebullient and articulate, amusing and outgoing would be a knock-out artist for a residency, and that the nature and free-wheeling quality of his work would be of great appeal to children.[44]

They chose a grammar school for a ten-day residency, where William encouraged children to approach their work with freedom. Bob watched them learning that 'art can be amusing and down to earth as well as inventive and highly skilled.'[45] More residencies followed. Bob purchased a set of twelve of William's woodcuts to be displayed for a term at a time in Devon schools. Aged thirty, William had his first solo exhibition, at Spacex in Exeter, and the next year he showed paintings and sculptures alongside Peter Bartlett in Taunton. He would have nearly fifty solo exhibitions in twenty-five years.

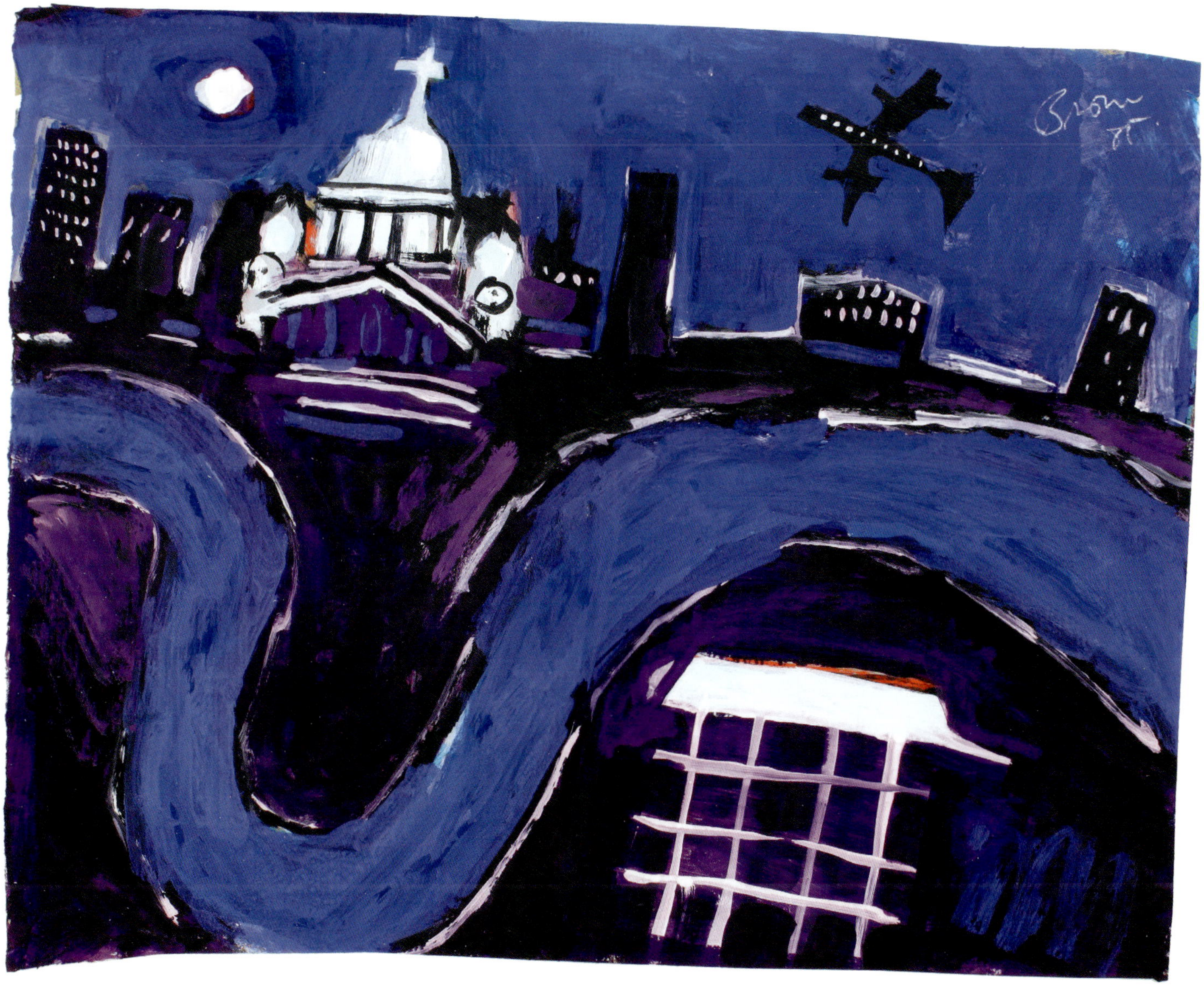

Untitled (River Thames with St Paul's and the Cutty Sark), 1985, mixed media on paper, 50 x 60 cm

William married again in December 1983, this time disastrously, to a Devon girl called Ruth. They moved to south London, where he rented flats variously at New Cross and Upper Brockley Road, and he worked as a painter and decorator, but the relationship broke down immediately and they divorced. William made map-like drawings of the landmarks along a snake-like Thames [41] but it was an unhappy period. He told a story as emblematic as a dream: depressed at not being paid for a job, he barely noticed on an escalator in the Underground that a hole in his tool bag had started to drop screws and nails; he heard grinding as the escalator shuddered to a stop and he hurried off.[46]

He had taken out a lease on a ground-floor flat at 23 Leonard Street in the City of London when he was offered a place to stay back in Devon by Bernard Samuels, the inspirational director of Plymouth Arts Centre, who was credited with having given first exhibitions to both Beryl Cook and Ben Hartley. The dual location gave him a chance to develop projects such as the competition commission to make an artwork for a railway bridge in Reading and to continue his print workshops for children in Devon. At a school in Plympton in 1987 he met Carys Griffiths, the deputy-head. Carys had changed from secondary to primary education because she enjoyed a wide range of subjects, and when her school was offered an artist in residence, she accepted with alacrity. William appeared a few weeks later. Carys assigned an empty classroom to use half the time as a studio and half to take a group of children. Although she had to tell William off for going to the pub for lunch and returning past his best, the classes soon took off. The children had a lively time drawing and producing huge, spectacular

Press photograph after a workshop at Tavistock Primary School in around 1990

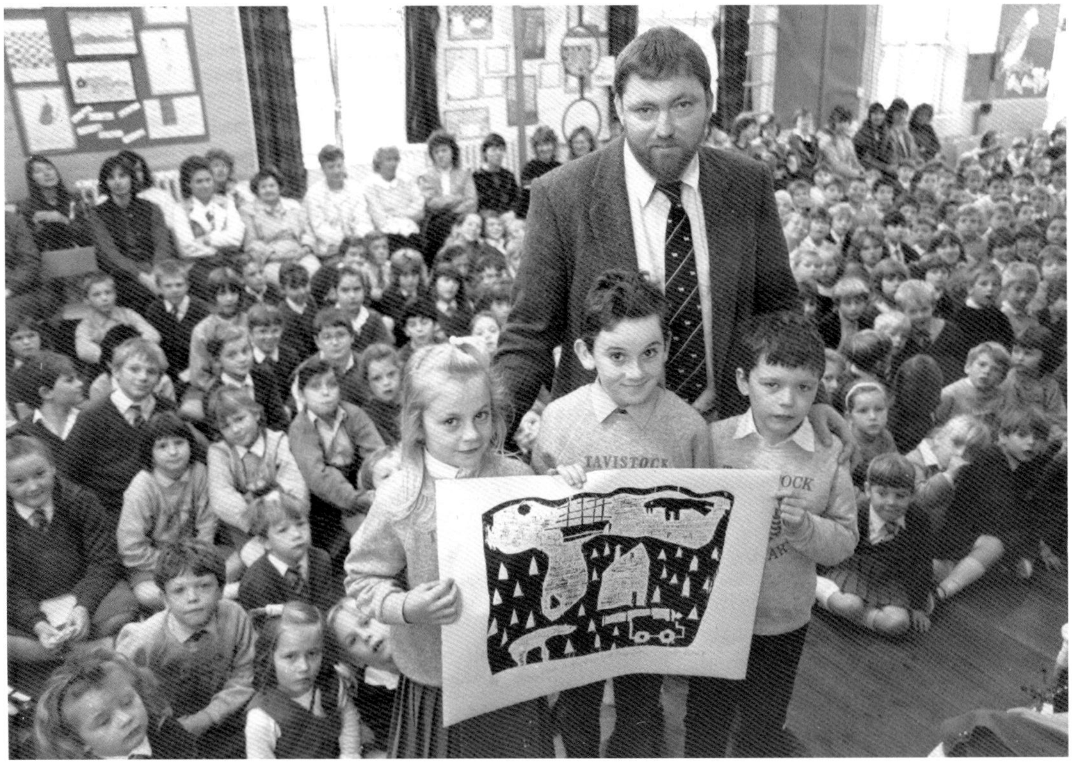

woodcuts. William's enjoyment in the directness of the imagery produced by the children began to spill over into his own work.[47]

One evening, Carys invited William for a drink. They walked together to Buckland Abbey and on to the beguilingly named Who'd Have Thought It Inn at Milton Combe. William was soon singing with the regulars and, as Carys described it, he was 'pretty merry' as they walked the mile and a half back through fields to her home at Winsbeer Cottages near Buckland Monachorum. She put him to bed with the help of her son Huw. The following night William asked to take Huw and Carys out for supper and remained presentable throughout.

Carys was thirteen years older than William, divorced and with two grown children – Huw then about to go to university and Sue training to be a doctor. They continued meeting when his residency ended, in London when Carys joined working groups for the national curriculum and in Devon when William came west. When he was flying to Canada for a family visit he asked Carys if she would like to join him. On the return plane he said he thought it would be a good idea to get married, which they did in July 1988.

Carys was preoccupied with looking after her parents in Bridgend, the other side of the Bristol Channel, a circuitous journey by motorway. She had been looking for a promotion in Devon when William suggested that she could try for one in south Wales. Her parents adored William, and he was already helping to take care of them. As to his painting, he said he could do that anywhere. Carys was soon offered the headship of Plasnewydd primary school in Maesteg.

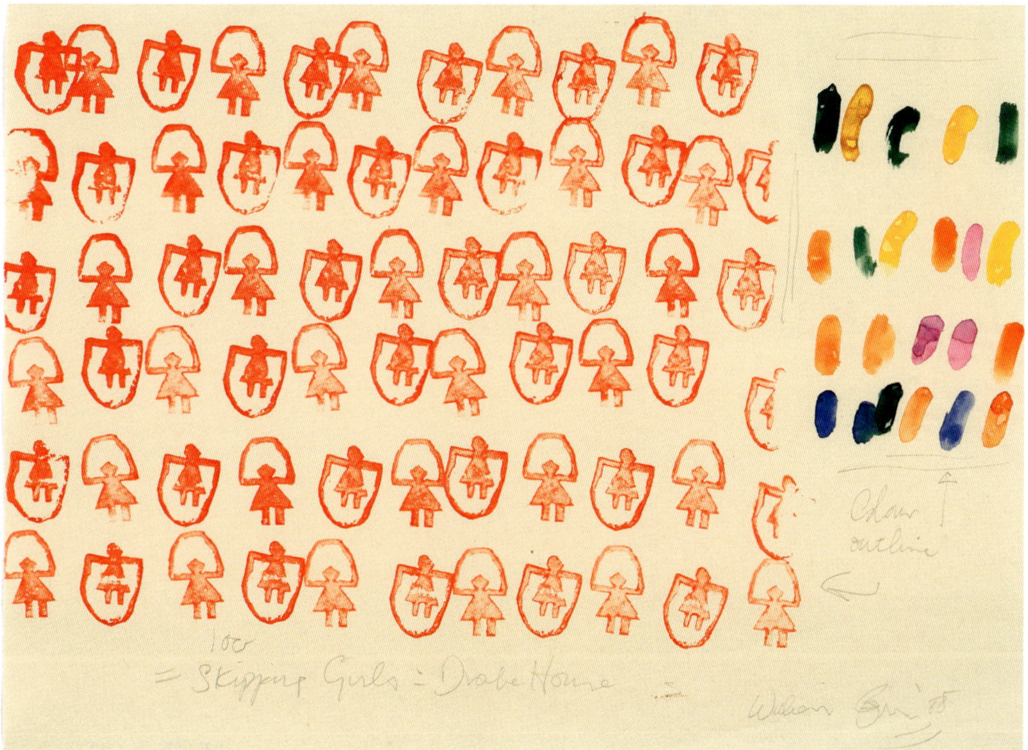

=100 Skipping Girls in Drake House, 1988, potato print, 48 x 64 cm

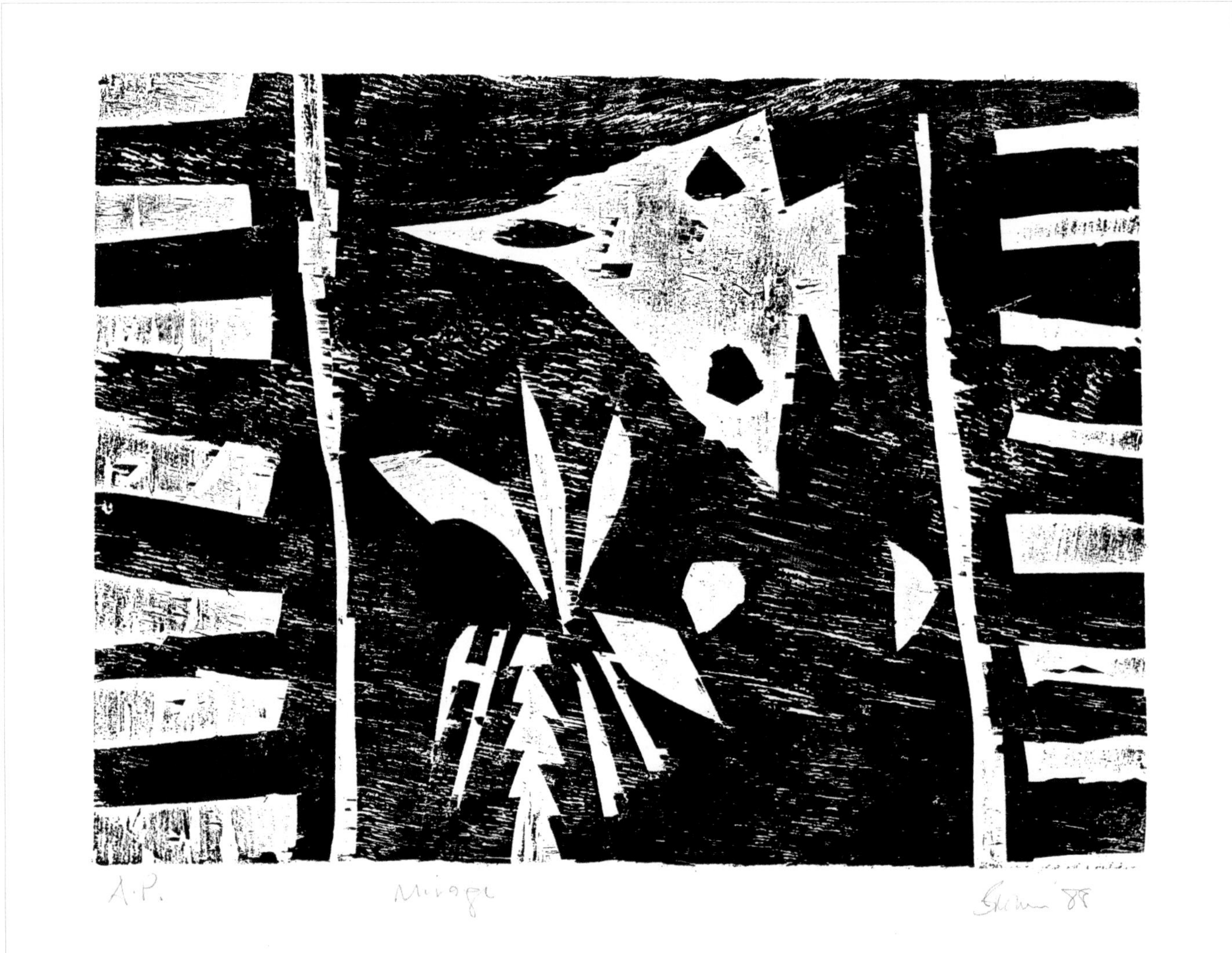

Mirage, 1988,
woodcut, 37 x 45 cm

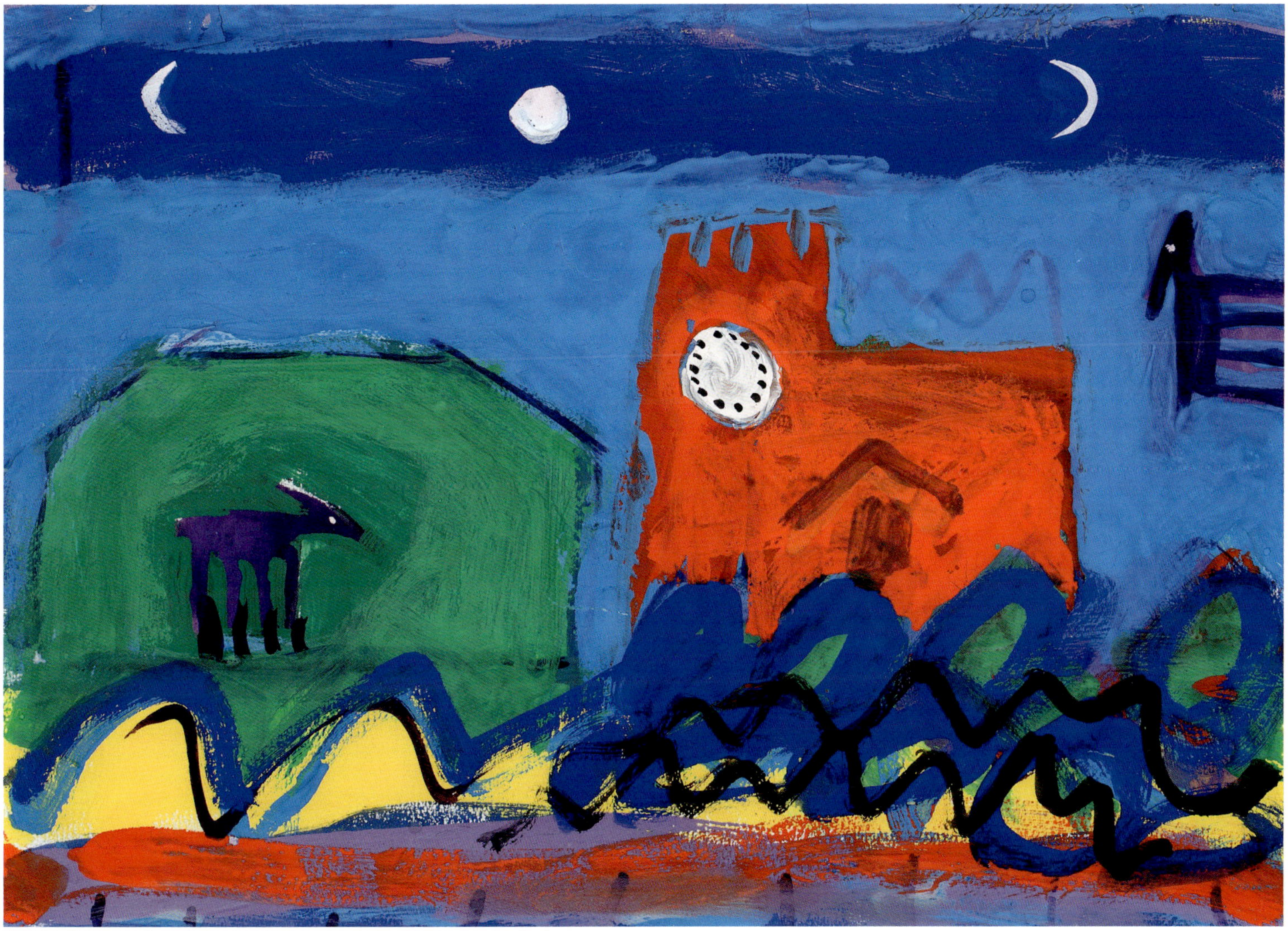

Buckland Abbey,
1989, acrylic on card,
35 x 40 cm

I am a narrative painter

… stories continue to enthral me.

Wales
1990–2008

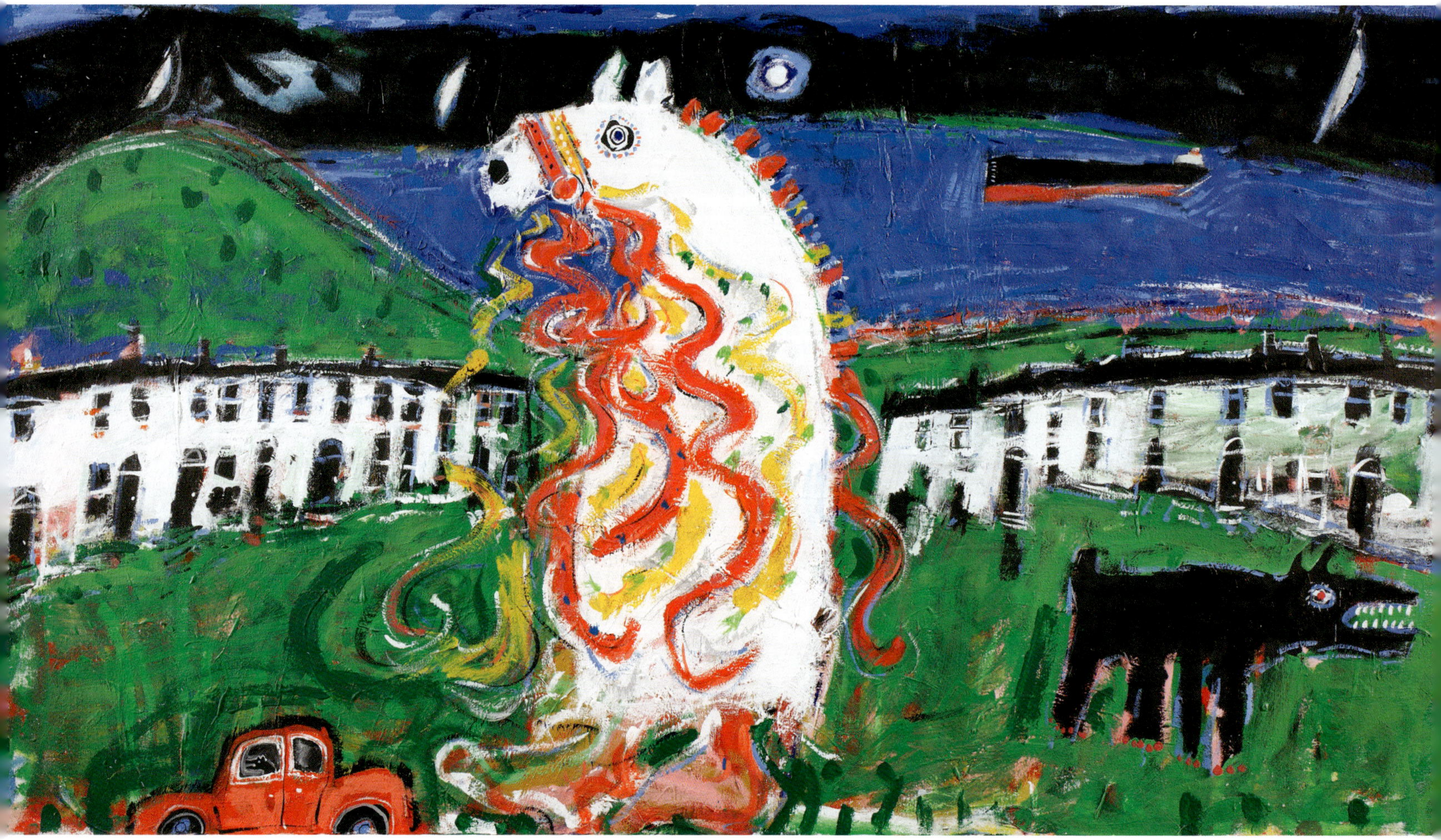

Mynd am Dro (Going for a Stroll), undated, *c.* 1996, acrylic on canvas, 94 x 173 cm

Perhaps William enjoyed a statelessness that let him belong anywhere, yet he seemed to find a special place among his fellow Celts when he made Wales his home. He quickly gained creative allies, one of whom was the poet Malcolm Parr, who said: 'The arrival of William Brown was one of the best things to ever happen to the arts in Wales'. Alison Bevan reiterates: 'what an incredible catalyst for good in the arts in Wales William was, bringing artists, poets and other creative people together; championing and supporting other artists; initiating projects and exhibitions.'[48]

Carys had grown up around Bridgend, where her father, Herbert Davies, had been a noted headmaster and her mother, Catherine, a teacher. She found a house close to her parents in Bridgend, jammed into the curving medieval street Newcastle Hill, halfway between the ancient bridge over the River Ogmore that gave the town its name and, higher up, the Norman castle and St Illtyd's Church. The house was comfortable and airy, with a courtyard garden at the back. William set about learning Welsh, which Carys had spoken in her childhood.

Carys asked William to do something about her new school's offering in art. He created a gallery in the basement, boarding the walls, patching up the floor and installing lighting, and invited some of the artists he had met already to show there, including Tony Goble, Adrian Metcalfe, and the 'Swansea Lowry', Jack Jones. The gallery was opened to the public on selected evenings and to the schoolchildren all day. His workshops were as popular as ever.

He gave printmaking classes and demonstrations at other schools in the area. The head of Garth primary at Maesteg, Terry L. Williams, said: 'William had the knack of getting the best out of all the pupils and making it look simple. The staff used to enjoy watching him and learn some new skills themselves.'[49] William sparkled at the interactions. At Gütersloh in Germany he provided similar workshops for the art educator Johannes Glaw at a grammar school and at the Symposium for Junge Kunst/Young Arts in 1993 and 2000, which brought students from Germany, Russia, Poland, the Czech Republic, France, the Netherlands and Peru. William 'infected the group with his brilliance and enthusiasm'. On a return trip to Canada his sister accompanied him for visits to primary schools at Niagara Falls organised by the local art college and saw a vignette of his interactions: 'There was a little boy who told Will that he could not draw. Will was very encouraging to this young fellow and said he should not worry about this and, believe it or not, this kid was drawing like a house on fire by the end of the first class.'[50]

Below, left: *Bridgend,* 1997, woodcut in two colours, 30 x 21 cm

William and Carys at Coney Beach, Porthcawl, in around 1995

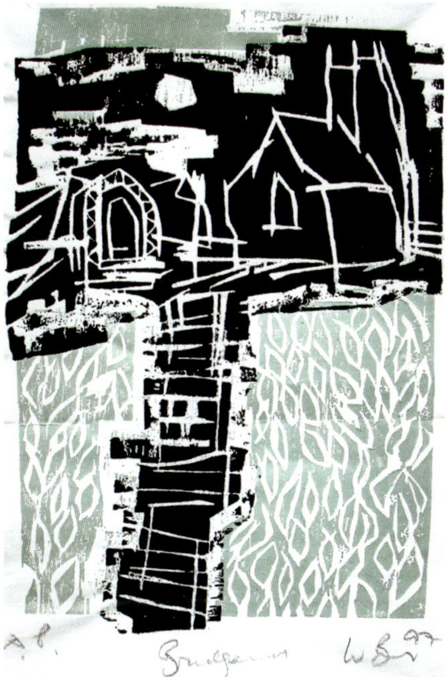

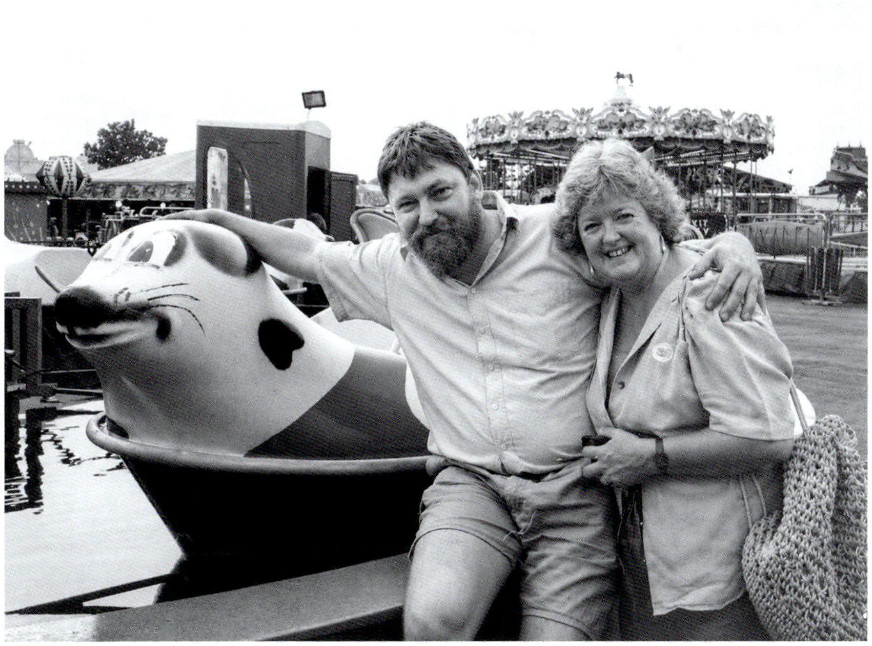

This joy in working with children would continue until around 2000, when William decided to keep more time for painting. He had less enthusiasm for working in art schools. When Robert Harding invited him to Carmarthen's, William was 'brilliant as a lecturer with all the fine art students but he obviously did not relish such situations as he turned down a repeat a couple of years later'.[51]

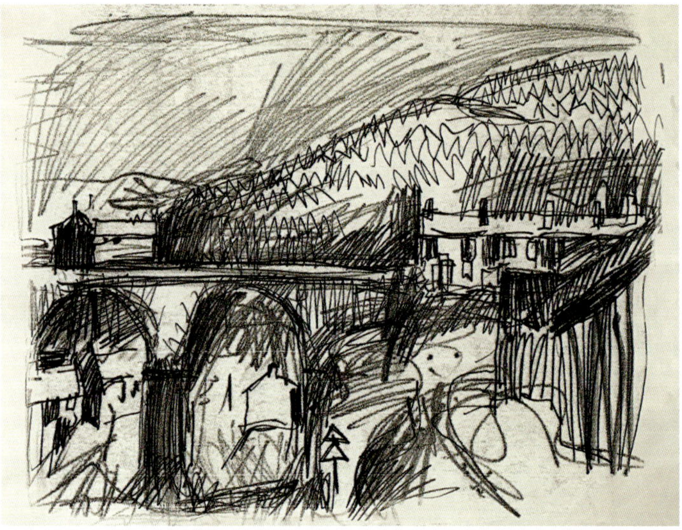

Untitled (South Wales landscape), undated, *c.* 1992, monoprint, 50 x 65 cm

Soon after relocating, William walked up the steps to the imposing Glynn Vivian Art Gallery, opposite the library and police station in Swansea. He met Keith Bayliss, artist and community arts officer, who would become a close collaborator. Keith offered William a role as a community artist with a project at Rhos in the Swansea valley. He noticed immediately William's facility to make friends of strangers and integrate into the community. 'It was as if he had always been there,' Keith said. An exhibition of the work produced was shown at the Glynn Vivian in 1990, titled *Tangled Roots*.[52] Keith, William and Malcolm Parr went on to work with five primary schools in the valley, explicitly introducing them to expressionist and surrealist approaches. This led in 1993 to an exhibition and a booklet titled *Image and Word: The Five Schools Project*.

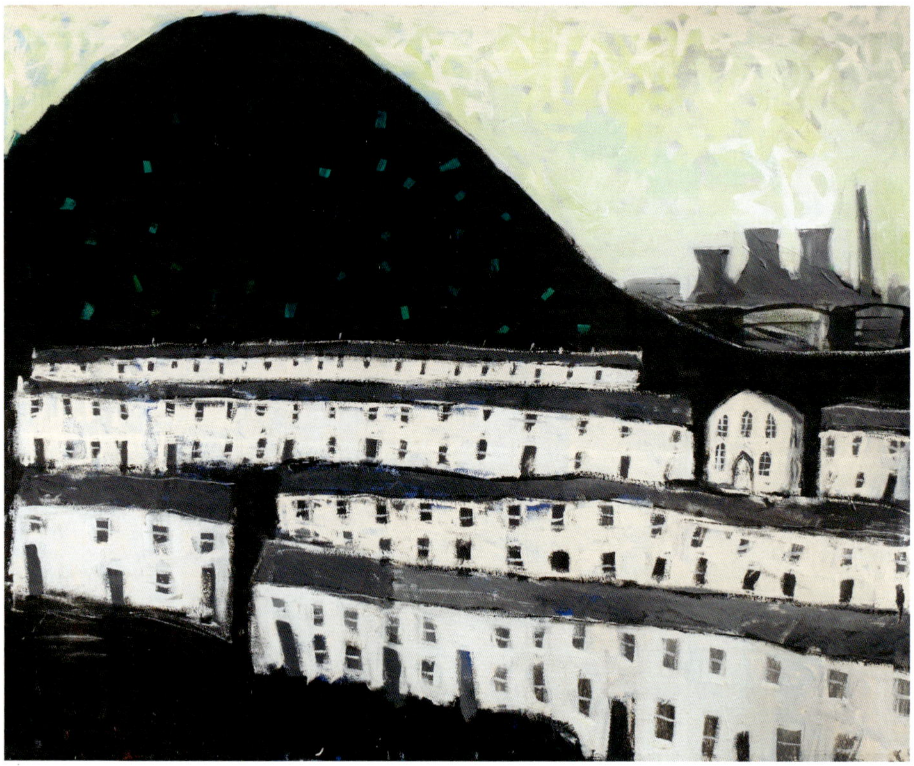

Bryncoch 1, 1992, oil on canvas, 126 x 150 cm

Working in the Swansea valley introduced him to farms and rolling hills but also to a landscape that was radically new to him. He began to apply the pictorial thinking he had developed in North Africa to his latest environment. The view towards Baglan from the village of Bryncoch where the road crossed from the Swansea valley to the Neath valley on the way home to Bridgend engaged him particularly with its contrasts of hills, houses and chapels with the behemoth of the chemical works on the coast beyond.

He found a studio in a building run by the Association of Artists and Designers in Wales (AADW) at Collingdon Road in Cardiff Bay, taking a room next to the painter Anthony Evans. From there he moved in 1992 to studio 2D on the second floor of Cardiff's Old Library, as central to the city as it was possible to be. He joined an eclectic community of some forty artists, laying the foundations for innumerable collaborative projects. He would explore the labyrinthine Victorian building and take visitors up a ladder to watch the life of the city from the roof. Its exhibition space was much visited by city-centre workers and William put on several shows in the next three years with the administrator Ron Adam.

A co-conspirator in printmaking was the American-born artist Paul Peter Piech, who had come to Britain as a GI at the end of the War and lived a few miles from Bridgend in Porthcawl. They curated an exhibition together at the Old Library in 1993, *Someday My Prints*, that showcased seventeen professional south Wales printmakers alongside work by students from South Glamorgan College of Education and the Llanover Hall adult education classes. William was a compassionate friend through hard times and they often editioned prints together until Piech's death in 1996. A photograph shows the two inky-fingered artists at a table with a glass plate and roller.

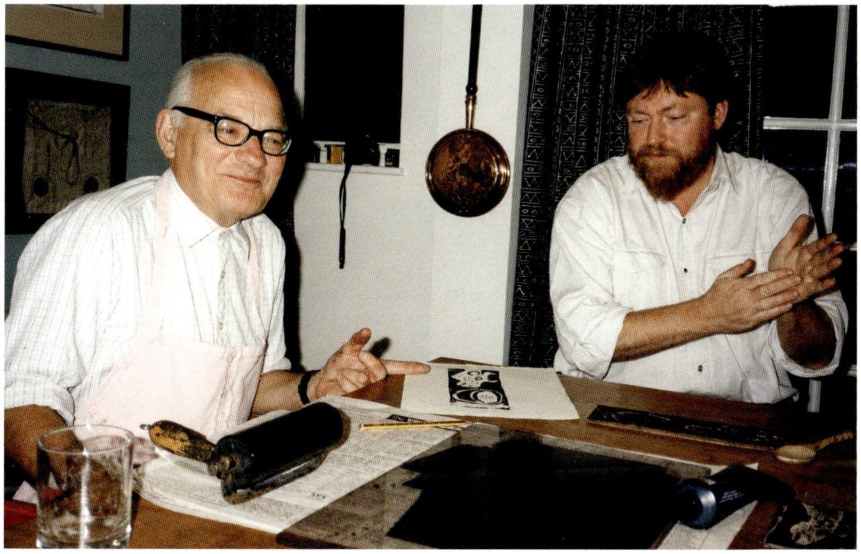

Poster by Paul Peter Piech for Ars Celtica exhibition, Swansea, 1993

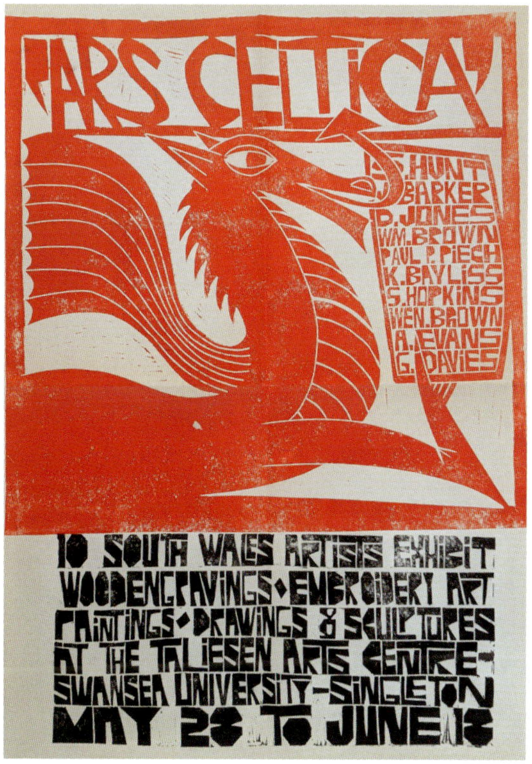

An impromptu printing session with Paul Peter Piech at the dining room table in Newcastle Hill, around 1994

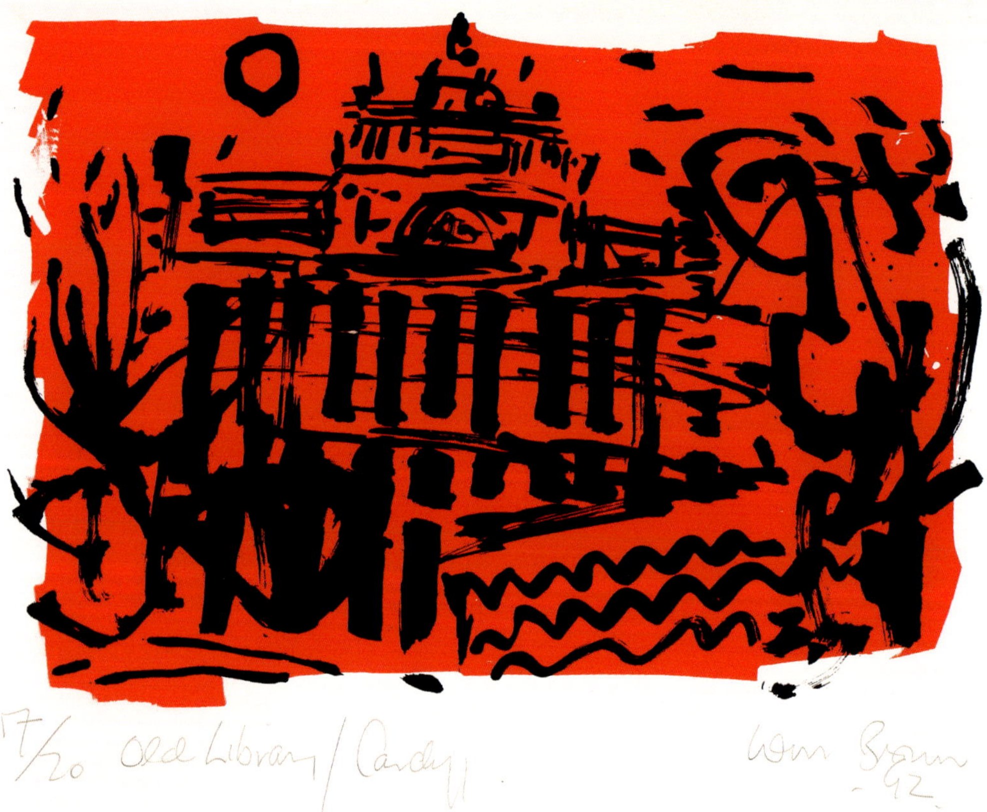

Old Library / Cardiff, 1992, screenprint, 40 x 45 cm

Poster with image by William for Contemporary Printmaking in Wales touring exhibition, 1993

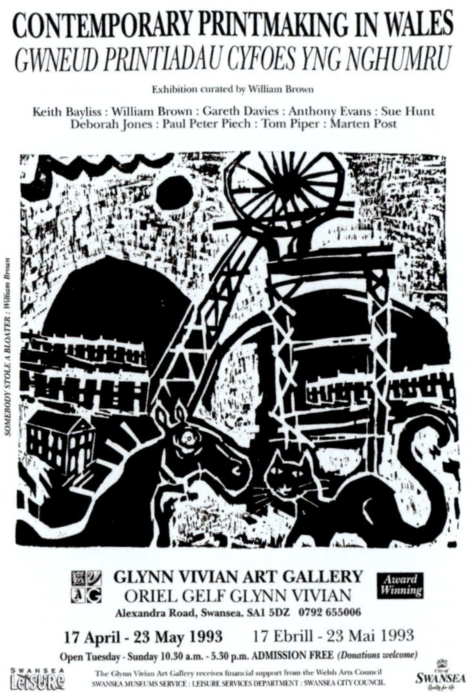

William curated another mixed exhibition, *Contemporary Printmaking in Wales*, which toured extensively in the early 1990s. In 1994, he organised with the ceramicist Peter Wills an exhibition called *6″ x 6″* that engaged with artists across the world to produce works 6 inches square. It began in Peter's home, along the street in Newcastle Hill, but the idea was embraced by other galleries as a touring show. It eventually included 120 artists. These efforts inspired Adrian Paul Metcalf to create a lively touring exhibition of box art in 1995, *Open Boxes*, in which William took part.

Despite this success at organising events, William was often impatient of arts organisations that seemed unable to act with similar speed and simplicity. In an aside he wrote, 'There is no sense of Urgency among the Salaried.'[53] It transpired that greater powers than the residents had designs on the Old Library and wanted it to become a glossily international contemporary art gallery. William battled for the rearguard but in January 1996 the new Centre for Visual Art evicted all its artists. (It opened in 1999 and closed a year later.)

For the next few months William borrowed a space in the studios of the ceramic sculptor Michael Flynn on Northcote Lane in the Roath district of Cardiff, with the sculptors Pete Bailey and Claire Curneen and the painter Tony Goble. Claire recalls of William: 'He was full of life, and that generation of artist felt like a dying breed. Burnt the candle at both ends, but seemed like a gentle kind soul and seemed highly intelligent. He filled the room.'[54]

For his next and ultimately most rewarding studio William was loaned St Stephen's church in the village of Llangynwyd, on the road between Bridgend and Maesteg. The building had been repurposed previously as a school and a hall but was disused and dilapidated. It was cold and damp in winter but it offered a huge space where William could work without interruption. He caught the bus from Bridgend, a commuter to his occupation. When the church was put up for auction, Carys bought it and William took the title of Abbot.

Curators saw the magnetism of William's work and offered major solo exhibitions. The first was at the Glynn Vivian, where Alison Lloyd (later Alison Bevan) gave him an exhibition in their spacious extension gallery and published a colour catalogue. He produced the largest paintings he had ever done, 2.3 metres wide. The new works included magnificent diptychs showing Berguette in northern France, threatened by the black wave of an approaching storm [102]. Other major paintings continued his North African and Canadian themes. However, the exhibition also began a breakthrough by bringing a new boldness of colour and extreme scale to tartan polar bears and first steps towards the exploration of beast-like bogeymen, the Mari Lwyd and loup-garou, which the title of the show alluded to: *What's Behind the Blanket?*

At Newport Museum and Art Gallery, Sandra Jackaman booked him for a similar show two years later. He made new work again, building on his interest in loup-garou and Mari Lwyd. Others among the new paintings were about Newport's distinctive landscape.

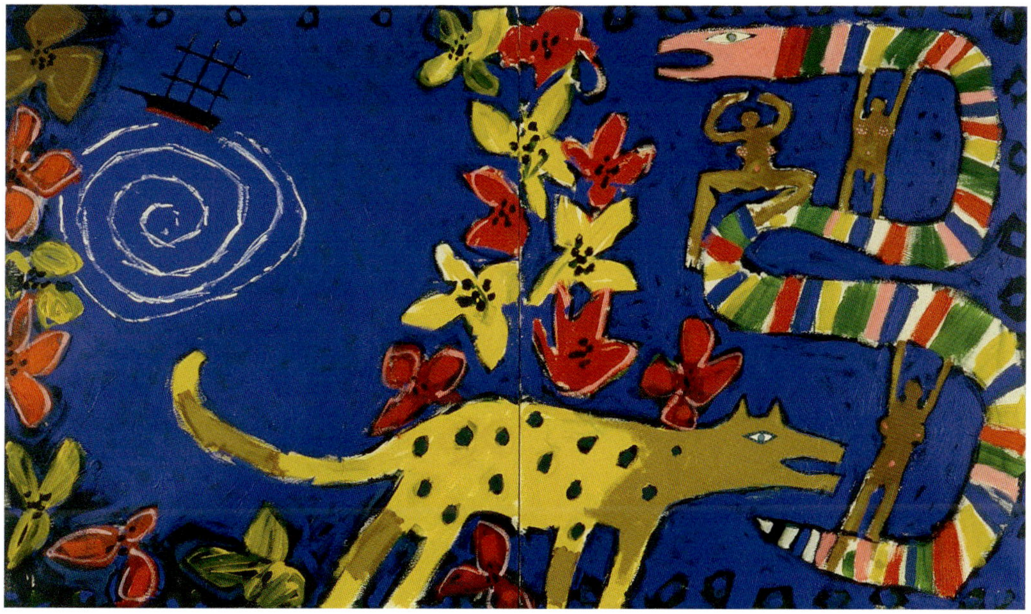

The Drunken Boat (diptych), 1996, oil on canvas, 152 x 228 cm

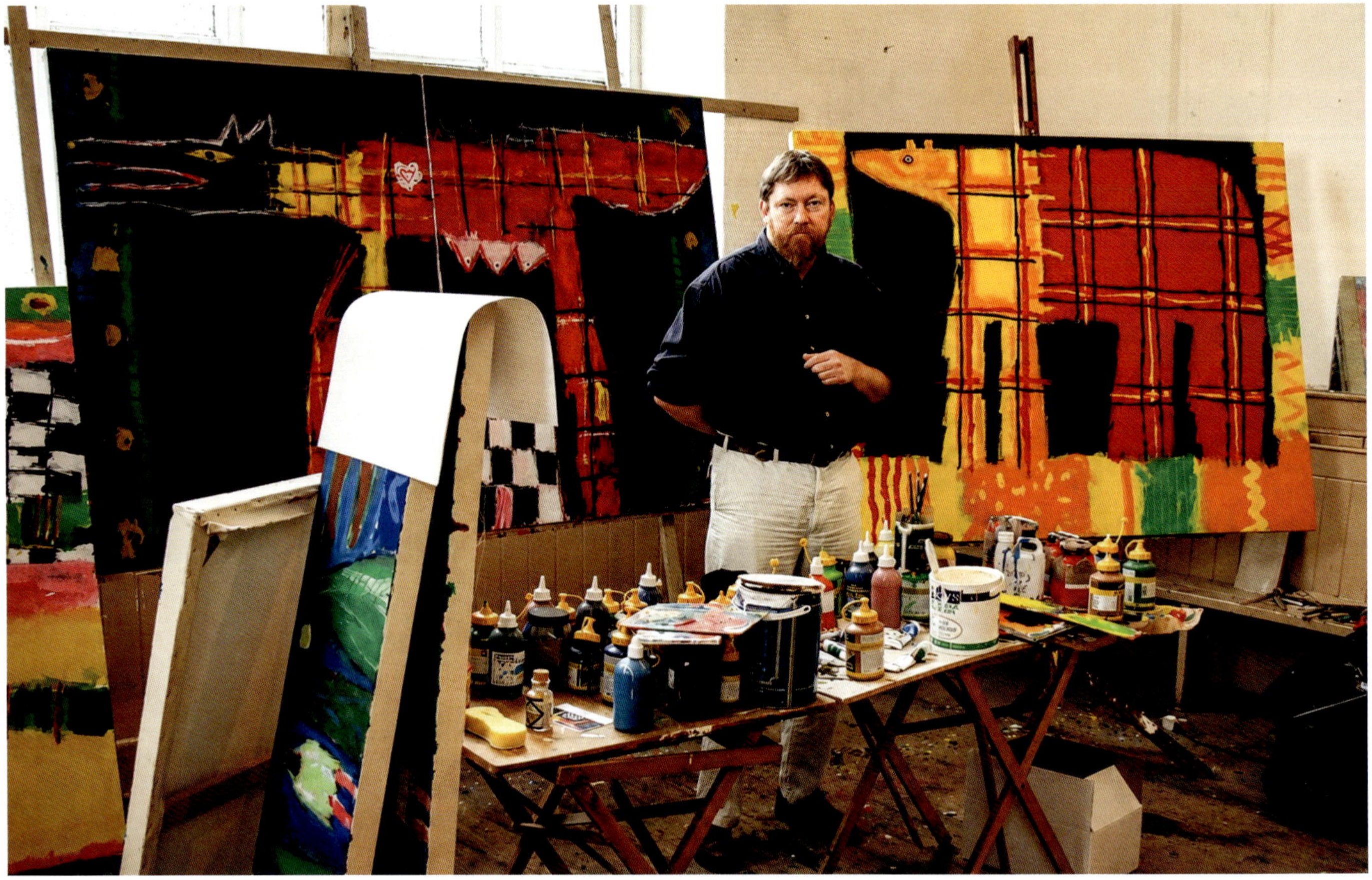

In the studio
at Llangynwyd.
Photo: Bernard
Mitchell

Valley's Challenge,
2008, acrylic on canvas,
122 x 122 cm

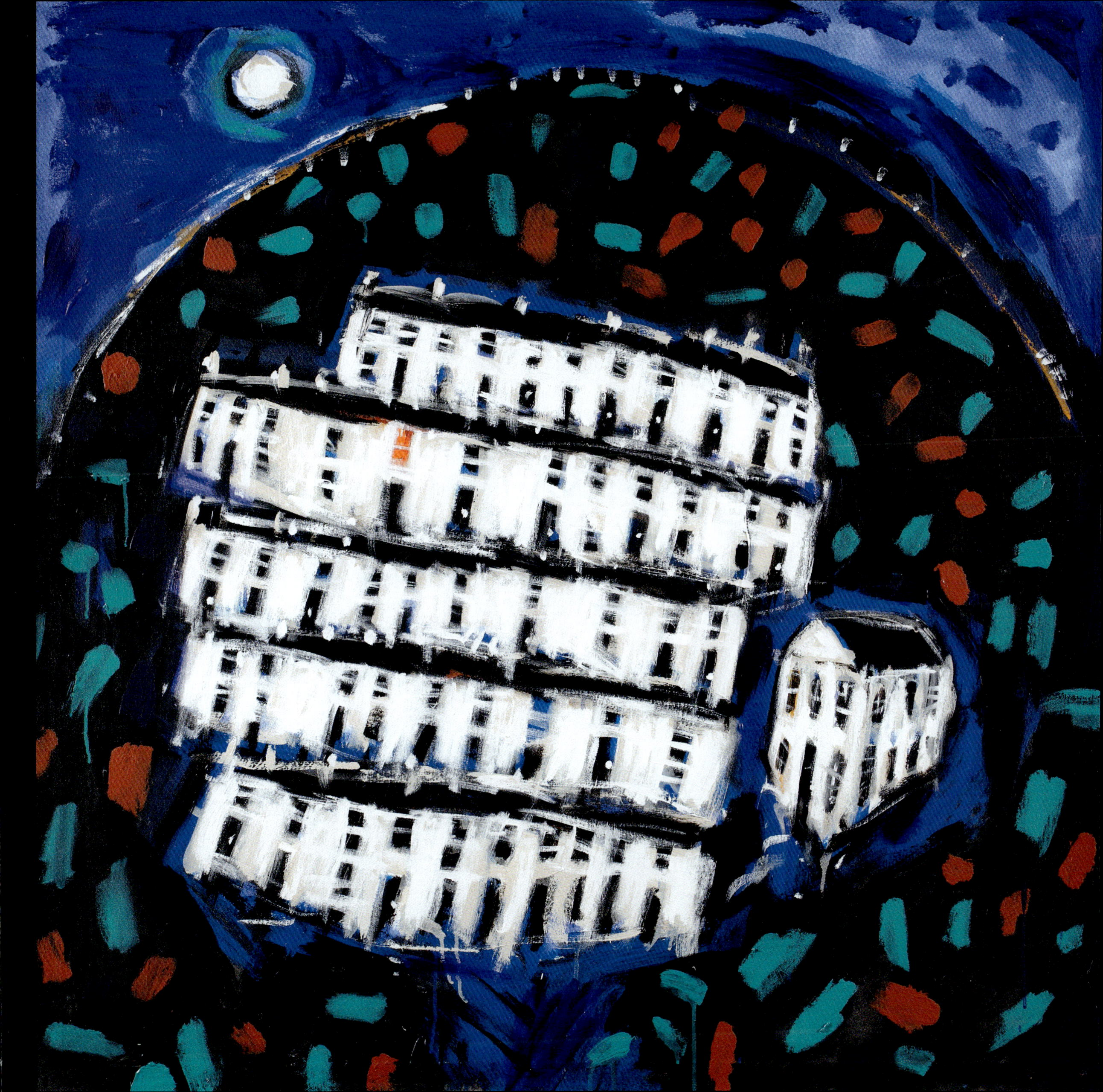

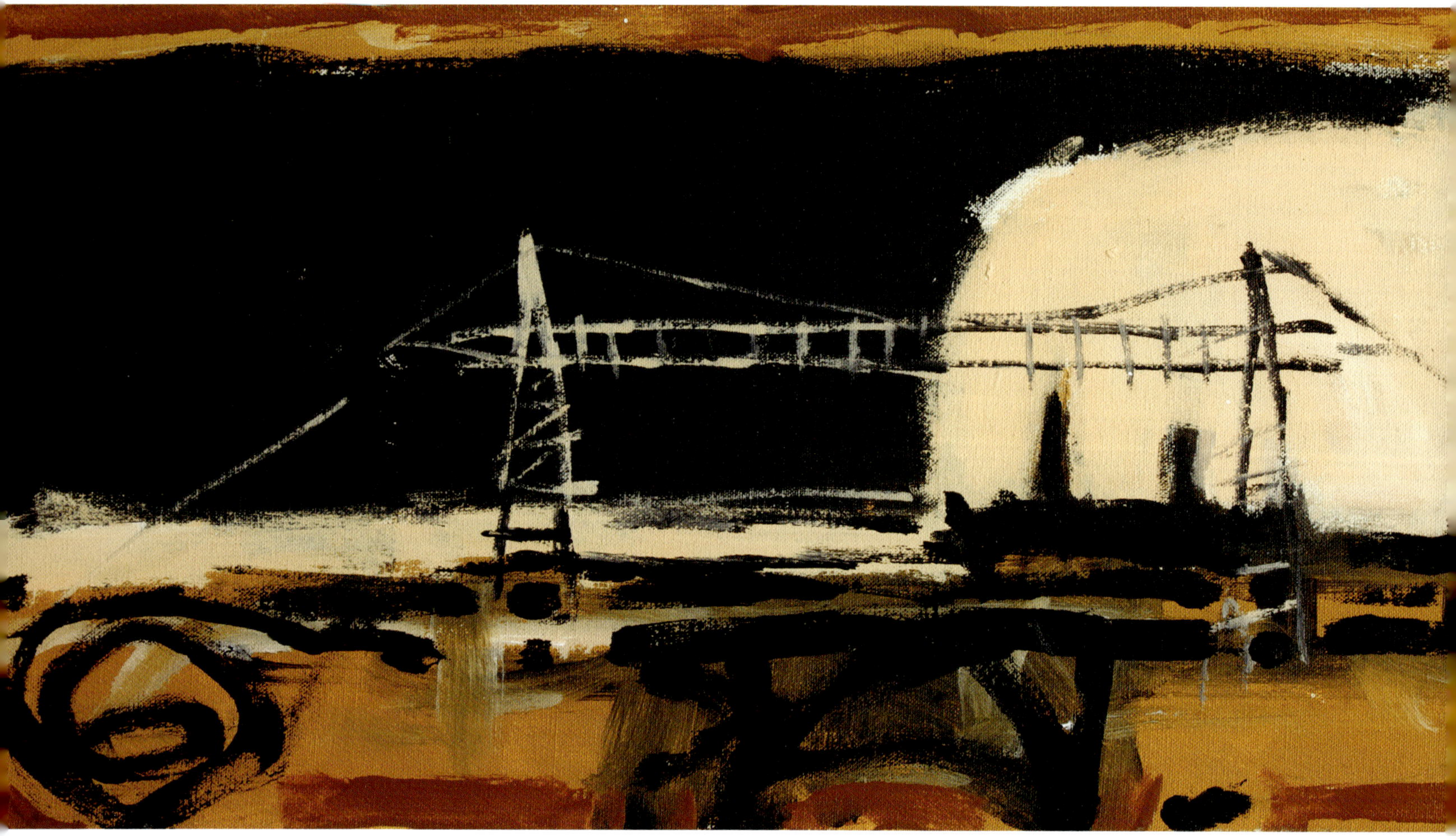

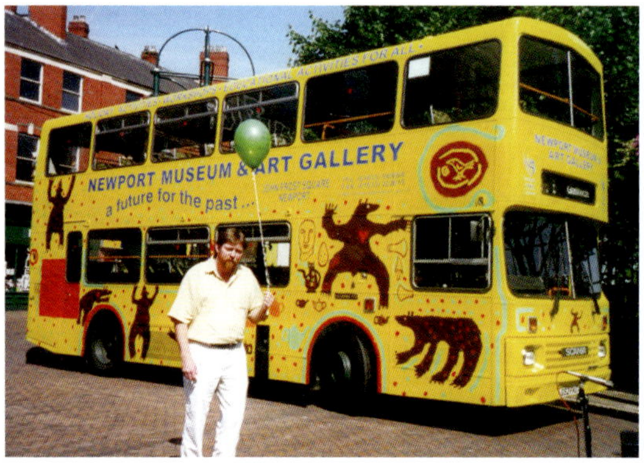

William with his Newport bus

Of all the subjects that he might have responded to, it was naturally the towering beast of the town, the Transporter Bridge, that caught his attention, stepping across the muddy banks of the tidal River Usk against the backdrop of dockside cranes and the Bristol Channel. He made one huge painting in the gallery itself so that visitors could come and see the artist at work. Commissioned to paint a double-decker bus to promote the gallery, William worked for fourteen days at the bus depot, covering the vehicle with a base coat of garish yellow and adding a dozen climbing brown bears.

A flowering of solo exhibitions followed. In 1997 he began to be represented in London by East West Gallery, the directors of which had written to him after seeing his Glynn Vivian exhibition catalogue. East West Gallery had been established seven years earlier in Blenheim Crescent, just off the Portobello Road in Notting Hill, by David Solomon and Jill Morgan. Portobello was a known gallery district with around forty independent dealers. David describes

his impression of both the artist and his works with the same words: 'sincere, friendly, unpretentious, honest'. Customers connected readily with the paintings, which were inexpensive in the London market and sold well. David and Jill found William professional and timely in supplying work. They scheduled an exhibition every two years, and in 2008 a tribute show to celebrate his life.[55]

William sometimes borrowed an oxymoron to describe himself: 'I have a whim of iron.' It conjured simultaneously his chaotic fancies and unwavering determination. Both qualities helped him when organising other artists, who might be preoccupied by their own work even as they enjoyed the opportunities that William catalysed. He did all his entrepreneurial 'fixing' without a computer or a typewriter, penning his cajoling, confusing letters by hand; but he had Carys to fall back on when a more businesslike letter was necessary. Carys, indeed, was a permanently stabilising force. William was only likely to go on pub crawls if they were apart and he felt her absence.[56]

He ploughed from one project to the next with never a fallow period or absence of ideas. A holiday was out of the question, he said, 'unless I'm painting or drawing; I get a nasty pain in my stomach.' Reflecting about an Easter holiday he wrote: '*Me Lobore orare Est* [to work is to pray] – I was in St Stephens. I find it impossible to disengage. Silly little faces. Horse-men loups-garoux – all haunt me.'[57]

In 1989 William had taken part in a mail-art project at Gütersloh in northern Germany organised by Johannes Glaw where he met the Czech poet Josef Janda. He began collaborations with Malcolm Parr and Lucien Suel. He then introduced Janda to Keith Bayliss and his fellow Swansea artist Jaroslav Mykisa, which led to an exhibition for Keith and William in Prague in 1996, an ongoing Wales-Czech collaboration, *Dreaming Awake*, and a tour of eight artists from Wales to Olomouc and the Terezin concentration camp memorial among other Czech venues. A vast exhibition at the Glynn Vivian of Czech Surrealists included the renowned filmmaker Jan Švankmajer. Keith Bayliss says William opened connections and put people into creative contact with one another:

Left:
Study of Transporter Bridge, undated, *c.* 1998, oil on canvas, 32 x 71 cm

> He was a catalyst, an engine, a dynamo in disguise [...] William's enthusiasm in bringing together sometimes a hybrid mixture of artists under the banner of an exhibition, proved a creative act in itself. William made things happen and by doing so encouraged others to make things happen.[58]

He joined established artists' groups, collecting memberships to enjoy the fellowship and validation as well as opportunities for exhibition. Unlike members who guarded their own creative time, he committed himself to organising and participating. The organisations included the long-established Welsh Group, the Association of Visual Artists in Wales, the Old Library Artists, the prestigious 56 Group Wales and, further afield, mail art groups, the Printmakers Council, the Leeds Surrealists and the BrUNIMA puppet society. His absorption into the fabric of Welsh art was signified when he was invited onto the visual art selection panel for the National Eisteddfod of Wales, which was coming to Bridgend in 1998. In the lead-up to the event, the artist Ivor Davies introduced William to the poet David Greenslade, who would become his continuing collaborator. They produced a spiral-bound book with eleven poems and eleven images on facing pages. The central subject was the Mari Lwyd and it was titled with the Welsh word *March* to suggest ironically a stallion. They sold books, paintings, prints and drawings in a stand on the Eisteddfod *maes* and split the proceeds from book sales and picture sales fifty-fifty – an indicator of William's generosity since only the book was a combined effort. Their stage-like Eisteddfod stand appeared in many paintings thereafter [134]. William and David went on to produce chapbooks and small publications in Welsh and English. David described their process:

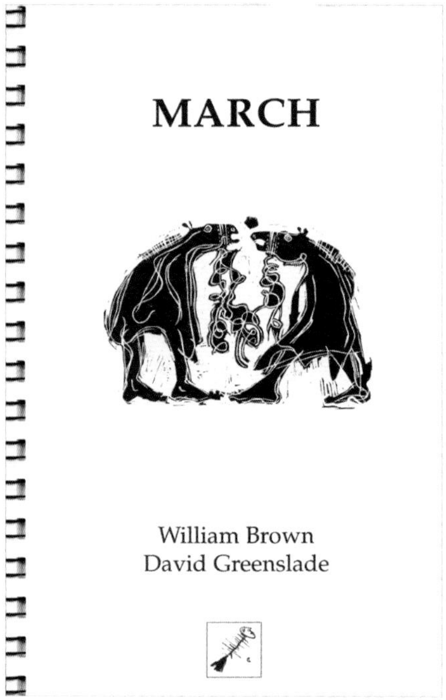

March, 1998

> I composed according to what I knew of him, his attitudes, his materials, his knowledge and his manners. When he knew more about me, it wasn't so much the verses that he responded to, but what I told him about a poem, how and why I made it, more than the (Welsh) language on the page. This is why the visual image of William Price [notorious bard and pioneer cremationist] features the famous bridge in Pontypridd, while the poem does not.[59]

For another joint project, a fantastical poem to be titled *Old Emulsion Customs*, William insisted on an unorthodox – even unheard of – way of working. He invited David to watch while he made the images for the book 'live'. He knew the poem already but asked questions about each passage and its sources while he worked on inked glass, burnished the prints with a spoon and hung them up on washing lines across his studio. David was left to choose which to reproduce. William used a similarly reactive approach with Colin Jones on the book *Elastic Black Dog*. His mind was so brim-full with ideas that not all projects could reach fruition. Peter Finch describes a book of haiku they were to make together that took tottering steps but then vanished.[60]

David says William 'put heart and soul into getting people together'. Their correspondence was full of arrangements for readings, collaborations and meetings.[61] In 2000, they were invited to attend the North American Festival of Wales when it was held at Ottawa. William took the opportunity to see more Inuit art and spent his fee on a sculpture of a polar bear in green stone. David recalls he took a bundle of watercolours to sell:

> At first the Welsh-Canadian / Welsh-American public didn't know what to make of them and nothing was being sold. I watched as William actually educated those who called by our sales table – how to look at a painting, assess what was in the painting and why owning a painting brought pleasure. It was very impressive and sure enough people started buying them. Gee I had no idea what was going on here said one visitor who bought more than one. We sold any number of *Old Emulsion Customs* as well – quite an achievement for a rather conservative event.[62]

Newcastle Hill, the studio at Llangynwyd and picnic haunts became a mobile salon thanks to William's facility for fellowship. The photographer Bernard Mitchell recalled collaborations were hatched in the Westbourne pub in Swansea on Wednesday evenings when William and a pack of writers and artists got together. Carys and William hosted afternoons at Newcastle Hill that were a creative who's who. In addition to regular collaborators such as Tony Goble, John Uzzell Edwards and Gareth Davies, visitors included Dorothee and Johannes Glaw, the artists David Rees Davies and Hervé Constant, the Czech translator Dagmar Štěpánková, writers Robert Rhys and Jon Gower, curator Alison Bevan and academics from Germany and Poland. William always did the cooking, an activity such as printmaking might be set up, and the party would continue for the rest of the day.[63]

An unexpected departure was William's work with the animation company Cinetig and its director Gerald Conn, who met William at Carys's school. He invited William to draw imagery for a video by the Welsh rock band Gorky's Zygotic Mynci. It was made through six weeks of intensive work at Chapter Arts Centre in 1999. The video followed a boy's journey from Wales to Spain. William worked rapidly, making hundreds of drawings.

While Wales had become William's permanent home he returned often to Canada, seeing his family in Ontario and heading north to wild country. He loved Inuit galleries, meeting the artists and buying sculptures. A favourite trip was by the Polar Express and powerboat to Moosonee. Another was to Lake Muskoka, 100 miles north of Toronto, where the stories of the indigenous Algonquin, Huron and Ojibwa peoples and those who came before them were told alongside those of the white settlement and the steamships. His sister Kathleen and her husband Boston by now owned a cottage on Loon Lake near Kierney, three hours north of the city. William would visit the nearby garbage heaps to draw the bears that came to scavenge. He poured plaster into pawprints in the mud and gave the casts to friends. Kathleen recalled their father's exasperated comment: 'Not another trip to the bloody dump!' But wild beasts were his richest and most enduring subject.[64]

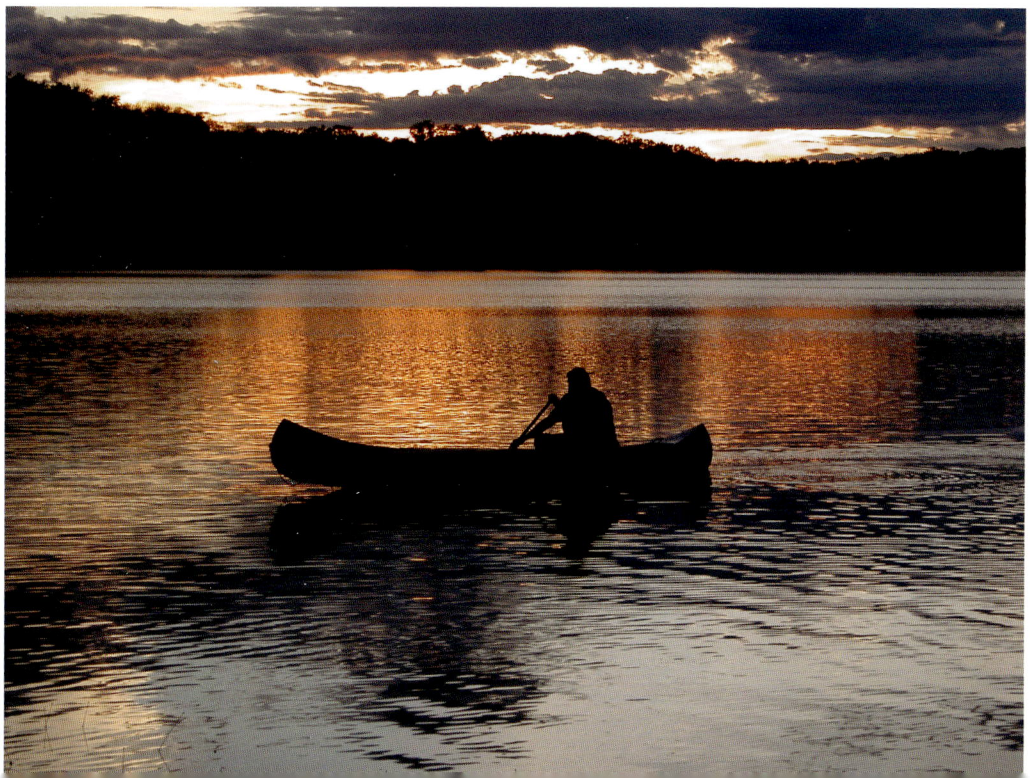

William canoeing in the Almaguin Highlands, Canada

A reminder of the animal in the human, powerful, cunning and unsophisticated.

Beasts

It was from the mid-1990s onwards that beasts reached their fullest expression in William's art, in bright, vital paintings, bold prints and literary collaborations. Bears, loups-garoux and the horse-man Mari Lwyd were everywhere, like squatters occupying his imagination. Other creatures came and went from his repertoire, commanding his attention for a time and then departing. Hannibal's elephants appeared briefly around 2005; seals, whales and walrus occupied his Arctic pictures. In 1997 he published with Lucien Suel *The new bestiary / Le nouveau bestiaire*, a pamphlet in black and white from Suel's own imprint, Station Underground d'Emerveillement Littéraire. Suel wrote poems to each image and William made free translations into English – he called them 'transladapations'. The book brought together a panoply of William's favourite beasts. On the front cover a puffin strolled nonchalantly from the open mouth of a crocodile; on the back a Mari Lwyd strode through a Welsh valleys town. Inside were wolf, bear, beaver, camel, mouse, horse, seahorse, cat and kippers.

Perhaps all these in different ways represented the 'animal in the human' of which he spoke. In an article written while collaborating with William, David Greenslade noted that these characters were 'an affront to socialised behaviour. They leap, dance and cavort, they stare and pass indifferently by, they expose themselves, they puff themselves up. They don't care anything about the trouble they cause.' William announced, 'I want to do all the bogeymen in the world.'[65]

It probably started with the wolves, which appeared in William's paintings and prints before the shape-shifting variety of werewolf, loup-garou, which had been enlisted by parents to frighten generations of children in France and Canada. In a pamphlet for Welsh primary schools, *Let's Look at Loup-Garou: The Work of William Brown*, he explained: 'It's a bogey man. It's what's behind the curtain or under the blanket.' He remembered a real wolf, 'caught by my headlights on a Northern Ontario road sometime in the '70s'. A painting redolent of this memory and probably made in the mid-1980s is more monstrous for the light of the moon, which throws shadows from the wolf's legs, as though it stands on stilts; an idea that William repeated in sculptures and paintings of camels, moose and wolves.[66]

Animals in that Country, undated, mid-1980s, oil on canvas, 114 x 90 cm

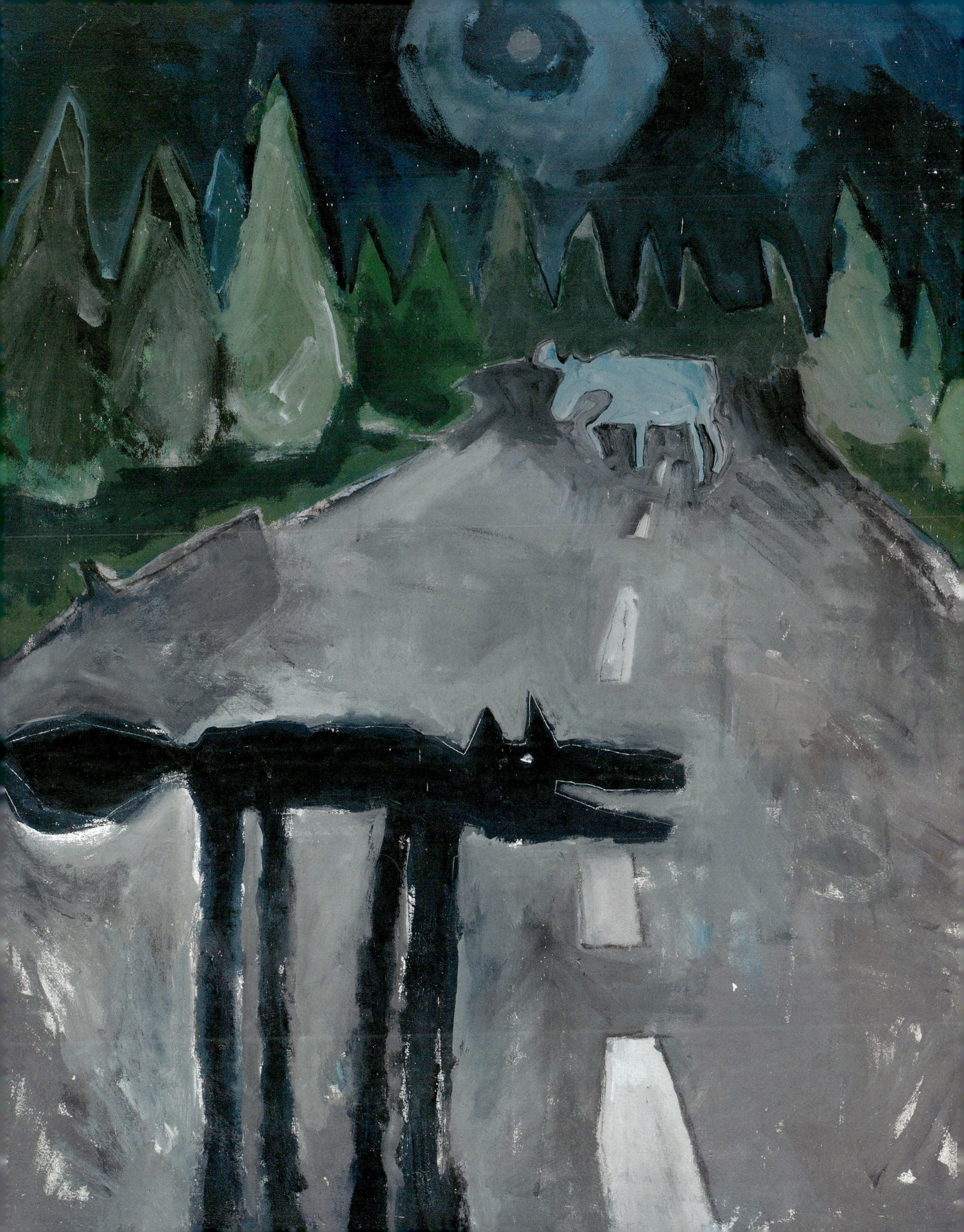

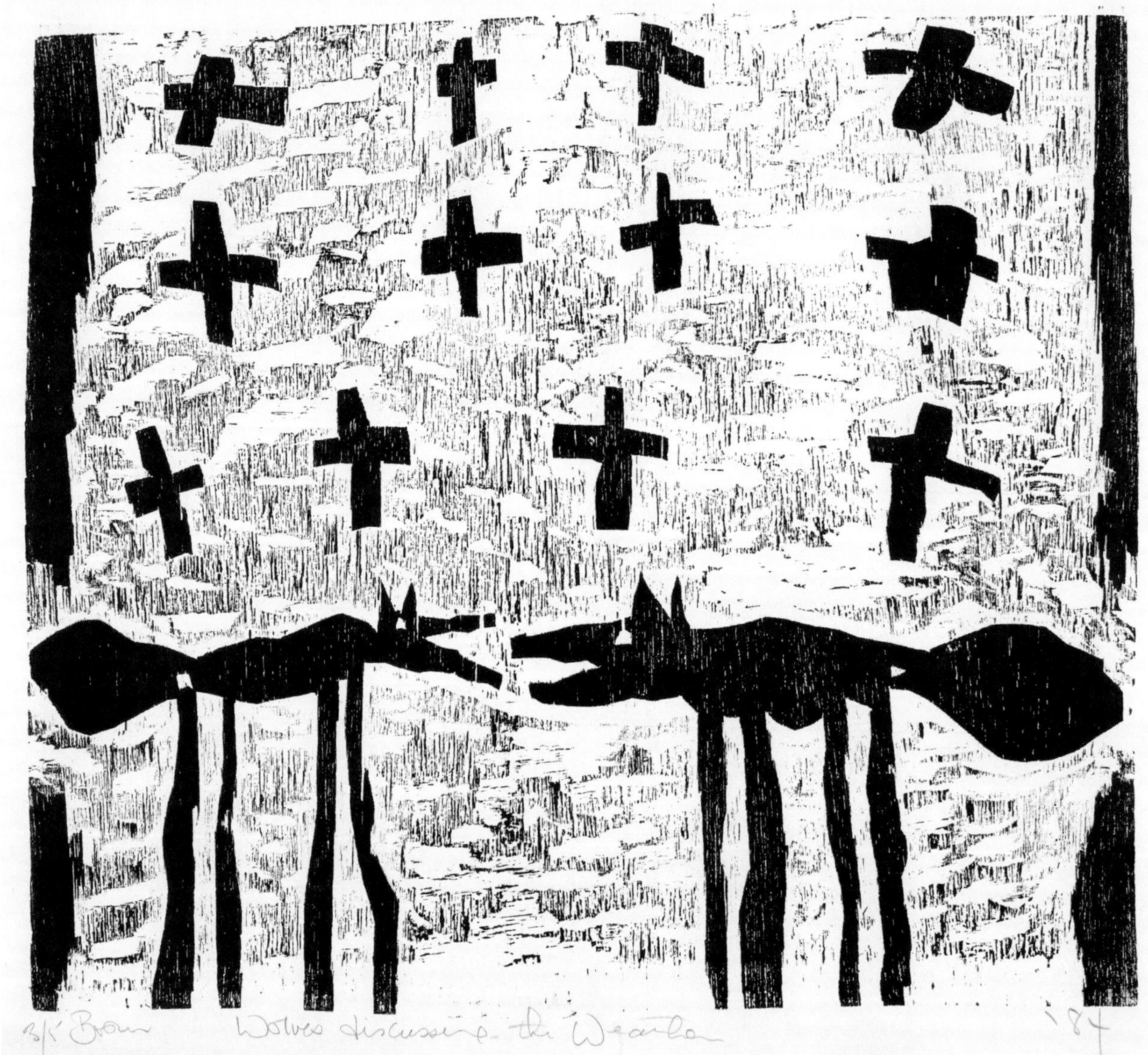

Wolves Discussing the Weather, 1984, woodcut, 50 x 50 cm

In the exhibition of artists' self-portraits curated by Alison Bevan at the Glynn Vivian Art Gallery in 1995, loup-garou has stepped out of its wolf's clothing to be seen as the mythical beast it is. William chose a large loup-garou to represent himself [62–3]. All the paintings in this series showed she-wolves, vividly coloured in tartan, set in a black void over a chequerboard floor with stripes of colour at their sides. The straight snout and mouth was like an alligator's and loup-garou had a bright eye and beating heart. He wrote:

> There are intense cultural resonances in the various forms of anthropomorphism. Loup-Garou, the spectre of the forest and bayou is common to Carib, Cajun and Canadian cultures. Here he is dressed in Tartan! The startingly yellow and black one is in fact that of the McClures … my own. His business is to patrol the human

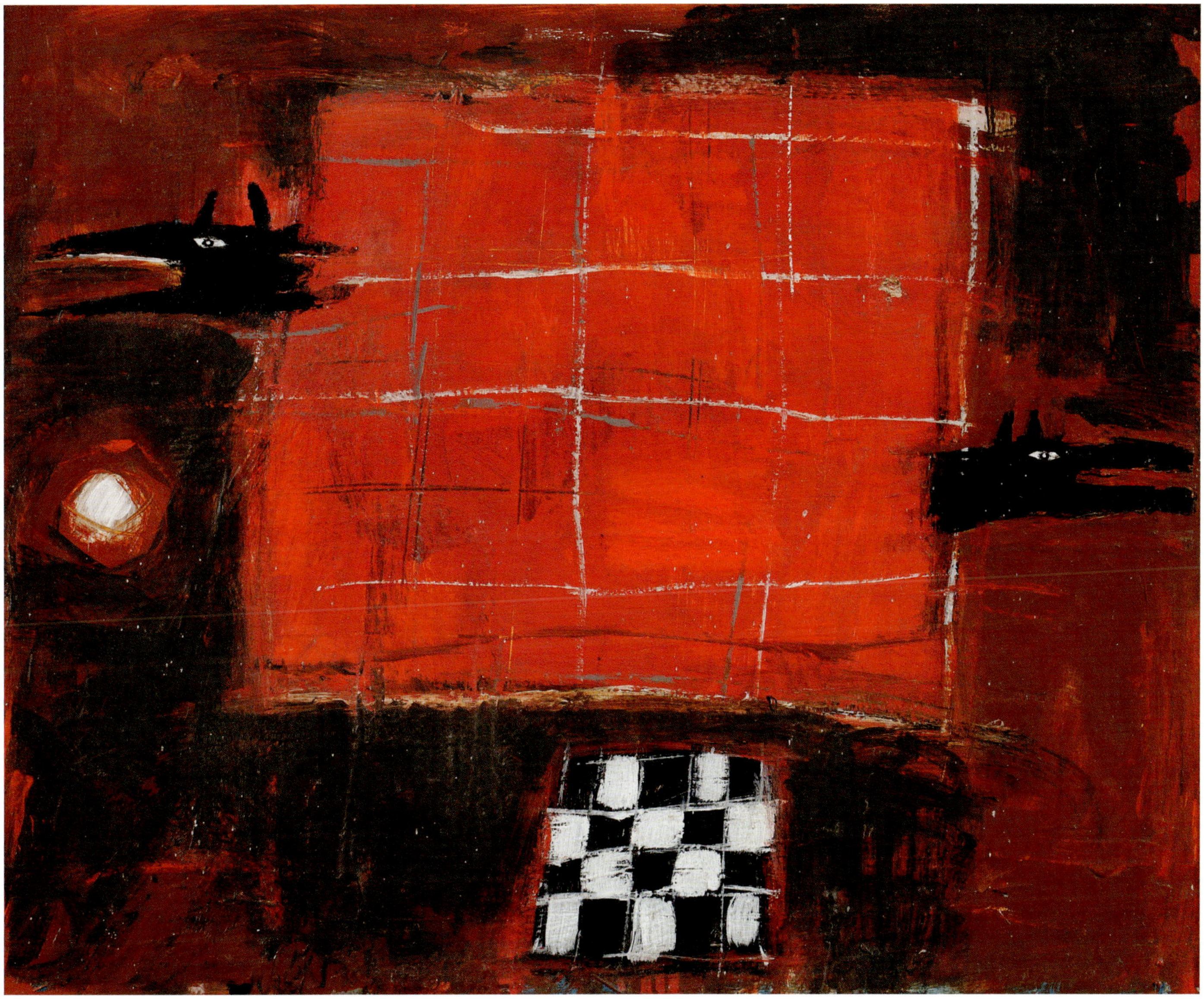

margins of the psyche and he serves here as both an intimate and self-portrait. This identification with the animal was briefly and brilliantly expressed in a letter to Pierre Matisse from the Italian sculptor Giacometti in which he describes a sculpture of a dog. "Un jour je me voyais. Dans la rue, un chien, sous la pluie. C'etait moi."[67]

What's Behind the Blanket, undated, *c.* 1999, acrylic on canvas, 51 x 61 cm

In subsequent paintings, loup-garou appeared from behind the eponymous blanket or menaced other creatures, putting its head into frame unnoticed to observe its prey [77]. Sometimes there could be more than one. In a letter to his regular correspondent Dagmar Štěpánková in Prague he mentioned: 'I observe that our new neighbours' young son has pointed ears, a long face and bright blue eyes. Also his back is covered with fur hair. I've decided that he is a loup-garoux bubaknik / werewolf. I have further proof too, because I left some

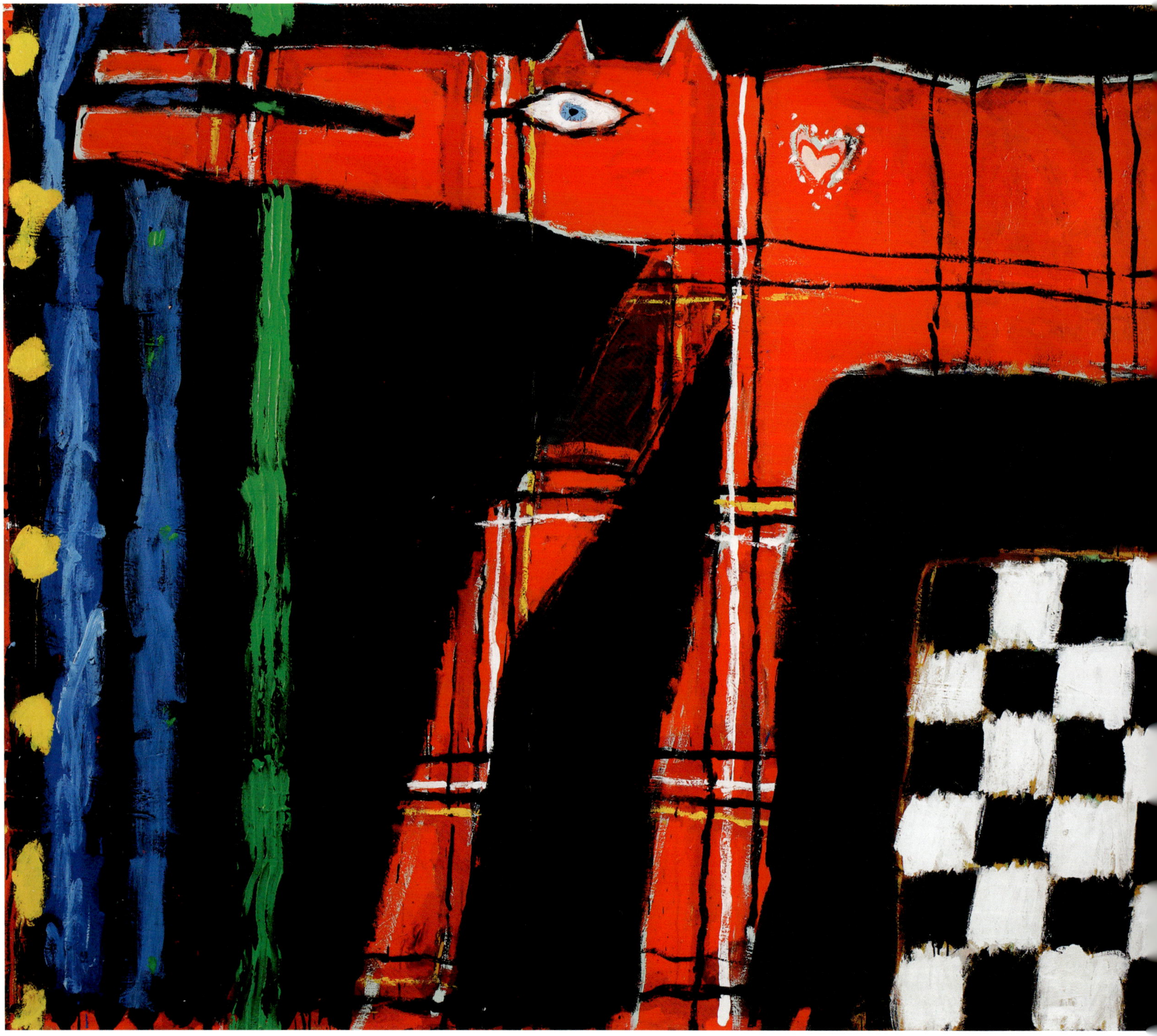

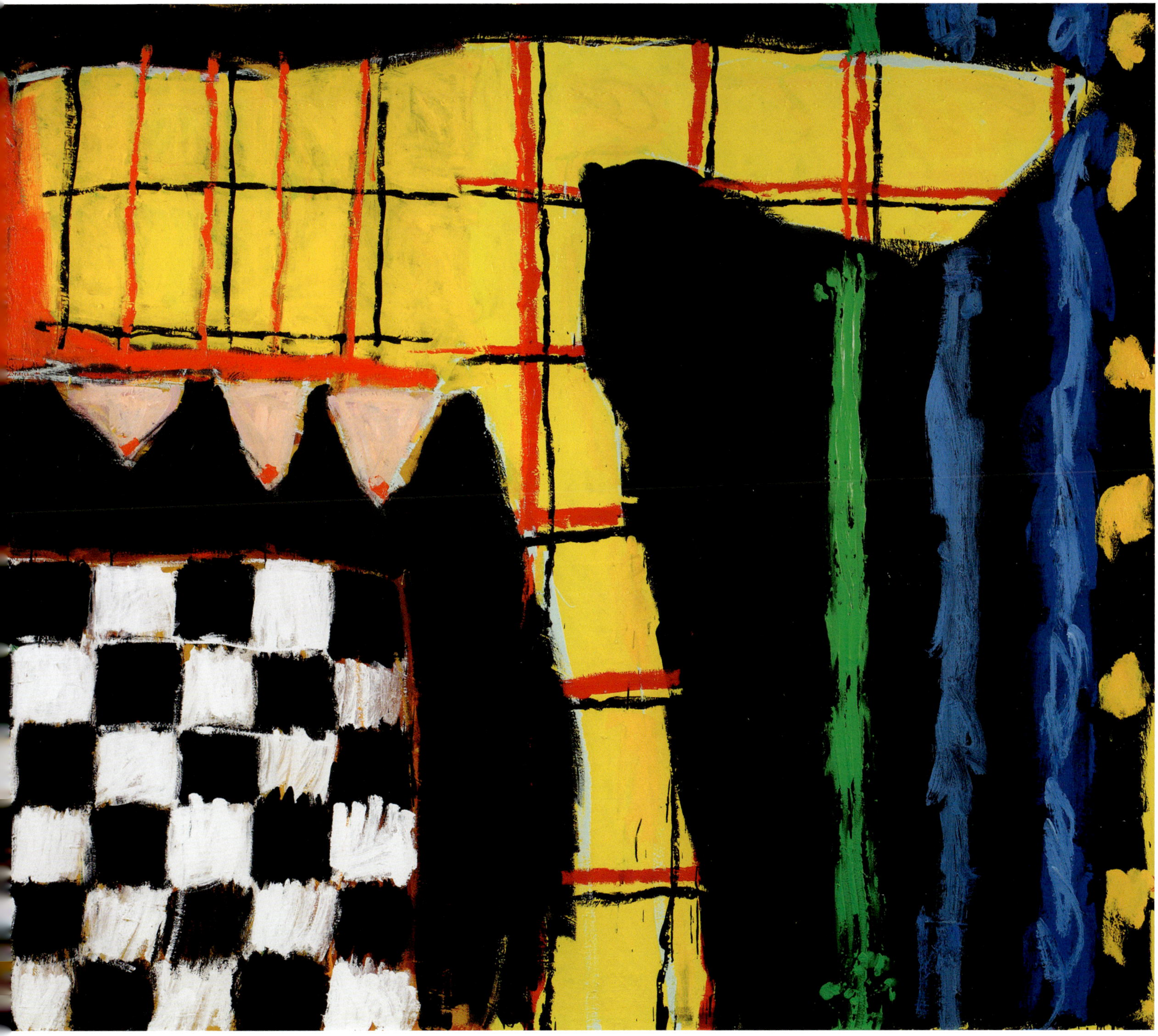

Loup Garou (diptych),
1996, oil on canvas,
188 x 426

chicken bones at the back door of their home and they were all missing the following morning – a full moon that night.' And while he would never have described himself as a performance artist, he would appear on stage or among friends as a wolf-man in a mask and gloves. Lucien Suel recalled his *succès de théâtre* on stage in Lille. They went on to perform at live events in France and Britain.[68]

Dogs came back in many forms, cross-fertilised by experiences wherever William went. He invented the Magic Dog of Güstersloh in Germany, recorded the wolves of North Africa and reflected on the slaughtered Gelert in Wales.[69]

Personal encounters would combine with imagination, and perhaps a drink or two, to introduce other shape-shifting beasts, such as the bubák of Prague, which Malcolm Parr saw on a visit with William and Keith Bayliss in their apartment on the Street of the Czech and Slovak Army. It was the home of a Czech magazine editor and, Keith recalls, 'when we talked of this apparition the next evening our host went white and called his wife to hear the story, for

What's Behind the Blanket II, 1999, acrylic on canvas, 90 x 121 cm

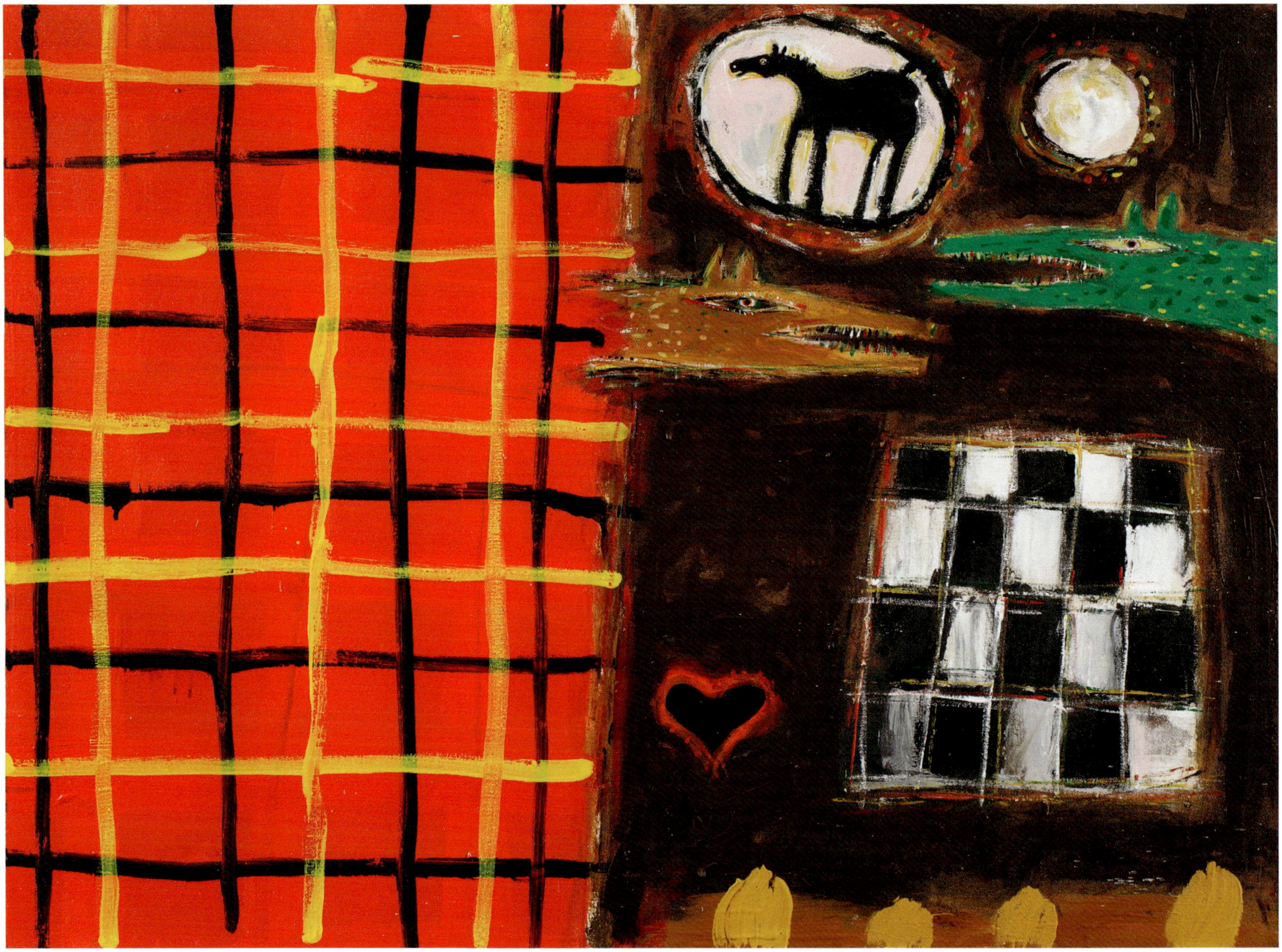

they had seen it on several occasions.'[70] This bogeyman or spirit in Czech folklore is described as a shapeshifter or like a scarecrow. However, as Malcolm thought he saw a green monkey, William showed the bubák as a green, somewhat bear-shaped monkey. He called one of the paintings *Something at the Window* and the bubák in the lamp-lit snowfall seemed as startled as its onlookers.

At the start of the millennium, he took up the idea of the 'mudman', a figure who like the Golem comes to life from clay. The paintings showed a pink, blotchy figure that was inspired by two friends. One was his North African travelling companion Mick Owens, who had contracted intestinal worms, and the other was a heavily tattooed, pierced and sunburned drinking acquaintance called Ted from Grangetown, whom William found in Cardiff pubs. The series *Ted's 40th* appeared around 2003. William teased both friends for their tortured bodies but perhaps he hoped for sympathetic magic by presenting them in paint. Certainly, magic was in the mix of his thinking as some painting titles included 'shaman' in brackets [66–7].

Something at the Window, 2006, acrylic on canvas, 43 x 86 cm

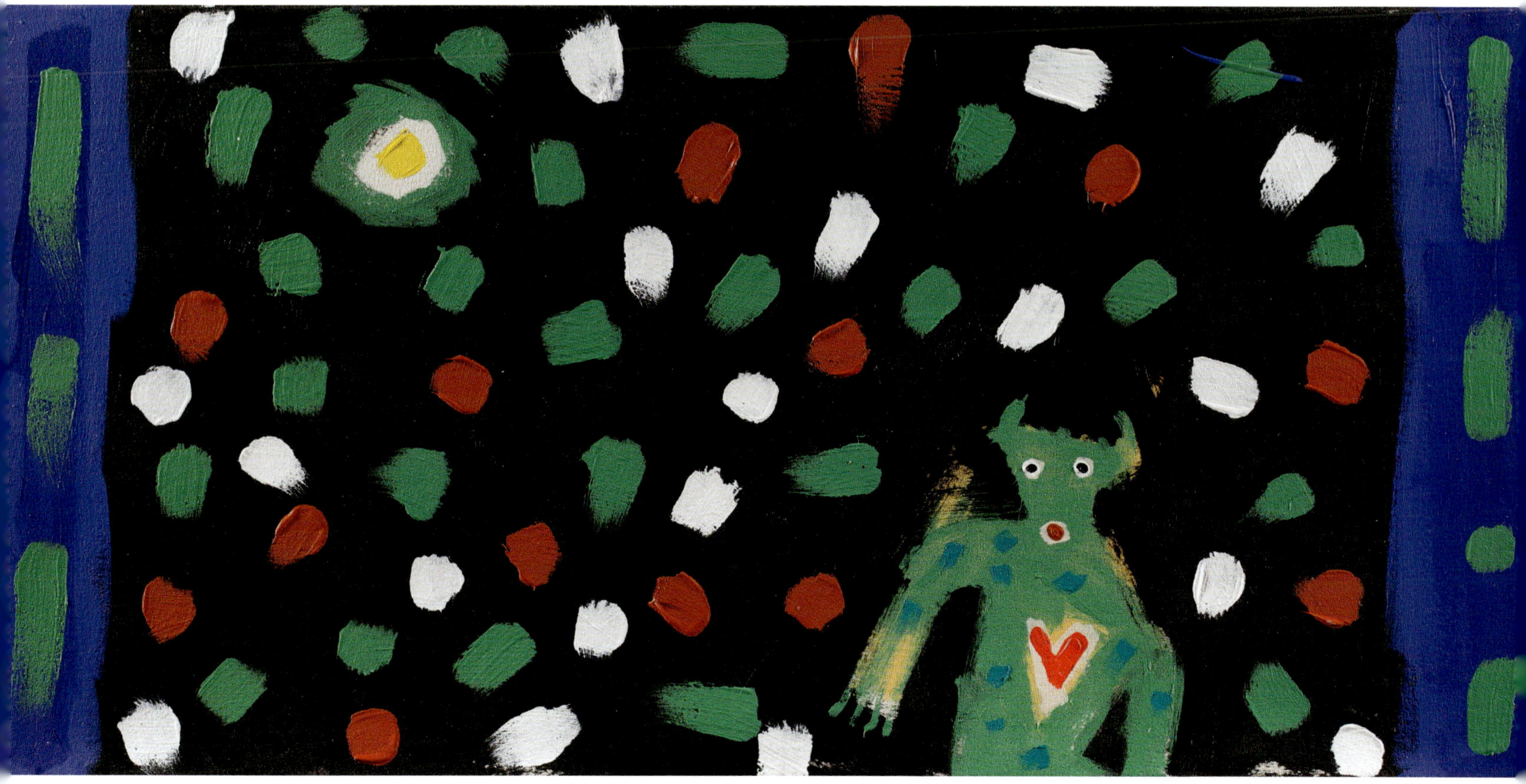

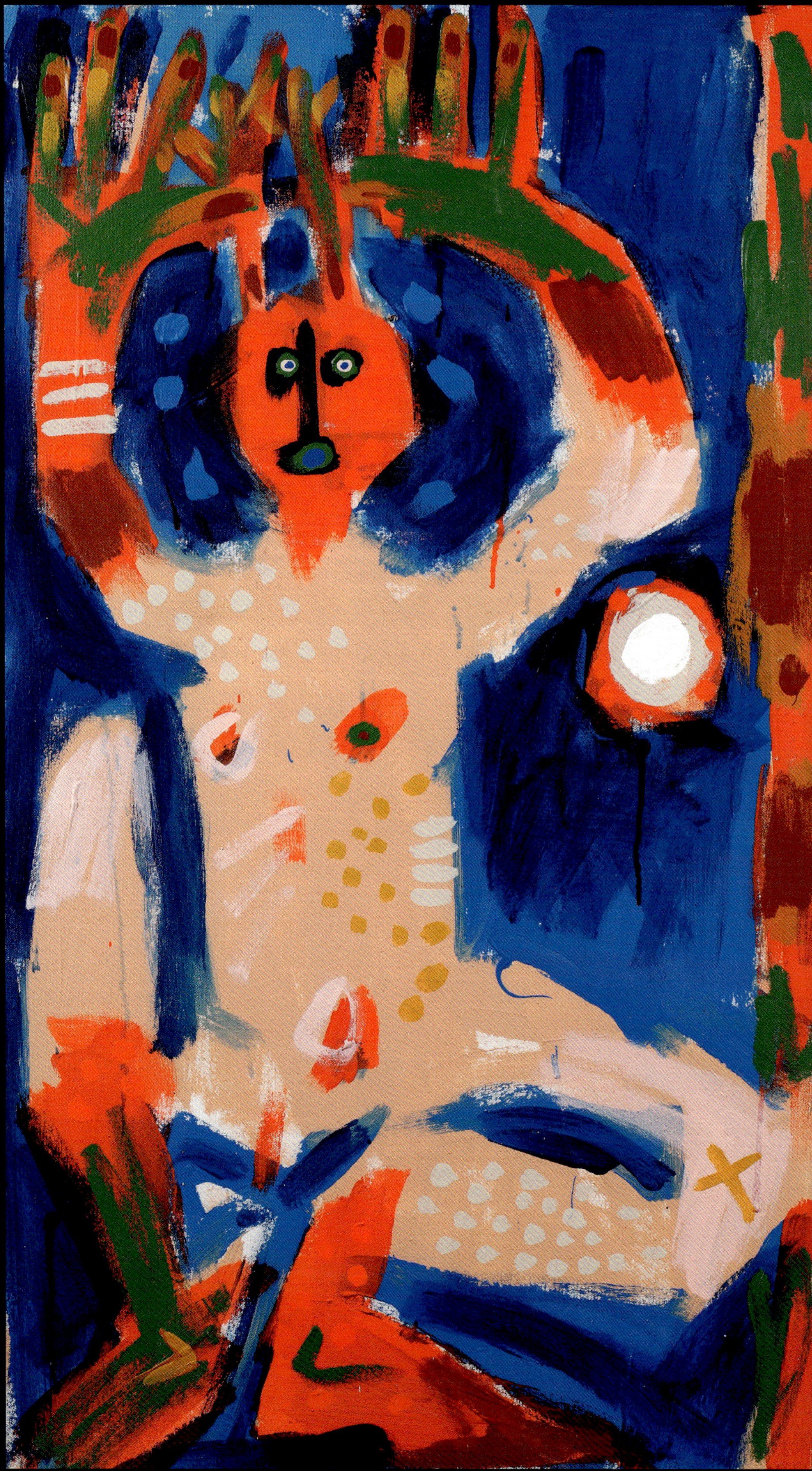

Mudman (Shaman 11), 2001, acrylic on canvas, 95 x 54 cm

Opposite:
Ted's 40th, 2005, acrylic on canvas, 39 x 29 cm

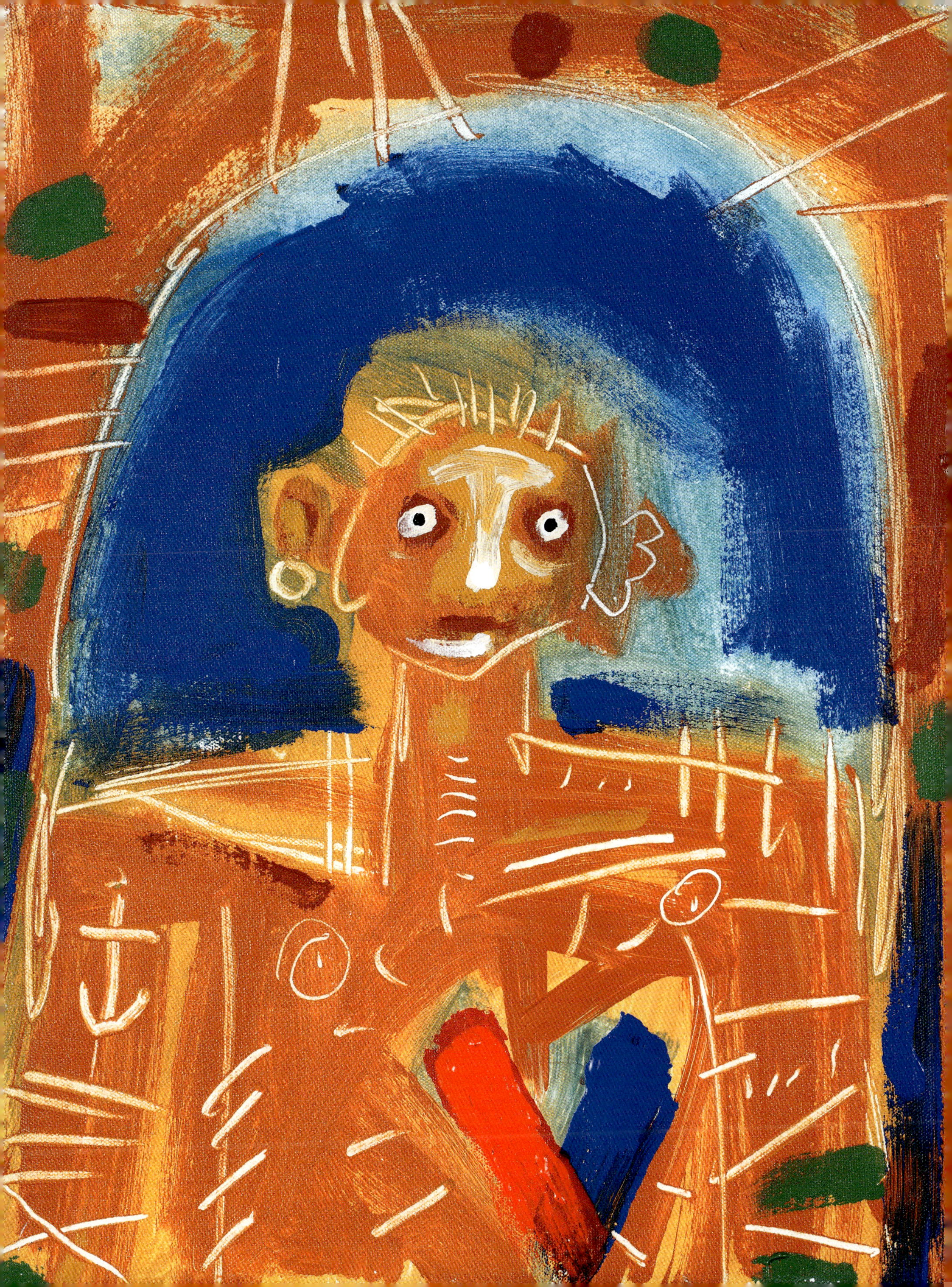

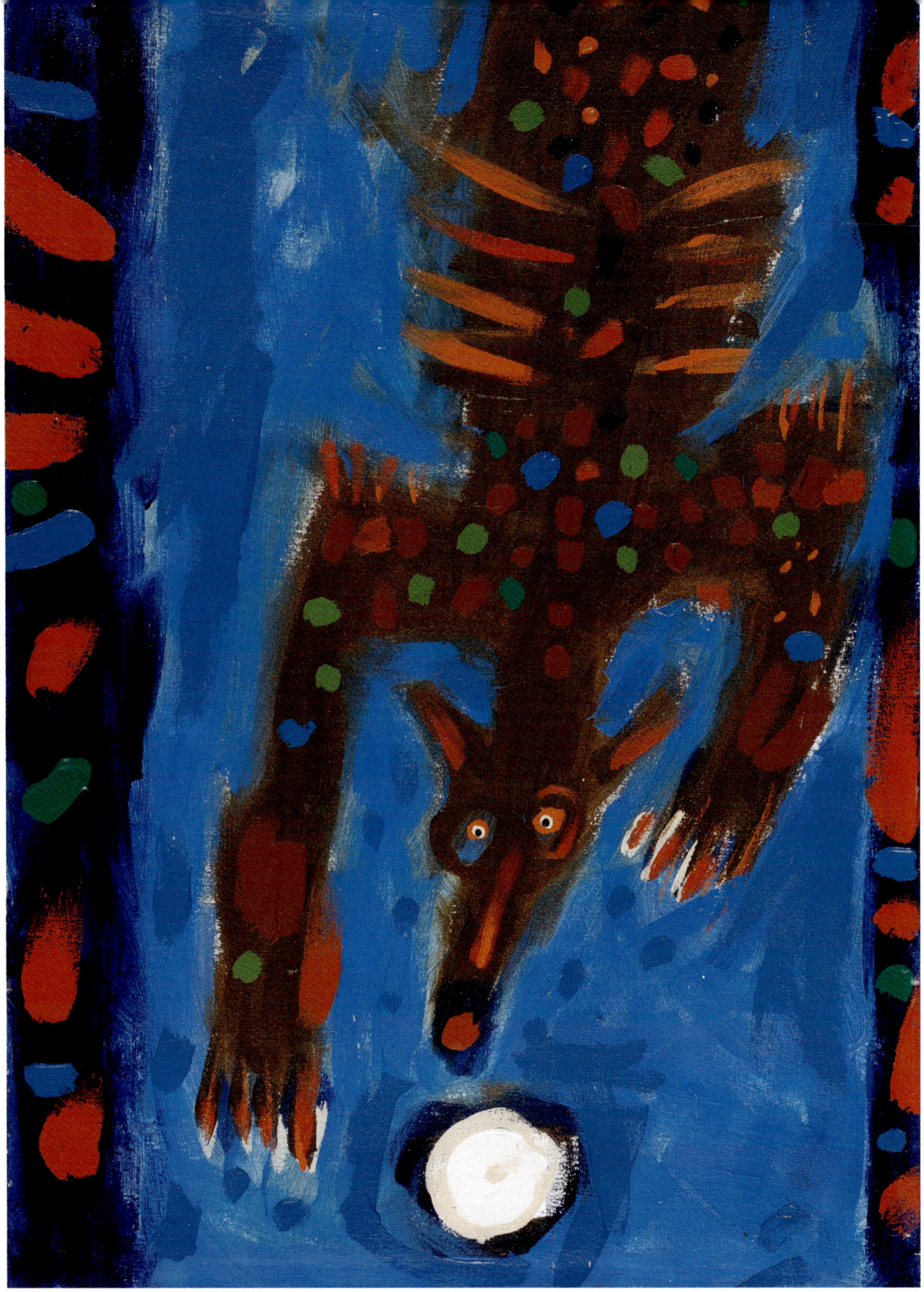

Claw Down the Moon to Yearn for..., undated, acrylic on canvas, 72 x 50 cm

William often talked about his first sighting of bears, when he was around five. In this case it was the humans who were the bogeymen, and William gave his sympathies to the bears:

> So it's nearly 40 years ago, and I am at a gas station in Ontario. Maybe not too far from Parry Sound – Pointe du Baril – I can't remember exactly ... anyway it's dry, hot August ... smell of gas. I noticed a car with American plates ... New York State ... and a big dead bear strapped across the hood. Near the pump, I tried to feed some Cheezies to a little bear chained up. He was too busy trying to scrape the worms out of his ass. To this day, I remember him scooting around the gravel.[71]

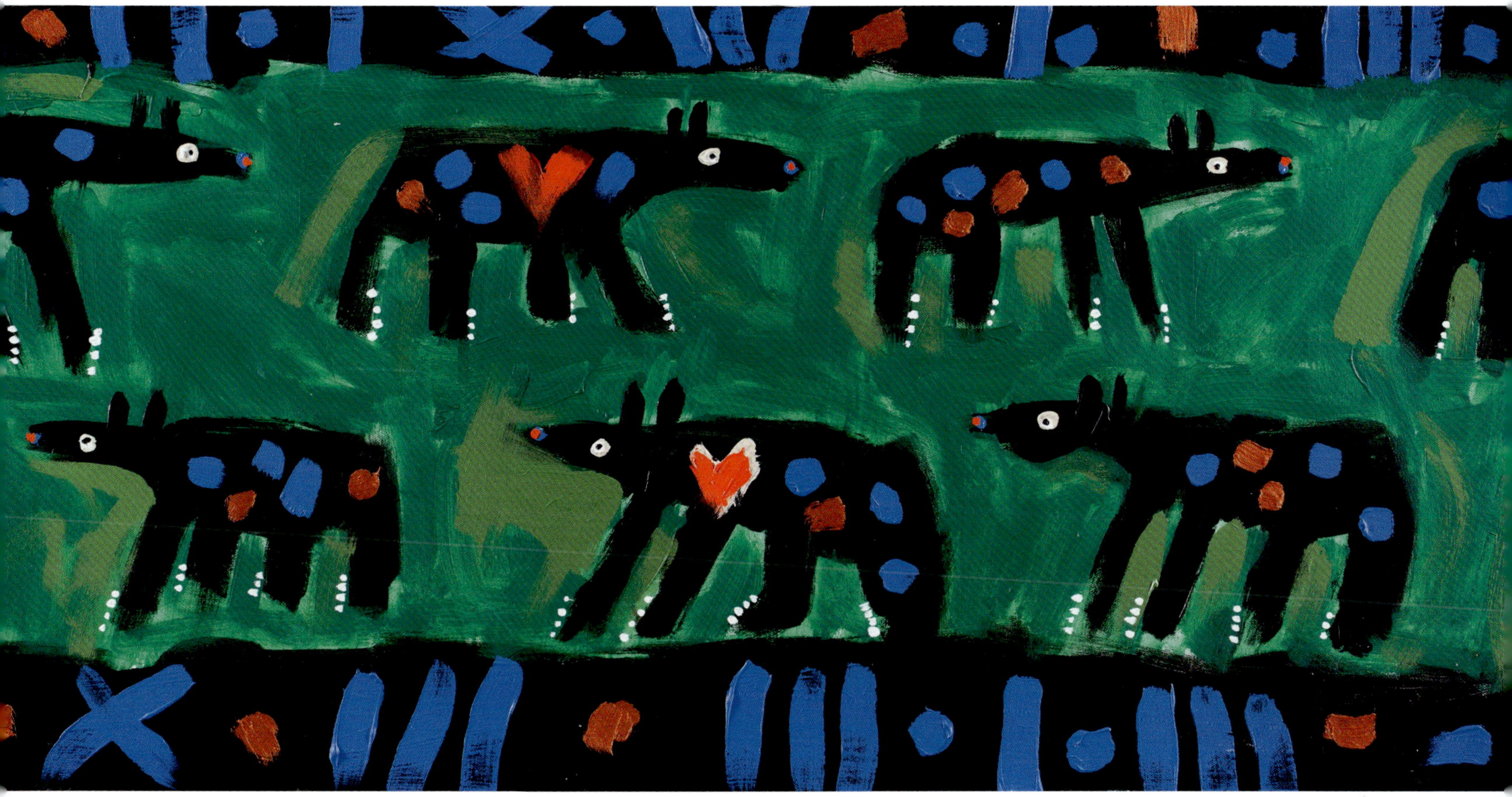

Whenever visiting Ontario he would head off to margin country where bears and people mixed and would sit in a car all night watching them. On one occasion when he took his young nephew along for the ride, one of his quarries appeared suddenly from the tree above their car. During an excursion to the Great North Woods he took David Greenslade to watch bears at Kearney refuse transfer station. David froze with primal fear at the sudden musky stench of danger, but William was elated.

Five and Two Half Bears, undated, acrylic on canvas, 100 x 60 cm

The bears in his paintings and prints are narrow of head compared with the black bears he would observe most often. His sightings of polar bears on occasional visits to the sub-Arctic regions seem to have inflected his imagery. The variety of ways in which William depicted bears expresses his obsession with them. Some pictures showed natural habitats – black bears walking on all fours in forests or polar bears under clear skies. In *Muskoka* [70–1], titled for the wild district 100 miles north of Toronto, a highway like the road to Loon Lake that William was so familiar with bisects nature in a straight line to the horizon, but the bears wander crosswise. Sometimes they become emblematic – almost abstract patterns. *Five and Two Half Bears* shows caravans of black bears passing in opposite directions between patterned borders as though woven on a carpet. Their claws are signified by diamond-like spots of white, they are patterned with dabs of blue and red and two have vivid hearts. Bears half in frame like these

Next page
Muskoka, 2000, acrylic on canvas, 80 x 134 cm

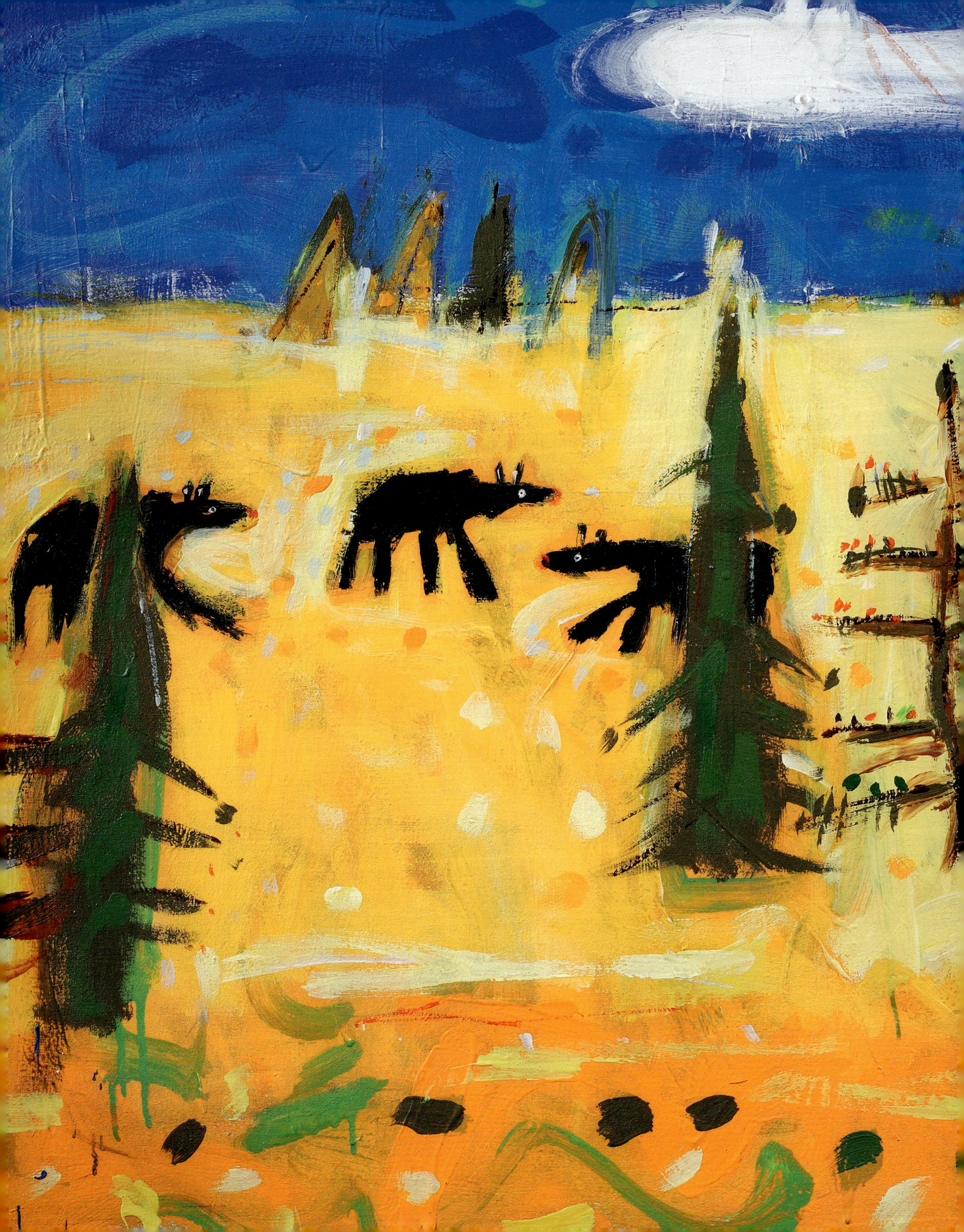

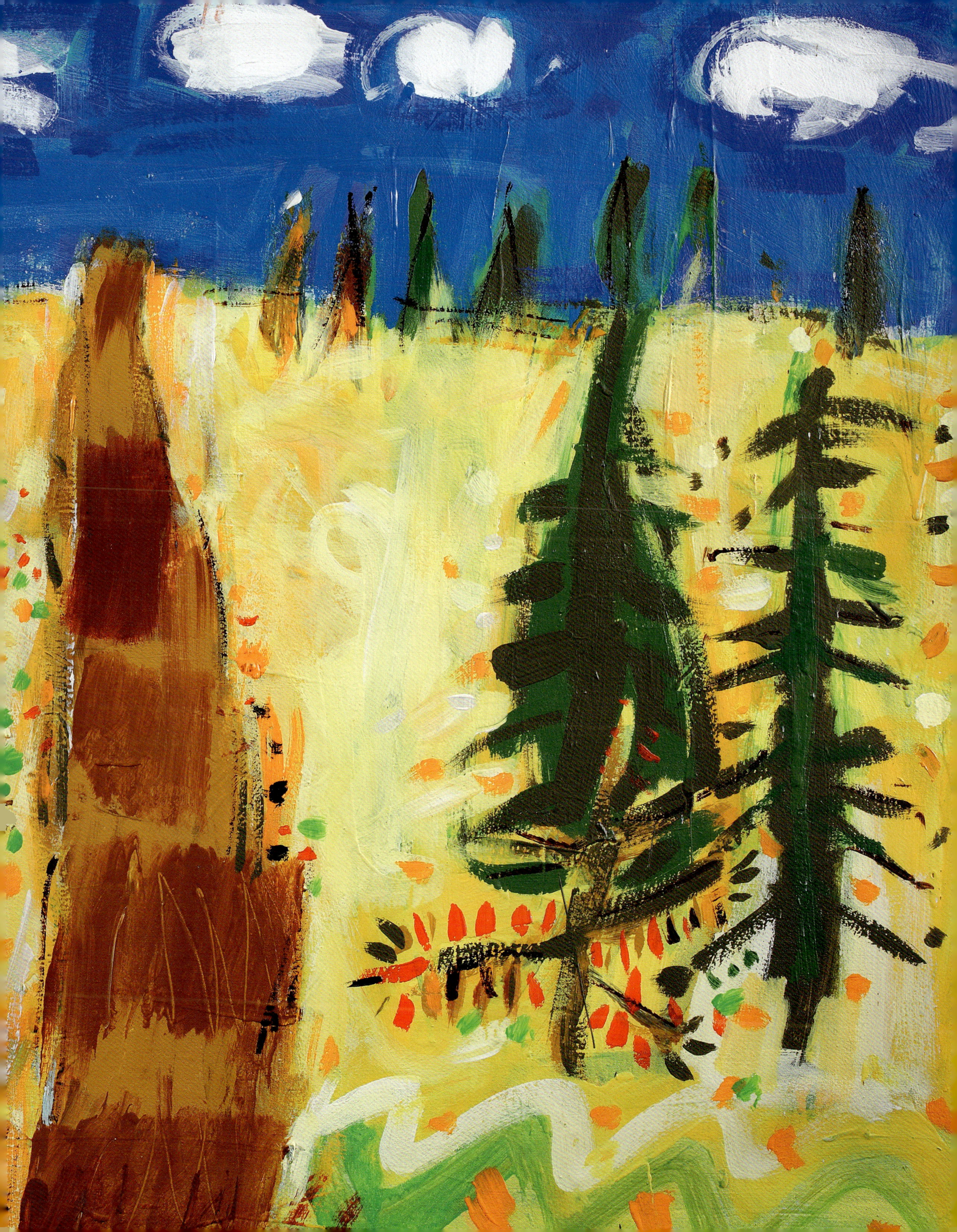

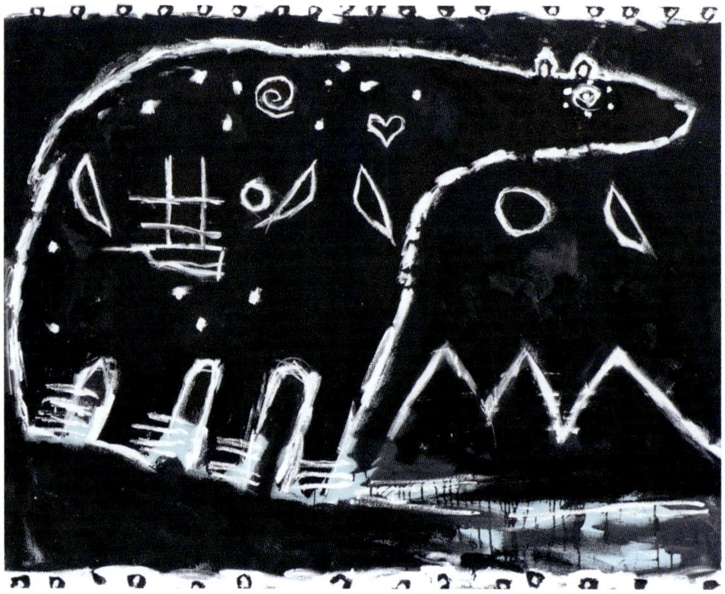

Untitled (polar bear), undated, c. 2000, acrylic on canvas, 122 x 152 cm

were prompted by news from Lucien Suel in France that a study had calculated 'eight and a half bears' remained in the Pyrenees.

William's creaturely empathy is clearest when he expresses the lonely plight of polar bears in a changing world. Though fast, powerful and aggressive, he shows them reflective and solitary: playing with snowballs (last reminders of the disappearing snows), alone under the stars or against the distinctive outline of Hudson Bay, or else walking apart, 'agreeing to differ'. For contrast, however, he brings a polar bear indoors to hide under his kitchen table, often with a souvenir snowball – a memento of its true home – in its paws or on the table overhead [18]. In some prints and paintings, the longing of the polar bear is depicted in memory-symbols of icebergs, the night sky, the first ship that came.

The Ferocity of the Returning Gael, 2007, acrylic on canvas, 60 x 100 cm

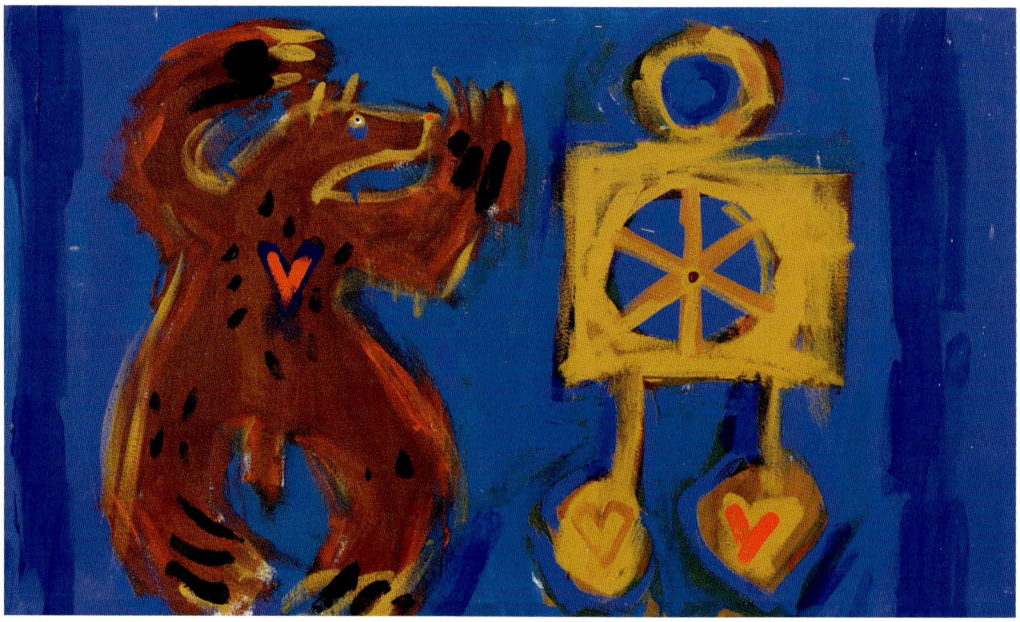

Another ursine outing is the dancing bears, which appear in crossovers of his many themes, pirouetting with love spoons, his Blaengwynfi Venus and other entities, their movements expressed by front legs raised, back legs kicking out and beating hearts. Historically, dancing bears were debased as fairground turns but William's interest came from recent Inuit culture, in which they represent happiness and a link between a shaman and a spirit-animal. He had a green serpentine carving of a dancing polar bear but his own dancing bears were black or brown. His wild colour, by contrast, is projected onto the narrow head, small eye and huge legs and rear of the polar bear. Many examples are decorated in tartan-style in his favourite combined colours – cobalt, ultramarine, yellow ochre, crimson. These bears are bright but are emphatically not clothed – the lines of colour cross them in a two-dimensional pattern as though projected on a theatre gauze.

McClure's Bear, undated, *c.* 1996, oil on canvas, 108 x 136 cm

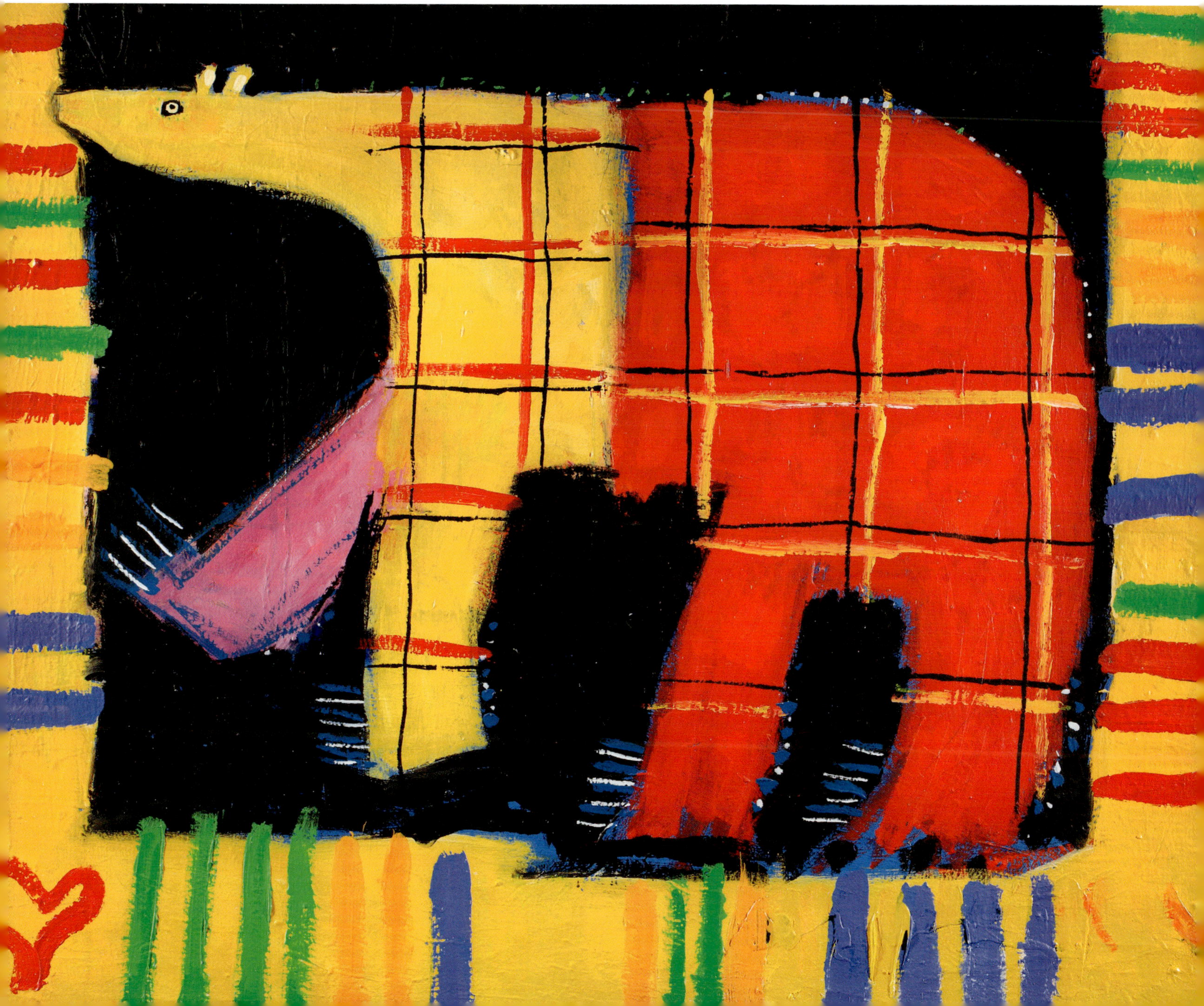

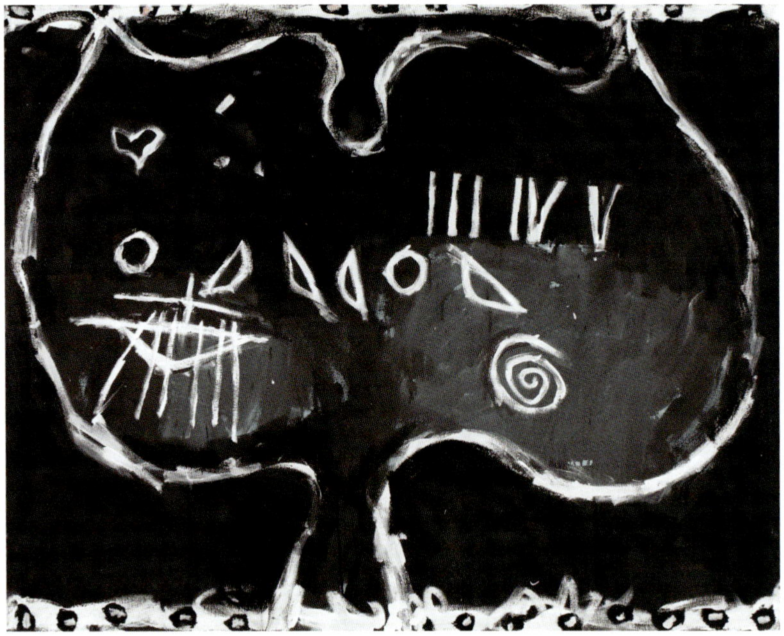

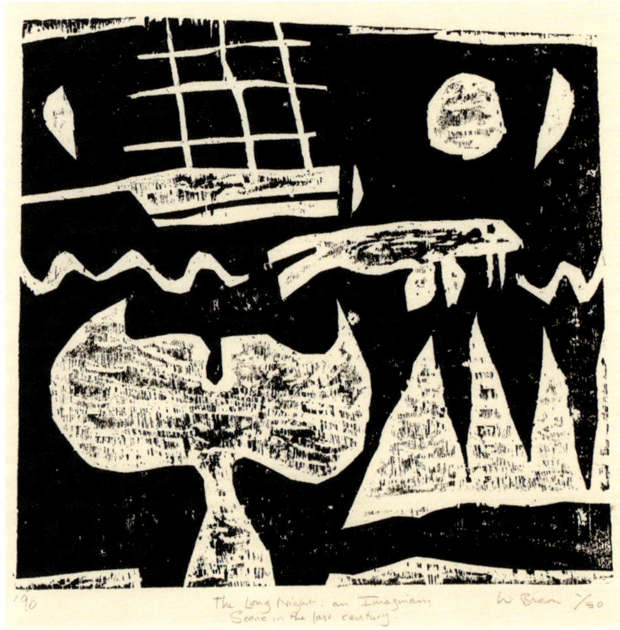

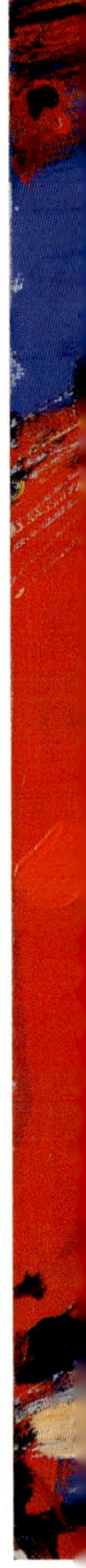

Untitled (whale's tail), undated, c. 2000, oil on canvas, 122 x 152 cm

Above right:
The Long Night: An Imaginary Scene in the Last Century, 1990, woodcut, 40 x 40 cm

Other animals of the Arctic suited a black or grisaille palette and printmaking as a medium. Seals, walruses and whales populated his imagery of Hudson Bay and the Northern Passage as silhouettes [90]. However, a whale's tailfin rising from the water is covered in marks of white on black. Rather than scars from harpoons or rocks, these are William's repertoire of symbols, written like a lesson on a blackboard – the spiral of the drunken ship, the heart, the prehistoric oared boat, ogham script and sun or moon. He titled some of these images *Call Me Ishmael* after the opening line of *Moby-Dick*.

He discovered the Mari Lwyd or 'grey mare' soon after arriving in Llangynwyd, where he made friends with Gwyn and Gill Evans, who ran Pont Rhyd-y-cyff Post Office next door to his studio and happened to keep the paraphernalia for performing the Mari of Llangynwyd under their bed. The custom was, in the words of David Greenslade, 'still rich enough in solemnity, absurdity, terror, ridicule, carnival and finesse to repay commitment and investigation.' William was entranced by the wassailing tradition's depth and vitality in the community but from around 1996 he transformed it into his own interpretation as a beast or bogeyman. He wrote: 'I have recently chosen to explore the very particular and peculiar South Walian story/drama/myth of the Mari Lwyd. This spectral horse/man and part tawdry 'carnie act', features in many recent paintings, prints and drawings. Here he is lurching 'ar y bryn coch' near Llangynwyd. A whodunnit in the making.'[72]

The mid-winter folk custom comprised a horse's skull on a pole manipulated by a man under a sheet who dances with a supporting troupe of mummers from house to house at night, knocking on doors and challenging the inhabitants to battles of wit and rhyme. William asked the Llangynwyd lollipop man who helped schoolchildren across the road to dress as

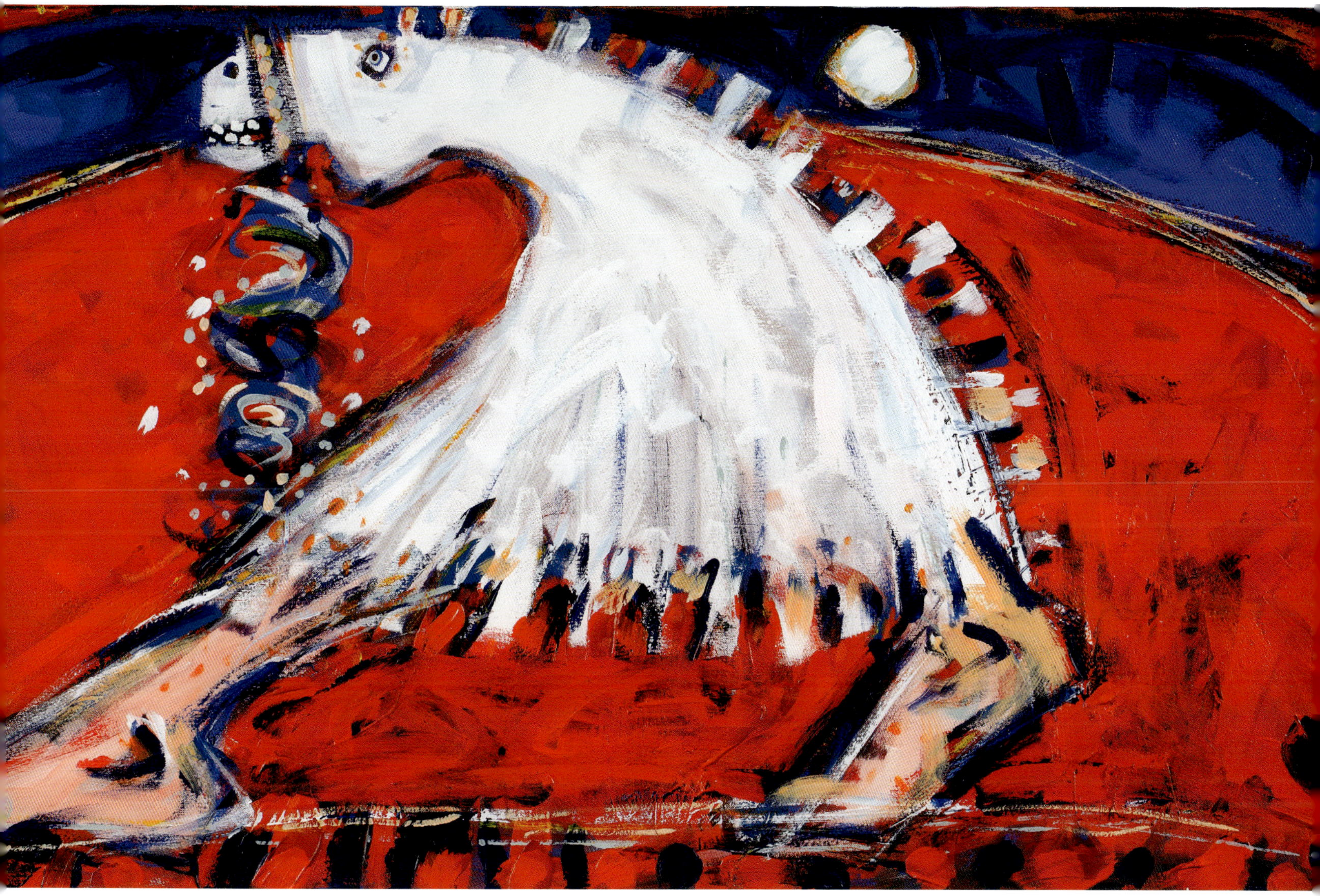

the Mari for him and proceeded to renew the custom rather than appropriate it. In his version, Greenslade says, 'The body is that of a human with exposed legs and enormous clown feet, while the visible head is that of a horse, not (as it would be in practice), a decorated horse's skull [...] enabling something extra to enter the ritualized picture frame.' Laura Gascoigne described the images as having 'the melancholy and mildly comic aspect of a revenant Eeyore crossed with a two-legged pantomime horse.'[73] William called the series '*Yr Ymwelydd* (the Visitor)'.

Mari Lwyd, 1999, acrylic on canvas, 68 x 116 cm

He sometimes Canadianised the Mari Lwyd to paint 'the Moose Lwyd'. It was a creature even more troubled by its lonely and inexplicable existence – a horse with antlers and a sheet [151]. He had seen moose in the wild in his childhood. The animals were generally unthreatening but enormous. A story in the family was that as a child William had told his

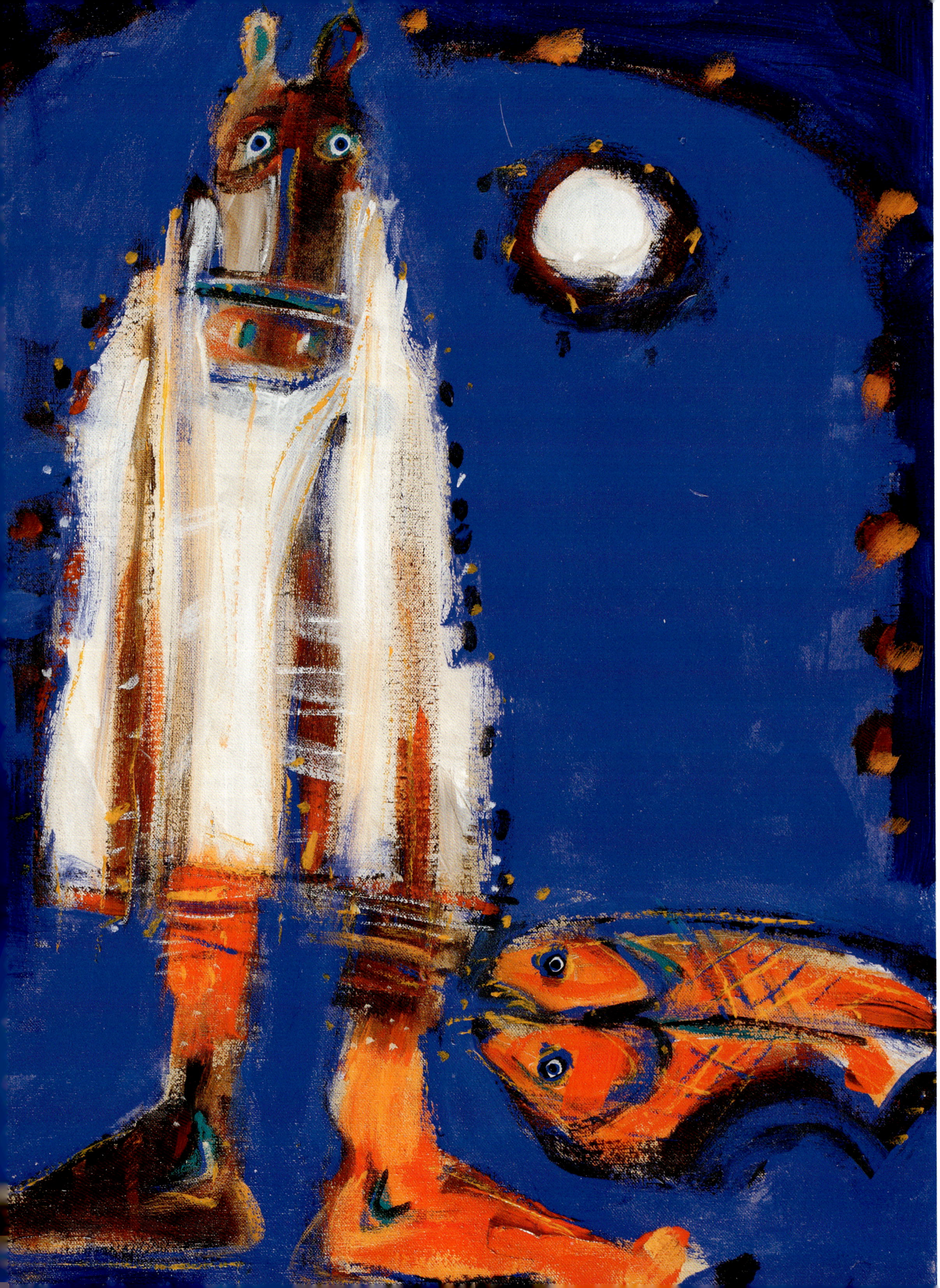

father he was driving too fast on a road through the wilds and asked him to slow down. As it happened, he said this just before they came round a corner to find a twelve-foot bull moose in the middle of the road. They managed to stop in time.[74] That may be the moose behind the wolf in his earlier painting [59]. William was not an artist who might paint a grand portrait like Landseer's *Monarch of the Glen*, but sometimes his moose appeared in the wild. In *Peek a Boo Loup Garou*, a moose is in the forest snow but the wolfman is watching and waiting.

Beasts of different kinds were redolent of his travels and his imaginary worlds. He painted horses on the moors of Devon, whales in the Arctic, and in North Africa, camels, snakes, dogs and the pervasive beast of violence, the fighter jet.

Left:
Yr Ymwelydd, 2006,
acrylic on canvas,
41 x 31 cm

Peek a Boo Loup Garou,
1998, oil on canvas,
76cm x 109cm

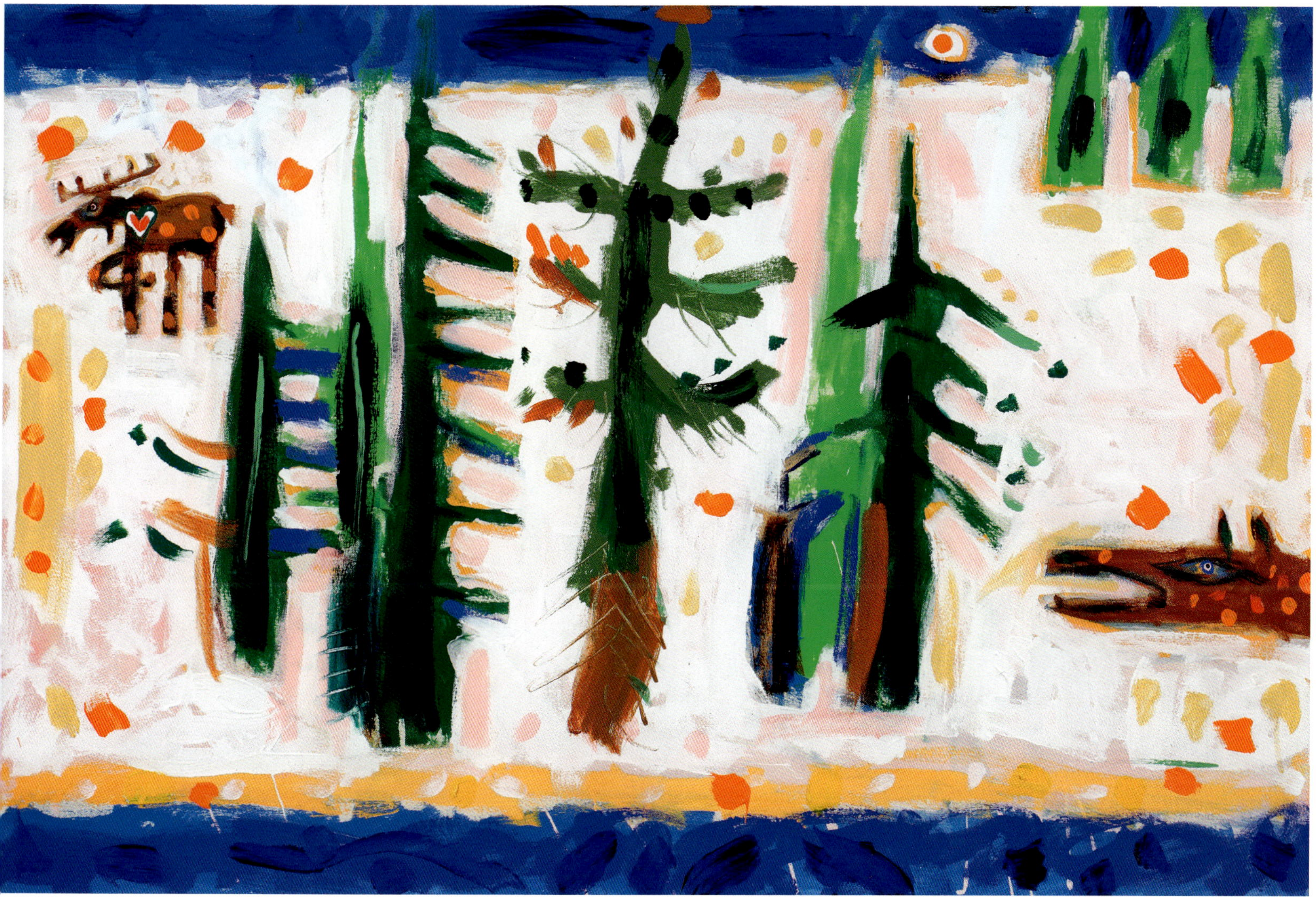

A beautiful and inspiring country.

Explorations

William was an explorer all his life. The landscapes, monuments and cultures of North Africa held his imagination from his first visit in the early 1980s until he died. He returned numerous times, travelling on his own, with Mick Owens, with Carys or with other companions he could persuade along. He planned to go with the French artist Hervé Constant, who was born in Casablanca but had never seen it as an adult. William insisted: 'Hervé, that is your roots.

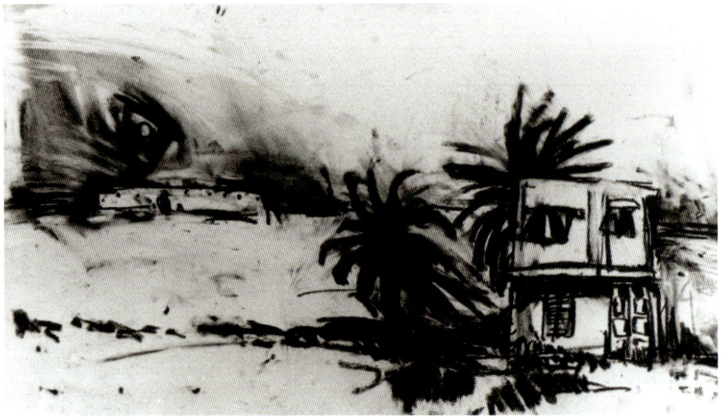

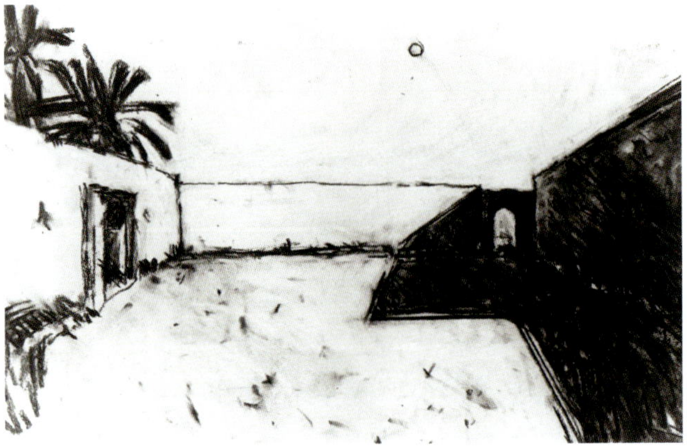

Algeria and untitled, both 1986, charcoal, 56 x 76 cm

You are born there. It is a beautiful and inspiring country you have to re-discover it.' He paid for Hervé to go when he was himself prevented by illness.

He took in Morocco, Algeria and Tunisia, travelling not only to the tourist spots but deeper into the life of the countries. His first drawings and paintings recorded what he saw but within a short time he had found a series of motifs that came together in many combinations – the ruins of Carthage and the huge amphitheatre of El Djem in Tunisia, Lixus in Morocco, date palms, cemeteries, camels, and incongruous visitors in the forms of passenger planes, ships and jets. A ringed snake, straight as a plank and with an open mouth, appeared in many pictures, reminding the viewer that these landscapes have their dangers.

He sought a palette and idiom to suit the region – the inverse of the snows and forests with which he had grown up. He began with spare charcoal drawings in Algeria that captured the empty yards faced by the blank walls of buildings designed for the desert climate. When he introduced colour it was vivid and hot: orange and blue to show heat and distant mountains or sea, and sporadic greens to suggest cacti, palms and circumscribed gardens and oases.

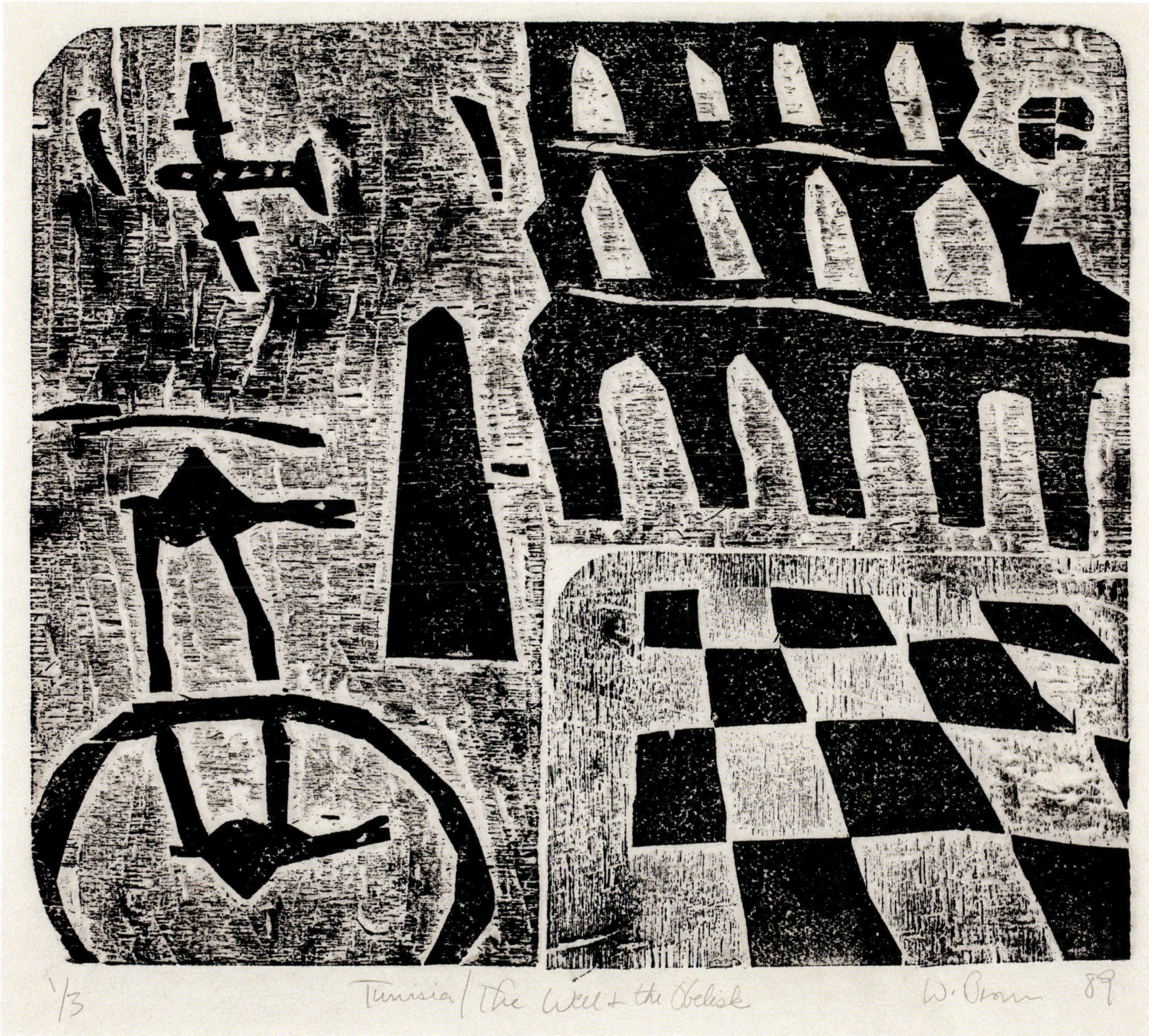

Tunisia / The Well & the Obelisk, 1989, woodcut, 50 x 50 cm

William filled sketchbooks on his journeys. He also carried miniature zinc etching plates, an inch or two across, with wax coatings that he could scribe while travelling and bring back to print, protected in scrunched-up tissue paper. The master-printmaker Pete Williams, when printing some on his behalf, asked how he had found studios for acid-etching on his travels. He replied, 'I just put them in a pot and pissed on them, left them for a few days and now you have them in your hands.'[75]

The Mirage jets were among the dangers visible. William was painting them by 1985. The next year he was in Tunis when the United States bombed Libya in an attempt to assassinate

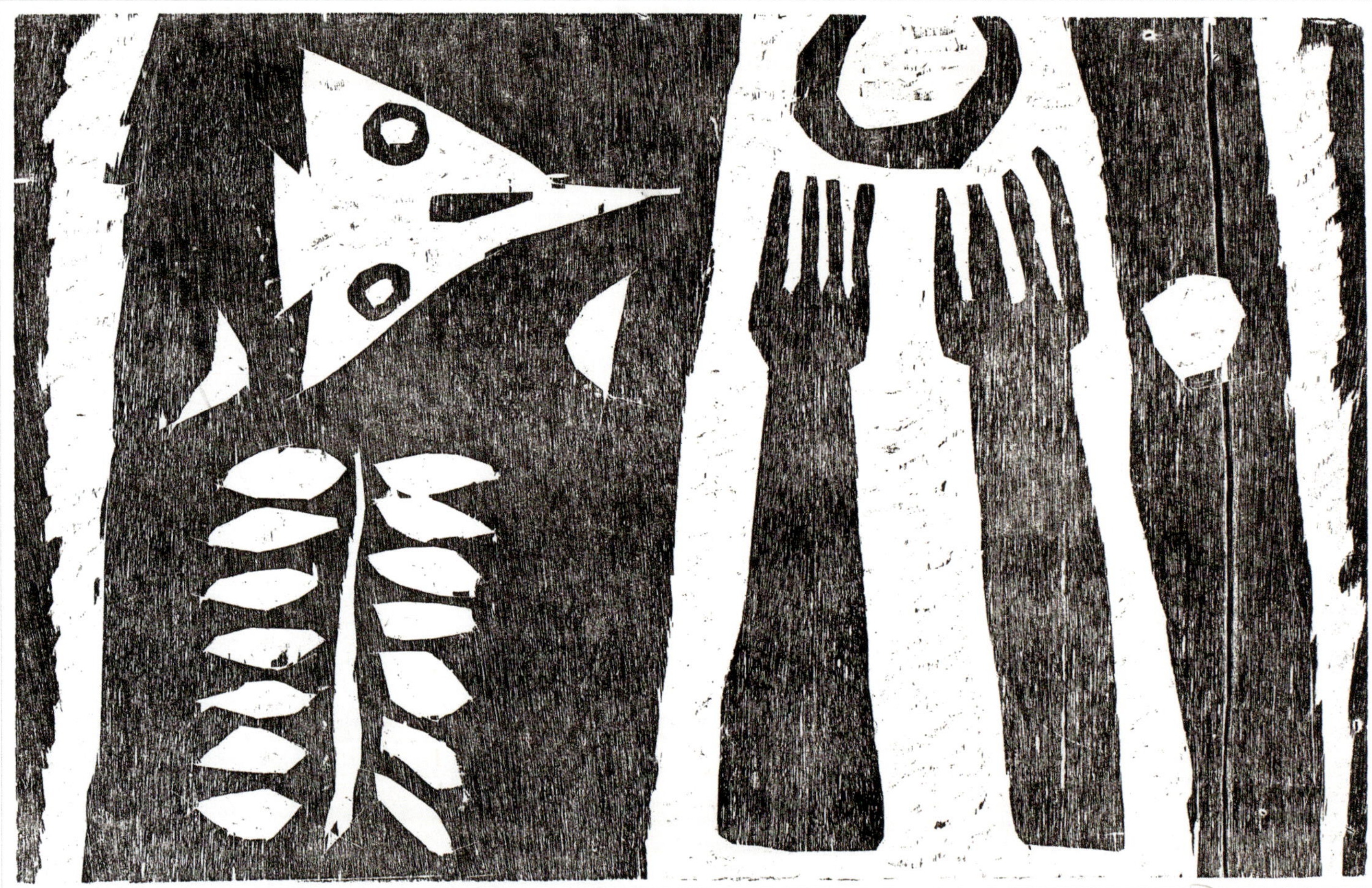

Punic Wars / Sousse, Tunisia, 1987, woodcut, 45 x 70 cm

General Gaddafi in Tripoli in the early hours of 15 April 1986. Nearly fifty aircraft flew down the Mediterranean between Tunis and Sicily. William declared he was in bed at the time but the jets shattering the night sky fired his imagination. He began a flurry of pictures that paired warplanes with palm trees.

He sought to put down statements on canvas and in editioned prints. The woodcut *Punic Wars, Sousse, Tunisia* showed a fighter jet with a palm frond and a pair of forks, or else

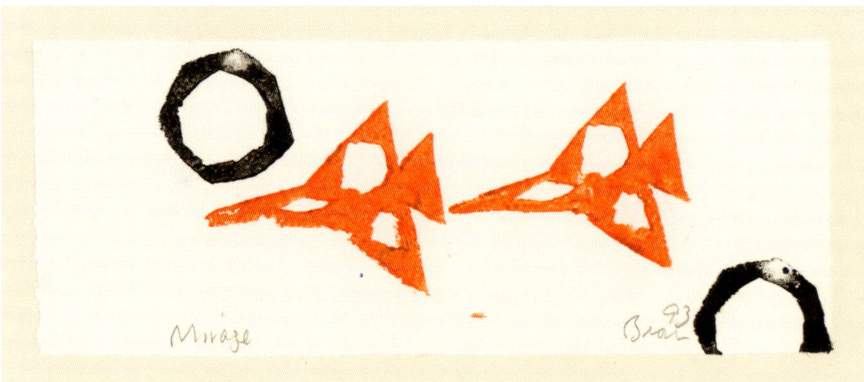

Mirage, 1993, potato print, 11 x 26 cm

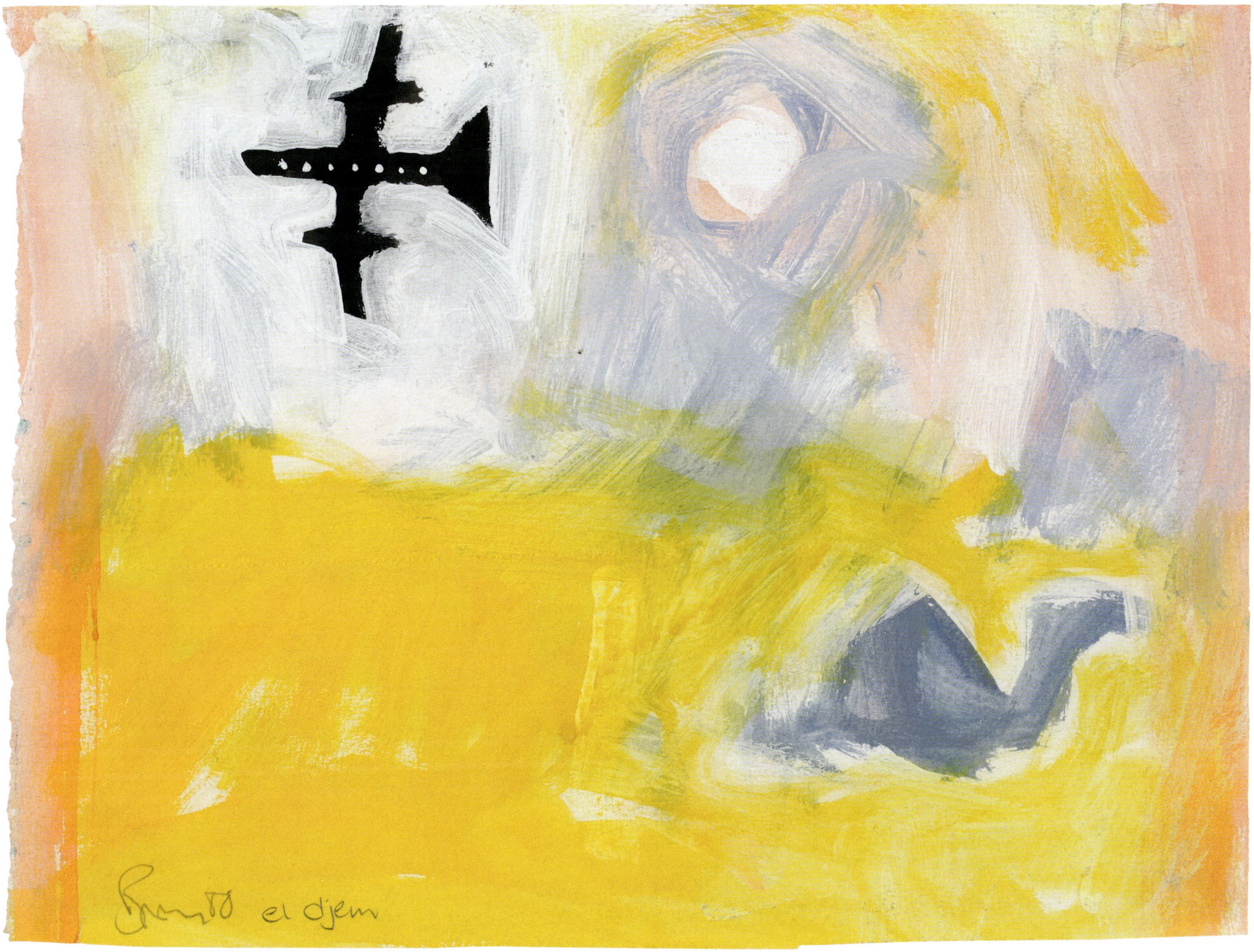

El Djem, 1988, gouache, 22 x 30 cm

dismembered arms, referencing modern warfare and the conflicts between Romans and Carthaginians two thousand years earlier. The jets returned in playful statements, too, such as a potato print of 1993 titled *Mirage*: two planes and two suns.

Shipping captured his attention equally. He watched the bulk carriers lumbering from the ports that transported phosphates mined in Morocco, the major global source of the material for fertilisers. The ships travelled along the Mediterranean to European ports or onwards through the Suez Canal. From further east in the Gulf of Sirte or Sidra, the downward curve in the north coast of Libya, came tankers exporting Libyan oil. The bulk carriers were distinguishable by the superstructures of cranes that lifted the materials from their holds.

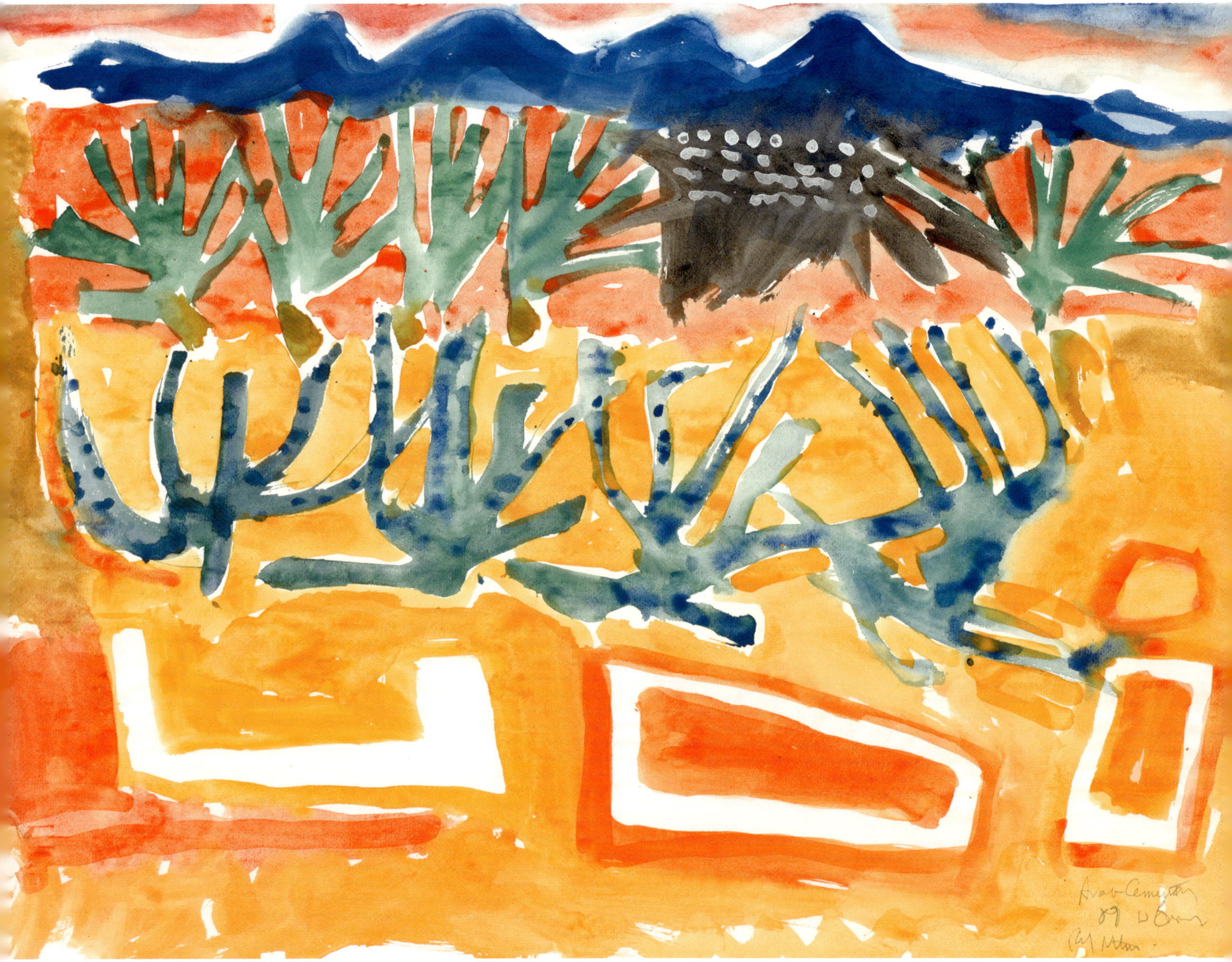

Arab Cemetery Rif Mtns, 1989,
watercolour,
47 x 64 cm

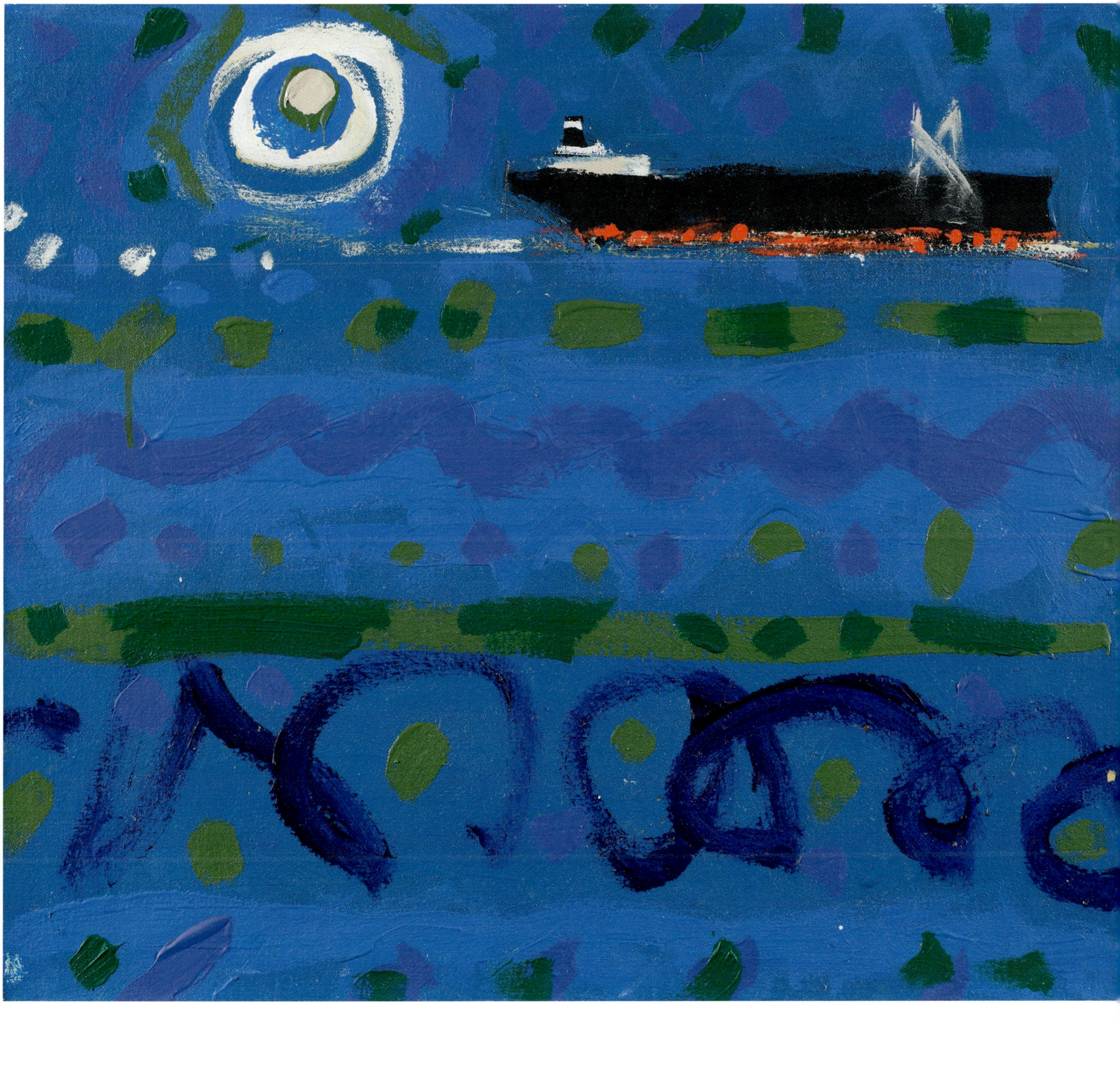

Shipping Gulf of Sirte, 2004, acrylic on canvas, 47 x 53 cm

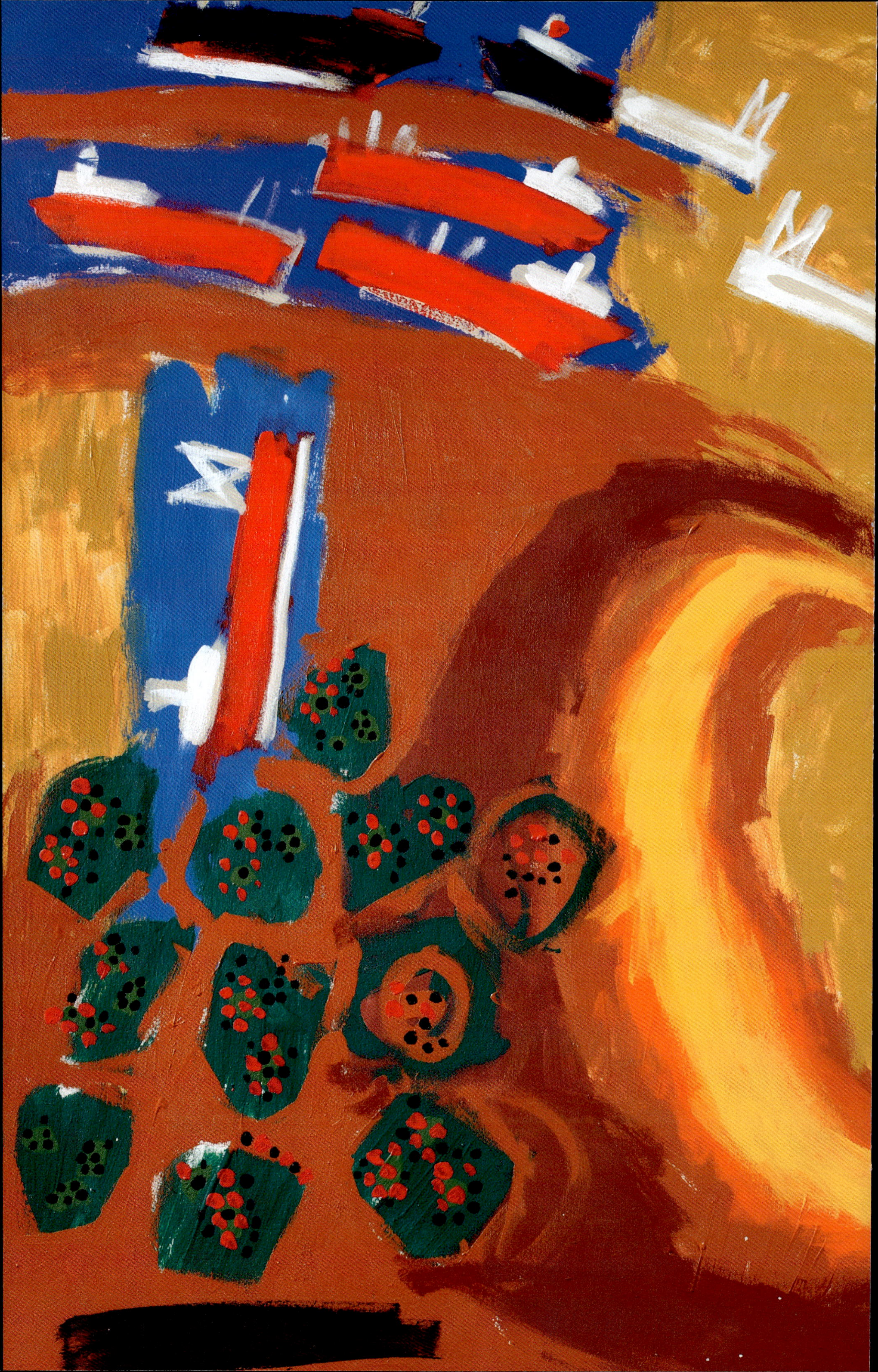

Barbary Coast IV,
2001, acrylic
on canvas,
123 x 180 cm

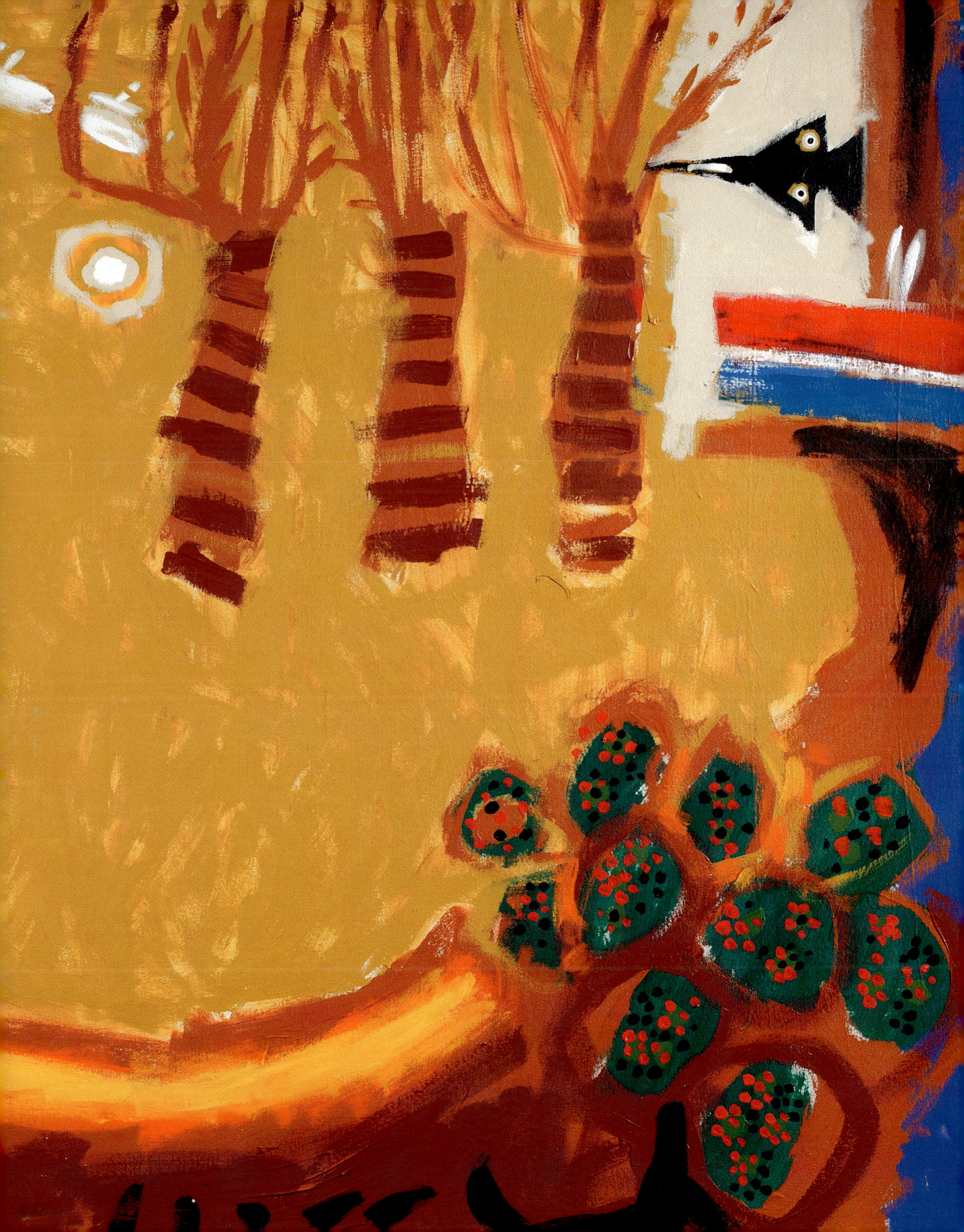

William's paintings at the millennium were map-like views that showed him fascinated and repelled by the mineral exploitation as part of a global system joining extraction and militarism. John Furse wrote in 2002 of:

> the severity of the current cycle of landscape paintings, conceived south of Casablanca in the Western Desert of Morocco, where the phosphate fields [...] become multi-national killing fields in the mind of their maker. There, open-cast mining is rape, ripping off what lies beneath the surface and leaving little or nothing of worth to the far-stretched local economy. The profit lies elsewhere. The well-stashed cargo-carriers put to sea.[76]

By contrast William celebrated the indigenously owned resources of North Africa. He often included palm trees in his paintings and wrote in 2006 for an exhibition in Oman with his friend Abbi Abbas:

> We cannot underestimate the importance of the date palm. "Les Deglets" as they are referred to, are an important crop – for income, domestic consumption, export etc. (amongst the "etceteras" is the notorious boukha distillate) prized by the Berbers,

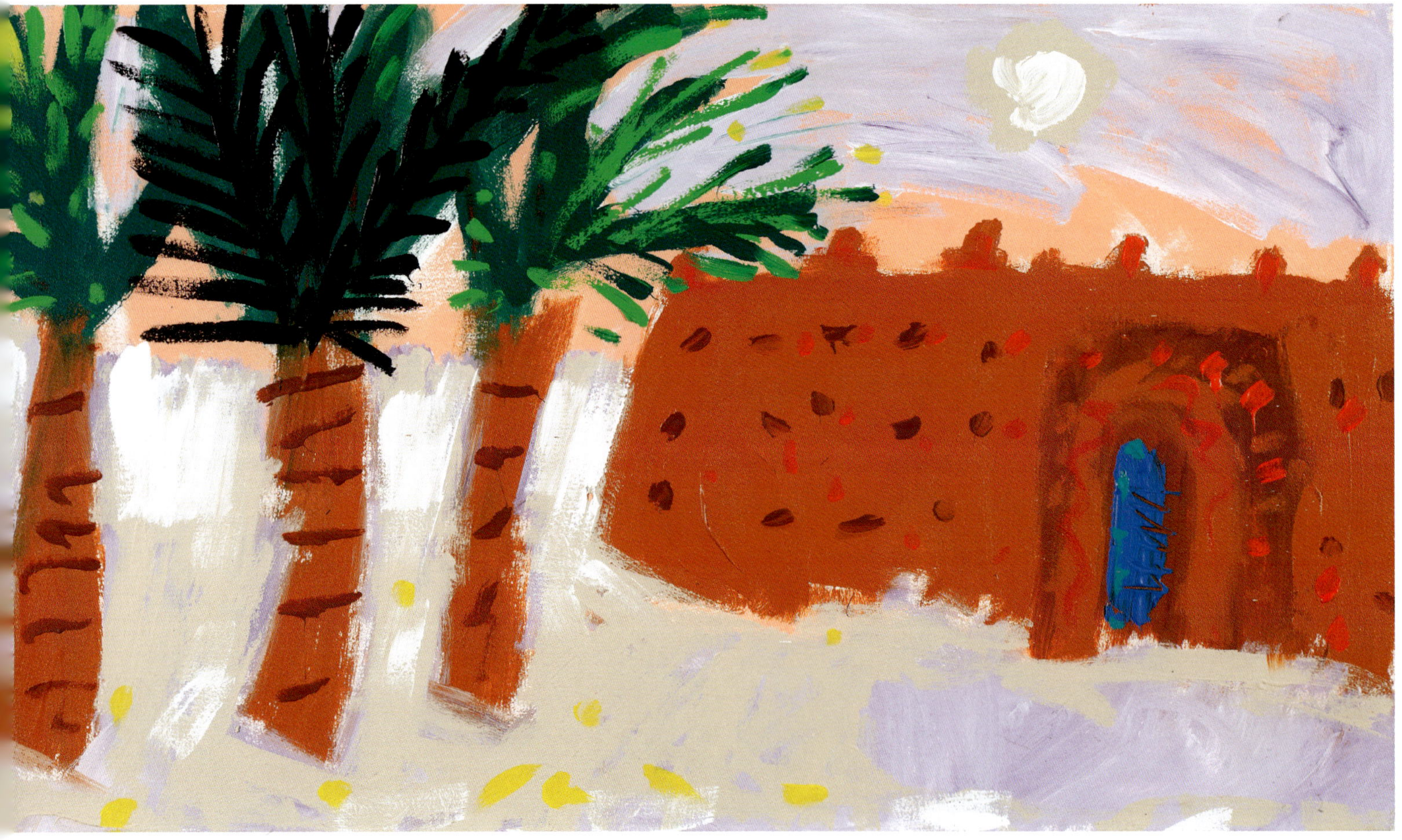

White Sun 4pm, 2001, acrylic on canvas, 68 x 101 cm

peoples of the Kabyle and the mountains of the Ma'ghrebe. Barakka is an Arabic word indicating "luck", "good fortune". The old uncle of a friend of mine Nouali Ali will inherit a palmery consisting of maybe 150,000 date palms in the Sahel.

This was the quality of environment William chose when representing the garden of Eden [88–9]. A colourfully ringed serpent rises between palm trees in an 's' shape on the left, while the right is a luxuriance of blood-red flowers. Above the skyline on the right is an airliner like a cross. Unlike traditional depictions of Eden, there is no Adam, no Eve, no apple.

Next page:
Eden (diptych), 1992, oil on canvas, 122 x 200 cm

The North of Canada was a vast region that William had explored since childhood. He viewed it with a combination of awe and irony, as he expressed in a note about his work in 1981: 'It is comprised mostly of lakes, northern lights and cedar bog. Beside mosquitoes and black flies there is a wonderfully unseen fauna – wolves can be heard.'[77]

The polar regions attracted William like a compass needle to magnetic north. He had travelled as far as James Bay, the southern cove of Hudson Bay, and made charcoal studies of the sea ice and the aurora borealis in 1982. He was drawn back by his pleasure in the deep-freeze winters of his youth, his awe at the unending vastness of the wastes, his admiration of Inuit art and his connection with the Arctic beasts, but the strongest attraction might have been the wealth of stories that he inherited.

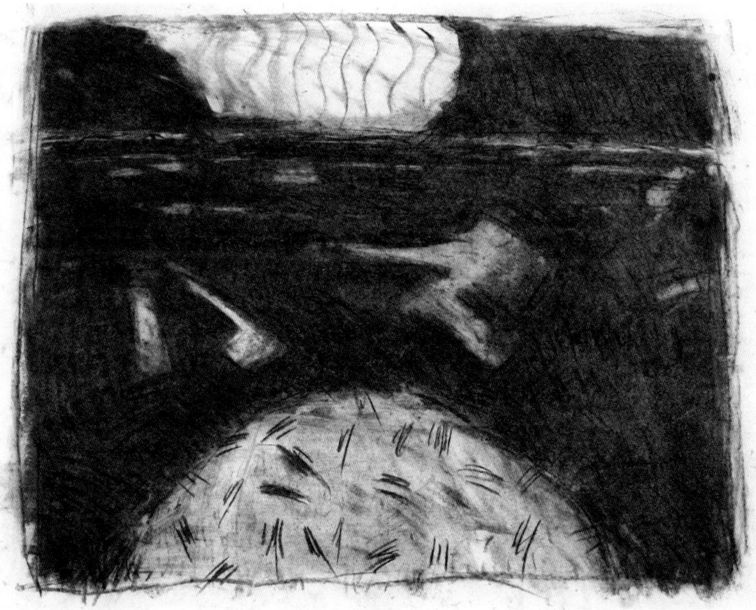

Sea ice, James Bay, Borealis, 1982, charcoal, 50 x 60 cm

Henry Hudson was one of the characters: the Jacobean explorer who sailed up the New York river that would be named after him and subsequently found the eponymous bay in 1611 before his mutinous crew cut him adrift in an open boat there, never to be seen again. Another was William's namesake Robert McClure, who in 1850 at last discovered the Northwest Passage through the Arctic Archipelago. The horrific 'lost expedition' of Sir John Franklin five years earlier was etched in William's imagination. It was later discovered that HMS *Erebus* and HMS *Terror* had been captured by the sea ice; no survivors were found. McClure's expedition set out to find Franklin and his men but his own ship, HMS *Investigator*, was locked in for three years before the crew eventually escaped across the ice.

In 1990, William wrote to the curator of Plymouth City Museum: 'I am completing at the moment an ambitious and assiduously researched / spurious set of woodcuts dealing with early Polar exploration. Featured is the luckless Henry Hudson in his eponymous Bay, etc. etc. I return to Canada this week for a month to complete the project.'[78] It was to be his most ambitious project in printmaking and a landmark in his career. He donated a set of prints

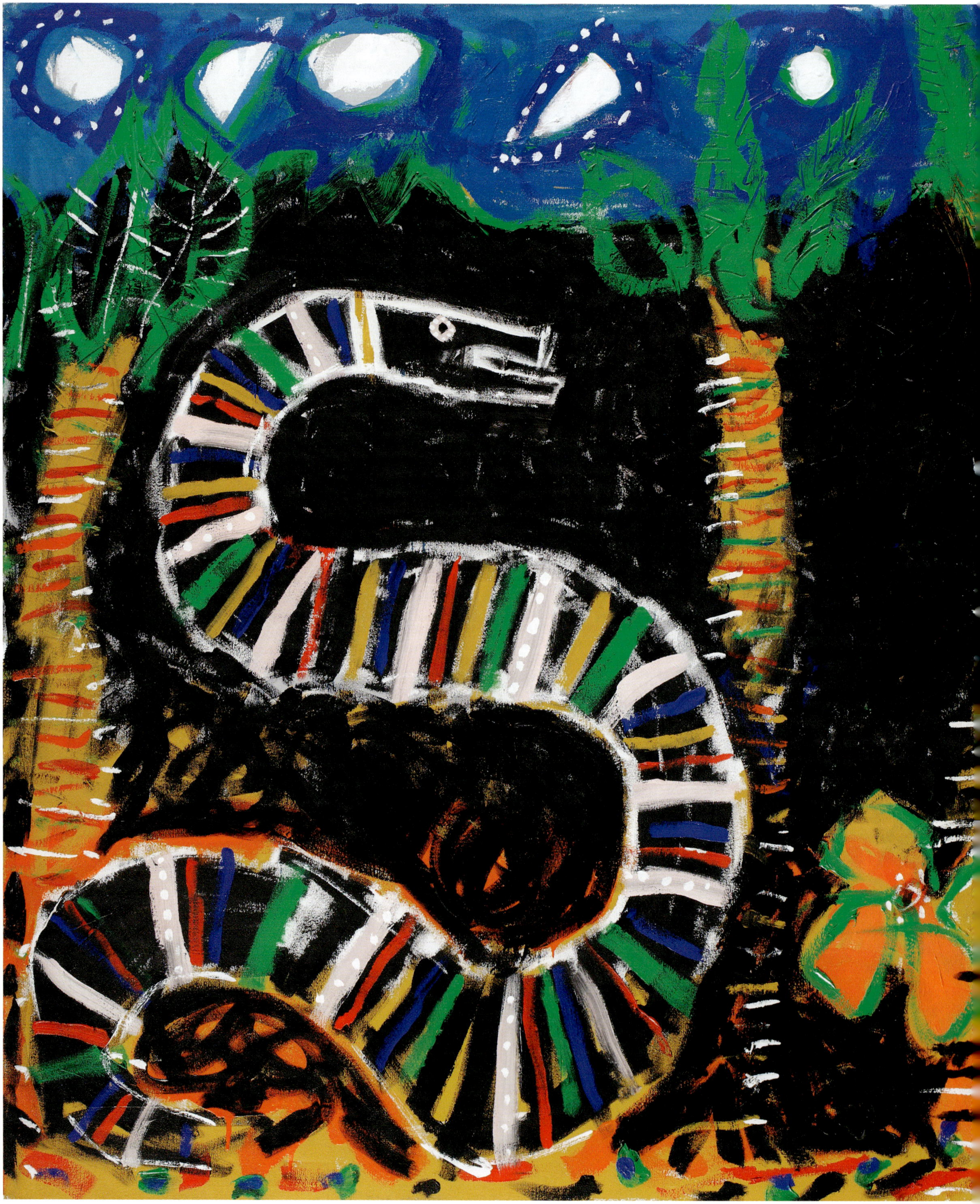

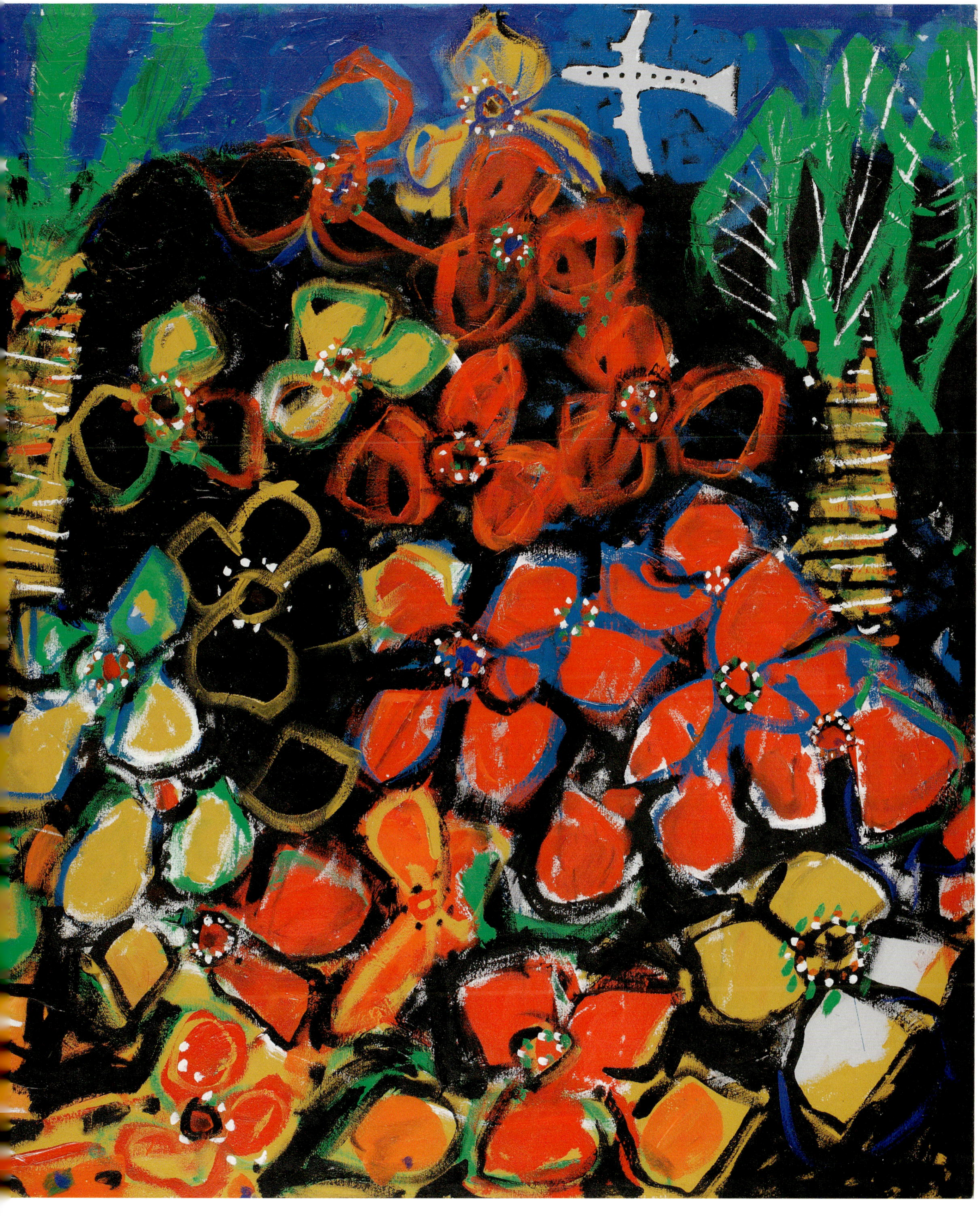

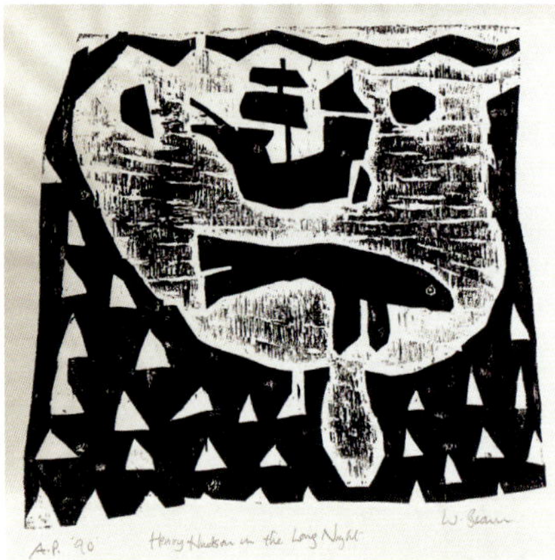

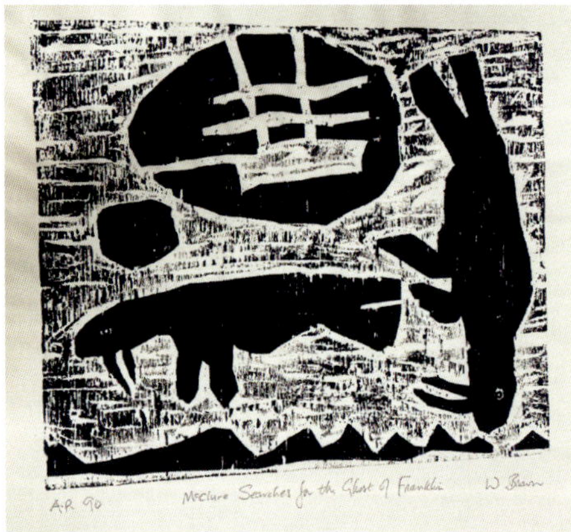

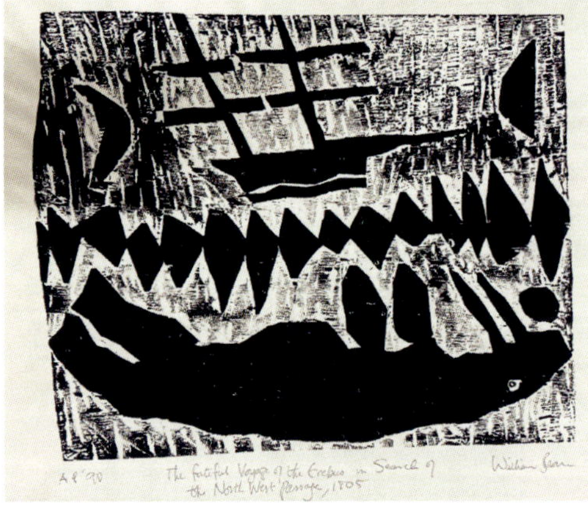

Left to right:

Henry Hudson in the Long Night, 1990, woodcut, 40 x 40 cm

McClure Searches for the Ghost of Franklin, 1990, woodcut, 40 x 40 cm

The Fateful Voyage of the Erebus in Search of the North West Passage, 1805, 1990, woodcut, 40 x 40 cm

Moose Factory / Asleep by a Frozen Sea, 1990, woodcut, 40 x 40 cm

to Plymouth. Copies of several images were also acquired by the National Maritime Museum (now Royal Museums Greenwich) and Peel Art Gallery and Museum in Ontario, where he showed them in 1991. Like his earlier woodcuts, the images were roughly cut on plywood so that texture came through in the lowered areas of white. The animals he depicted were the same as might be seen in Inuit art but the depictions were his own simplifications of their presence in the landscape.

Some of the print titles explicitly reference the stories that engrossed him: *The Fateful Voyage of the 'Erebus' in Search of the North West Passage, 1845* and *McClure Searches for the Ghost of Franklin*. Others capture a more general cultural and natural history of these Canadian regions, such as *The Arrival of the Orcadians at Hudson Bay*, marking the great role that men of Orkney played in the staffing of the Hudson Bay Company in the eighteenth century.

William's phrase 'assiduously researched / spurious' expresses the nature of his process, driven by imagination to create fictions from the stranger facts of polar history. His poetic iconography captures the essence of these stories of the far north.

Henry Hudson in the Long Night depicts a ship afloat in a pool that has the well-known shape of Hudson Bay. Half the space is filled up by a seal who swims oblivious to the arrival of intruders. On one side of the ship is the sun and on the other is a half-moon, a nod to the name of Henry Hudson's Dutch ship, *Halve Maen*. The caravel-shaped hull, like a curled leaf, entered his imagination, William recalled, when 'I was standing on the Clifton Suspension Bridge looking down at the tiny reconstructed *Matthew* as it passed. This beautiful little vessel made the journey across the Atlantic to Newfoundland 400 years ago. You could fit it in my studio in Llangynwyd!'[79]

Another woodcut expressed the exploitation of the north with imagery of the trading station or 'factory' of the Hudson Bay Company on an island at the mouth of the Moose River. William told the journalist Jennifer Gill in 1989, 'Moose Factory is a town that was founded in the 17th century on the Moose River where they made a living out of trapping beaver.' In *Moose Factory / Asleep by a Frozen Sea*, the shape of Hudson Bay appears again, with its near

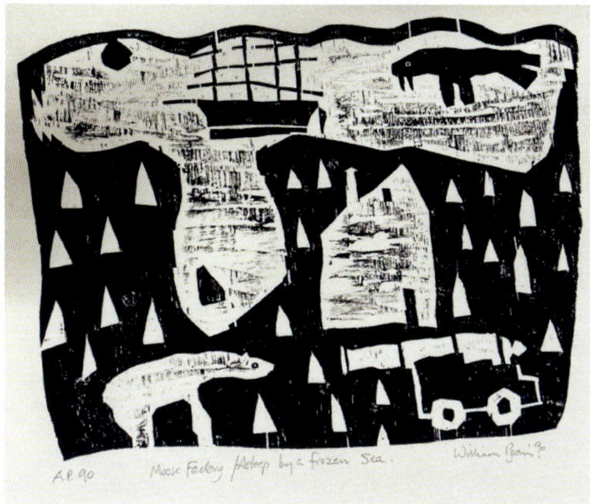

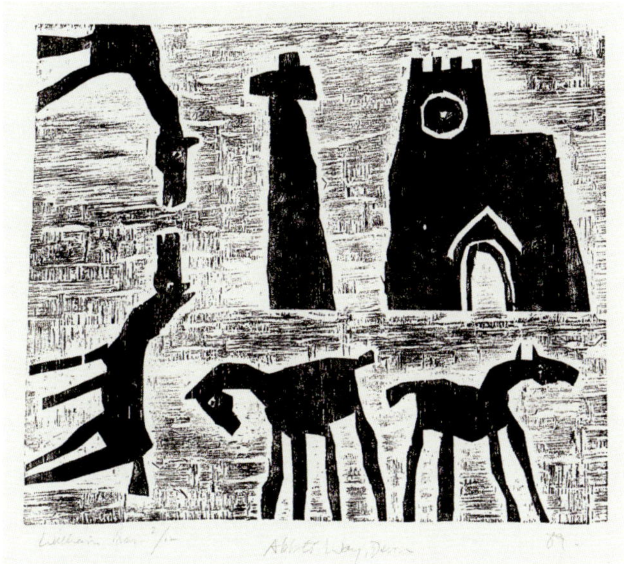

Abbot's Way, Devon, 1989, woodcut, 37 x 40 cm

extension of James Bay. The distinctive outlines of Staff House, a four-masted schooner and a cannon co-exist with a polar bear, a walrus and unending forests.

Between the sorties to North Africa and the returns to Canada, William explored the places where he lived. In south-west England in the 1980s he made images of landscapes and historic sites from Somerset to Cornwall. He enjoyed contrasts of motifs – ruined mines, high crosses, moorland horses, radiocommunication dishes and transatlantic jets. Princetown on Dartmoor and the Abbot's Way trail were among the places named in titles.

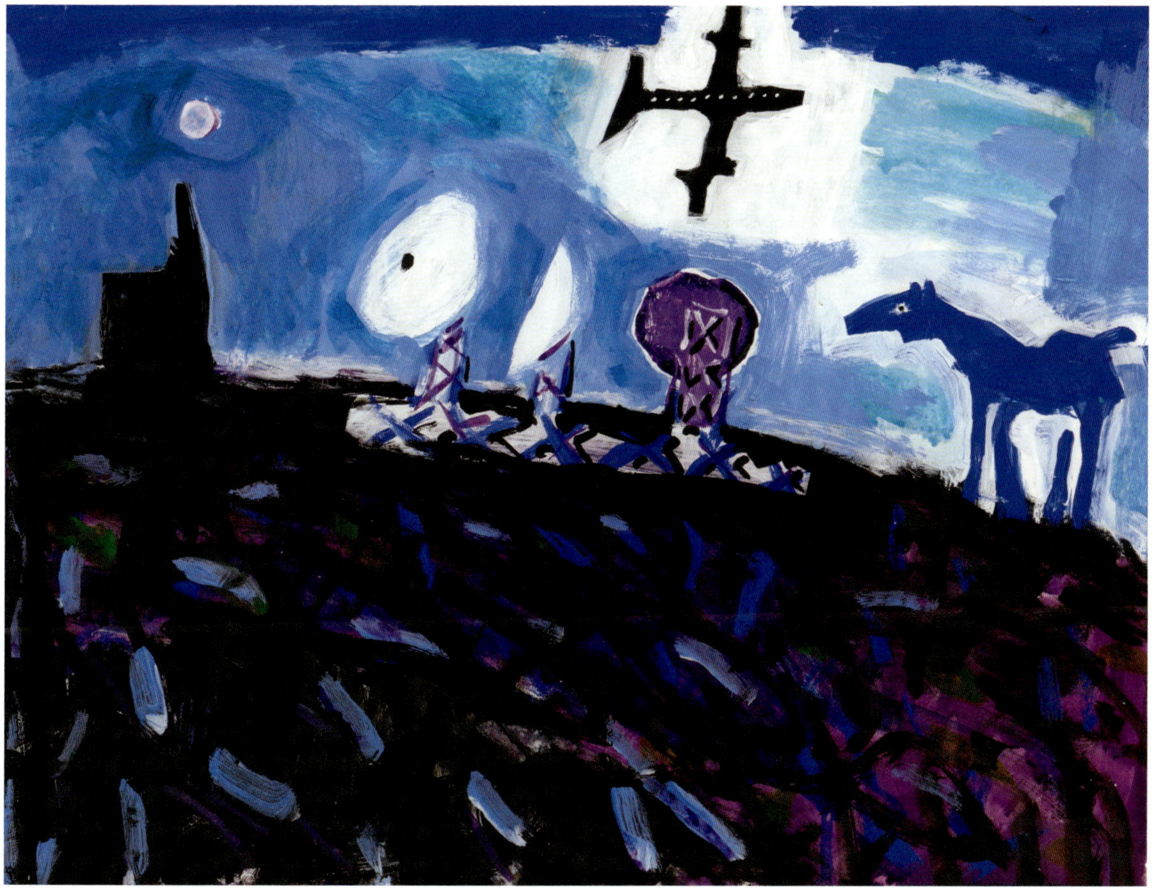

Untitled (Cornwall), undated, *c.* 1983, acrylic on paper, 29 x 38 cm

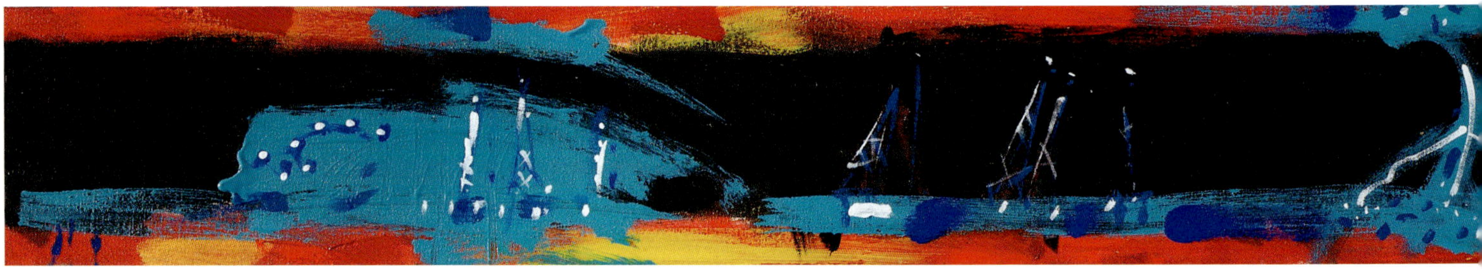

(Ar Hyd Y Nos) Vol du Nuit,
2001, acrylic on canvas,
53 x 77 cm

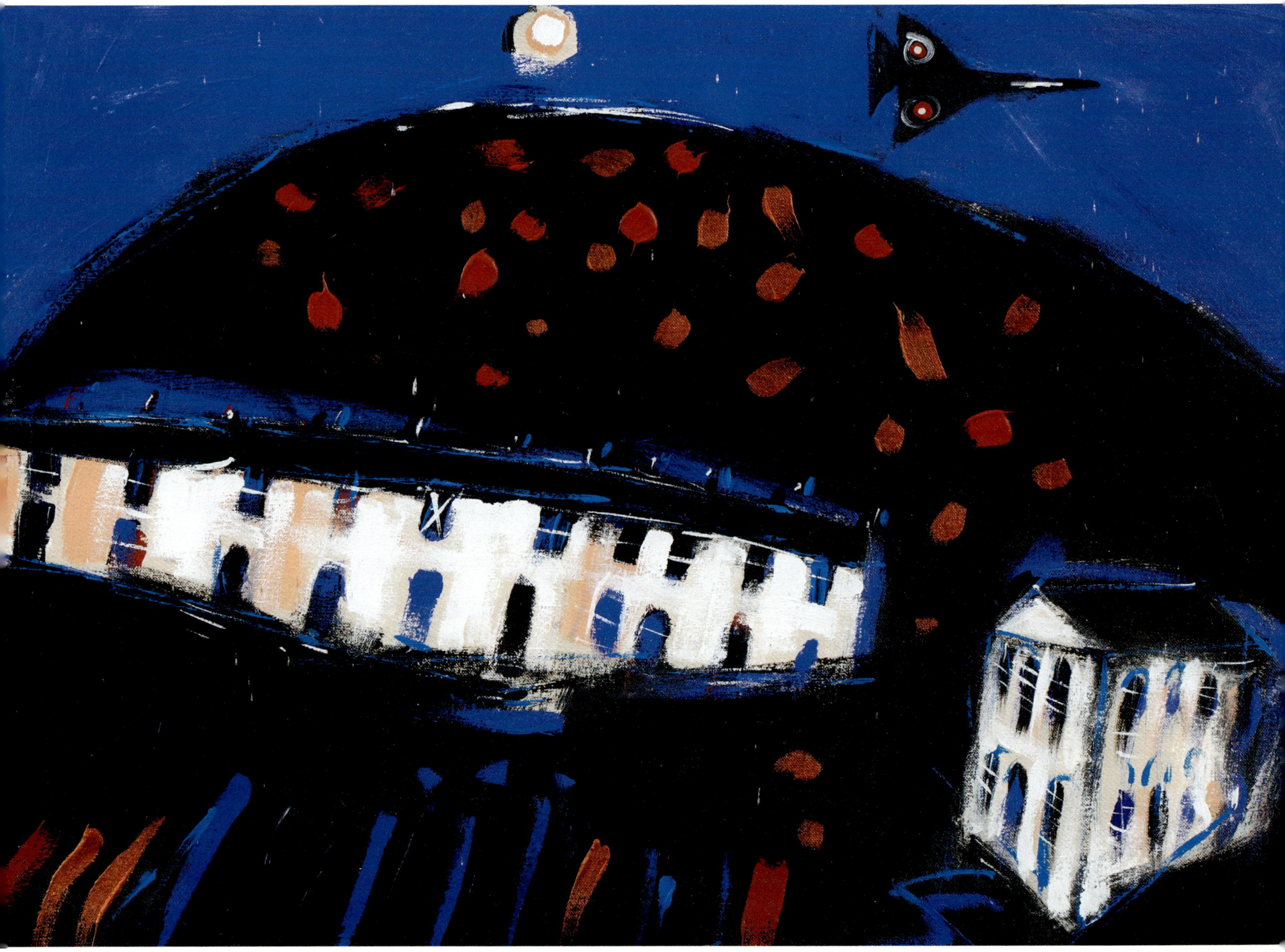

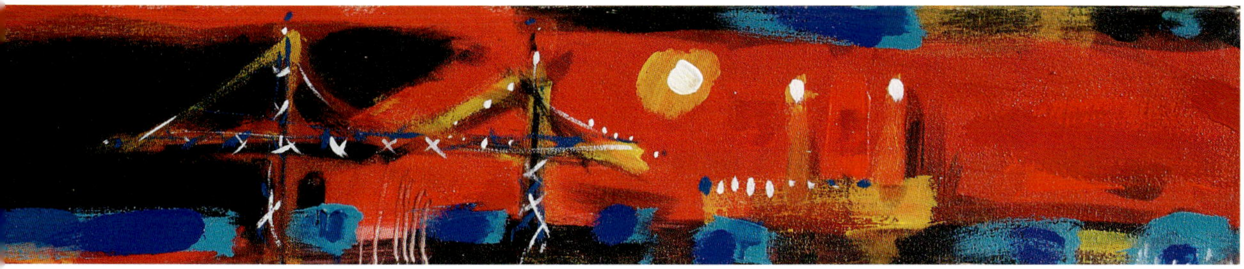

Newport – Approaching Storm – What's de Matter?, undated, *c.* 1998, oil on canvas, 16 x 180 cm

South Wales was a revelation when he began visiting with Carys and when they moved to Bridgend. He was struck by the verticality of mountain sides, the presence of the sea, the incongruity of cooling towers. His project with Keith Bayliss in the Swansea valley brought many drawings of the area into the collection of the Glynn Vivian. Malcolm Parr wrote about his exhibition at Pontardawe: 'these landscapes are as dramatic as any I have seen. Huge dark hills, like hump-backed whales, threaten to devour the straggling ribbons of terraced cottages. Yet these rows of tiny houses, vividly and fiercely painted, seem to have a life of their own.'[80]

William roamed along the coast to Swansea and found views from the hills back towards Swansea Bay and the Bristol Channel, with the hills of Somerset across the water [95]. In the early 1990s he still saw the landscape as an outsider; trying to pull the elements together for the first time but taking in the scene with freshness. He found a new palette once again, this time of black hills, white buildings, blue sea and emerald-green grass. Panoramic views took in the coastal strip with all its changing weather. As it transpired, many elements that so

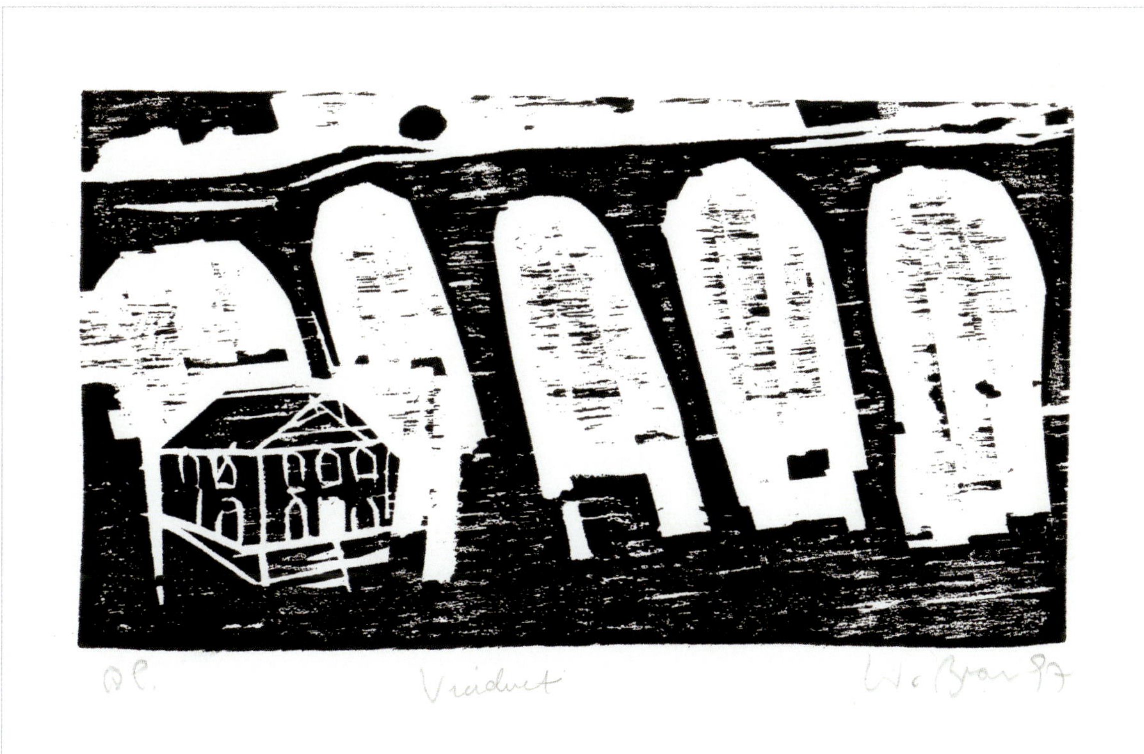

Viaduct, 1997, woodcut, 17 x 31 cm

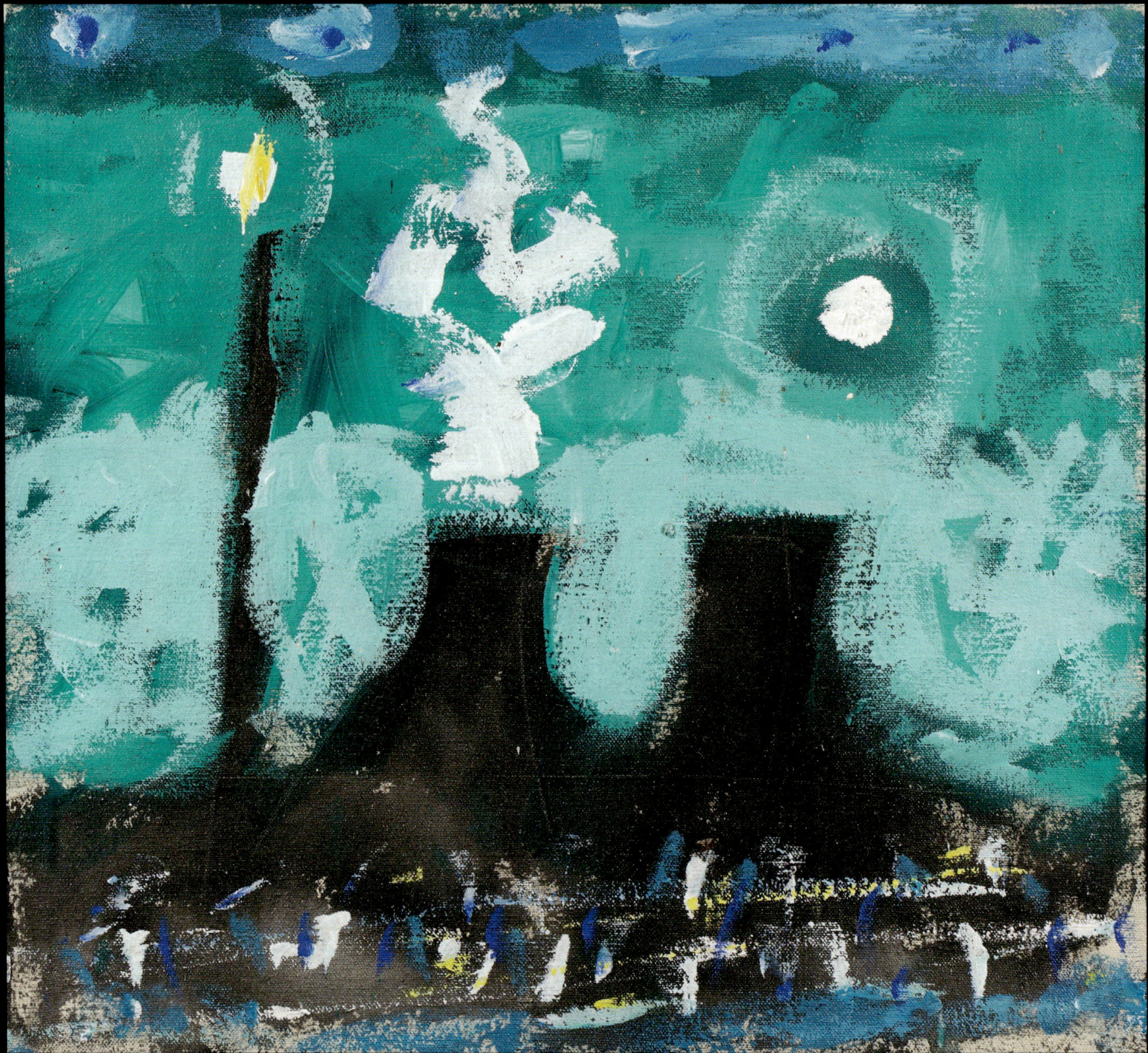

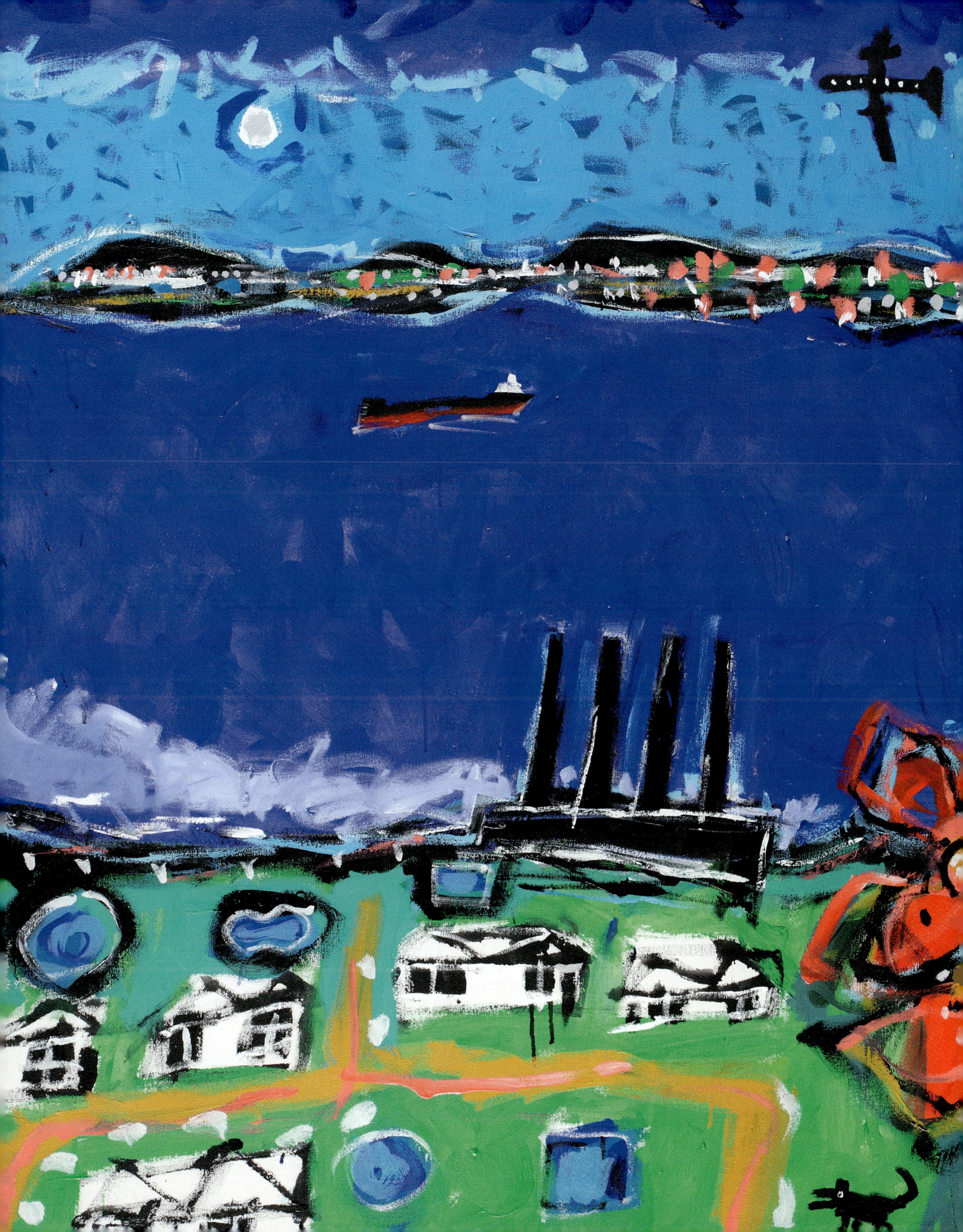

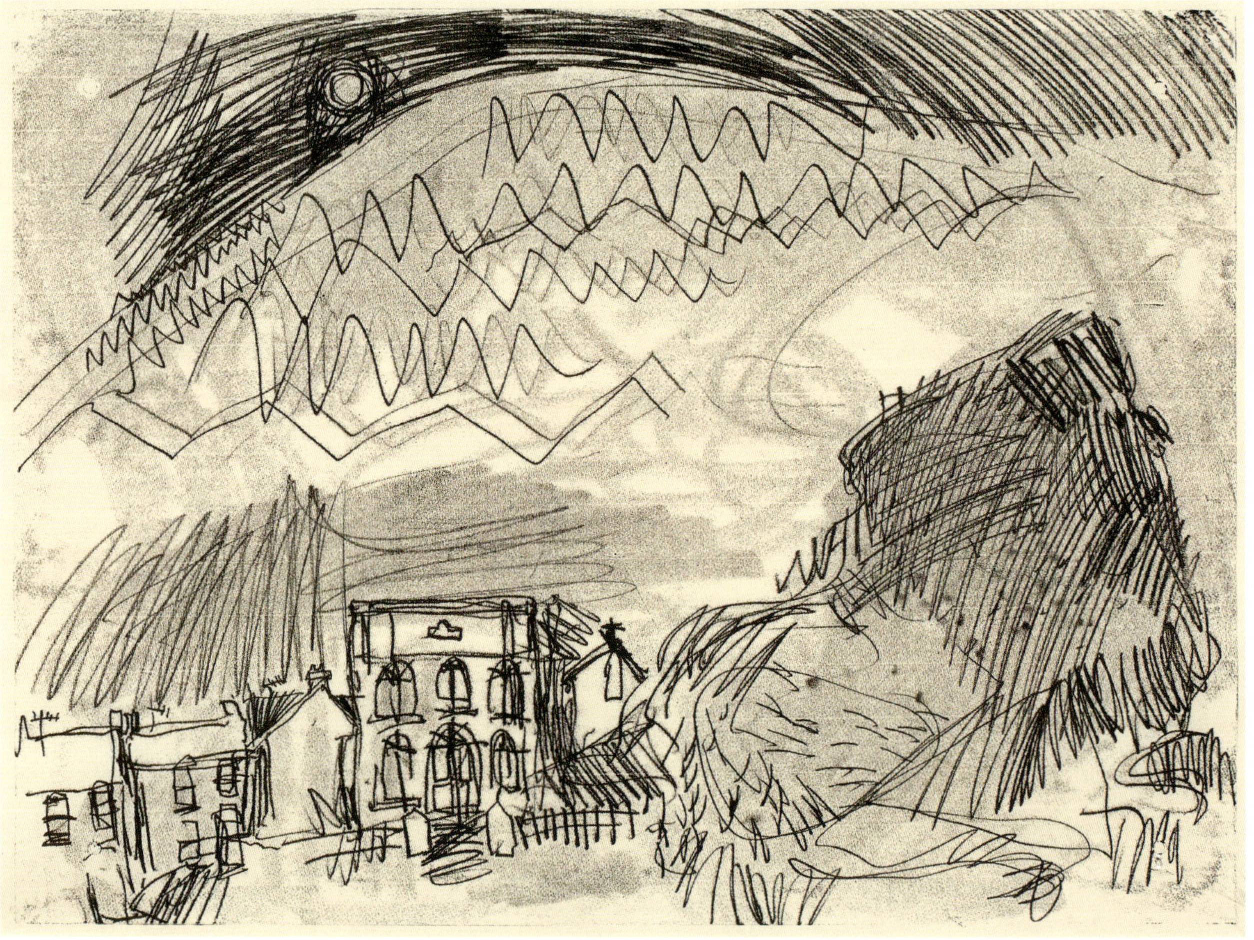

Untitled (Pontrhydyfen), undated, *c.* 1992, monoprint, 50 x 65 cm

struck him would shortly disappear from the landscape, including the vast cooling towers at Llandarcy oil refinery and Baglan chemical works.

In south Wales as elsewhere, William's interest was never in recording the topography. The point is demonstrated in an etching of a chapel sandwiched between terraced houses and a great rock – a distinctive location at Pontrhydyfen in the Afan valley. He drew it straight onto the plate so that it printed as a mirror image of reality. The incised valley above Port Talbot felt almost Alpine in its narrow, winding route surrounded by forests and crags but infilled by straggling former mining villages. He travelled along it to the end to find Blaengwynfi and the disused Rhondda railway tunnel.

Shorter visits were possible when travelling around Britain and Europe. In addition to the opportunities William took to hold exhibitions or attend events in the Czech Republic, Germany, the Netherlands and France, he and Carys embarked on successive holidays as legs of a 'Grand Tour'. William drew wherever he went and often exhibited the resulting watercolours. Florence, Venice, Prague, all appear in his sketchbooks. Pont-Aven in Brittany held a resonance as the sometime home of Paul Gauguin and he made several woodcuts of the town at night.

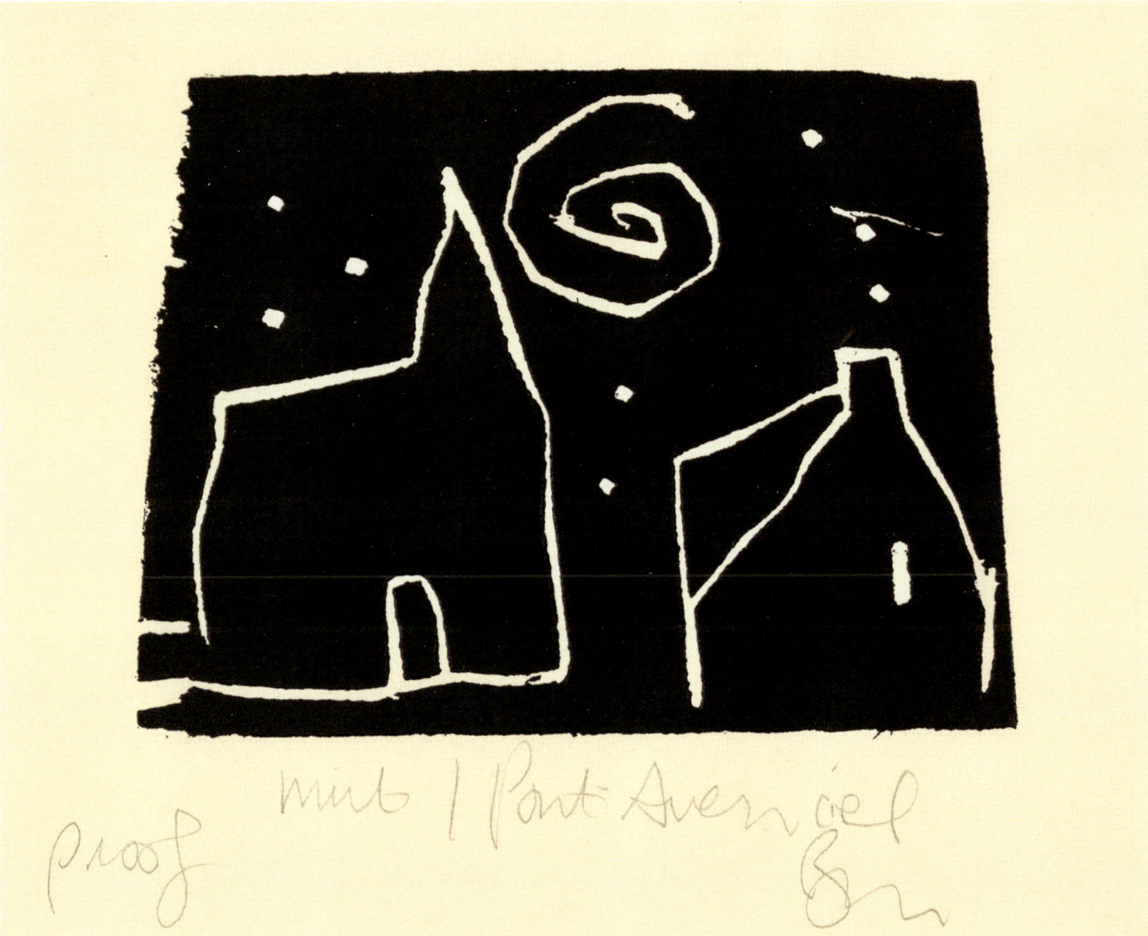

Nuit / Pont Aven Ciel, undated, woodcut, 15 x 18 cm

Below: *Ponte Vecchio, Florence*, 1998, watercolour, 15 x 30 cm

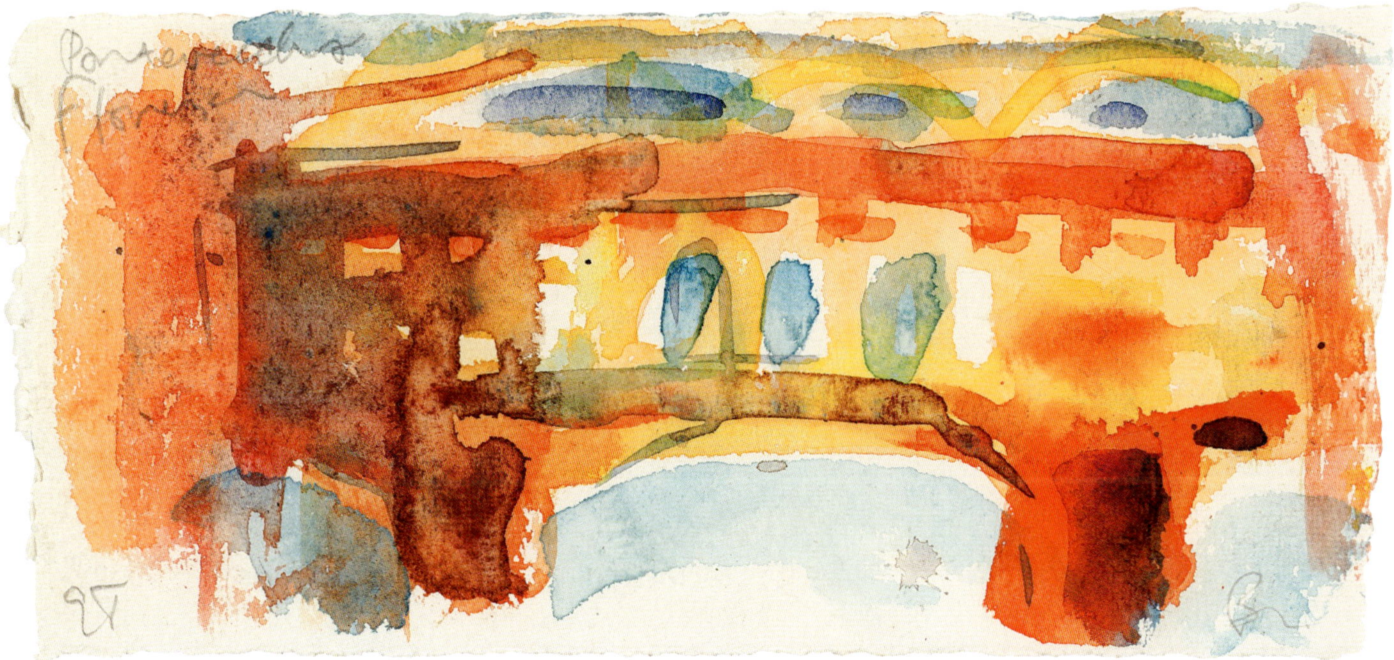

He went north in the British Isles, travelling to Orkney and Shetland several times in the 1990s. He set off first with Adrian Metcalf and a Welsh Arts Council travel grant, having said in his application that he hoped to research traditional links between the islands and the early exploration of North America.[81] He discovered an affinity with his Scottish roots and drew peat cuttings, crofts, and the famous red sandstone sea-stack, the Old Man of Hoy [100]. William and Carys went back many times to a rented cottage. They cooked live lobsters, but only after William had drawn them. In 1992, the Old Man of Hoy pictures were shown in London. A reviewer in the *Hampstead and Highgate Express* wrote: 'The cliffs of St Ola off Hoy Sound drop like a layer cake made for a gluttonous sea beast; vivid pink, striped with blue, green and white, spectacular and improbable; one of the works by which William Brown might become dramatically identified.'[82]

Creative projects took William to places that introduced him to new subjects. At Gütersloh with the Glaws he created images of a white church reflected in water [101]. With Lucien Suel, William was drawn to the group of conjoined towns in the Pas-de-Calais, Isbergues, Berguette and Guarbecque. Lucien and William had met through

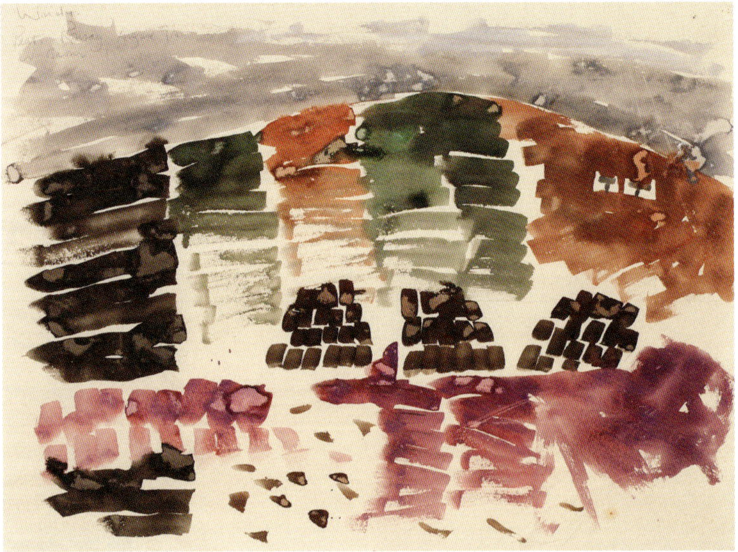

Windy. Peat. Rousay., 1996, gouache, 50 x 60 cm

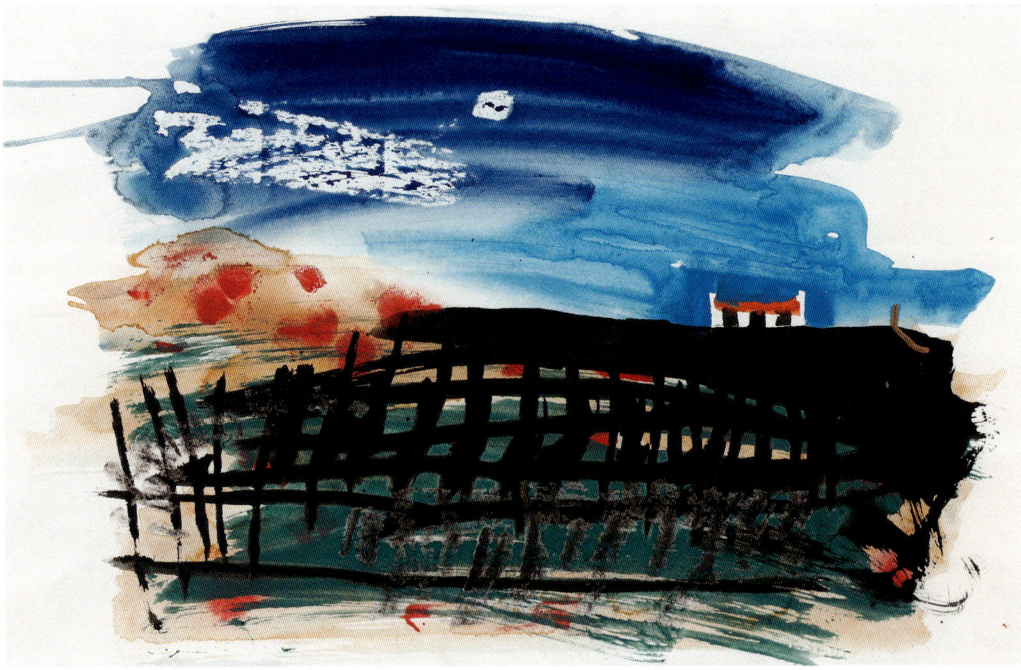

Untitled (Orkney), undated, 1996, gouache, 25 x 35 cm

Mail Art in 1989 and William came to visit in 1994. He found the landscape fascinating and familiar: a border region of France with Flemish influence, rural but with the scars of deindustrialisation and the conical spoil tips *les terrils*. He returned to have an exhibition at Isbergues in 1995, held in the town's exhibitions hall, attended by local dignitaries and well covered by the local press. William told a reporter that the place brought back memories of the intertwining of the rural, industrial and post-industrial.[83]

In 1996 he started to make huge diptychs of an approaching storm, each over 228 cm wide. The first versions were of Berguette, showing a black storm cloud advancing across the flat lands to the church of Saint-Nicholas at Guarbecque and a bow-like bridge across the ship canal at Isbergues [102]. He revisited the subject but relocated to Newport [103]. William was evasive when asked for explanations, even by close friends. Lucien Suel recorded a conversation for the catalogue at Newport Museum and Art Gallery. He asked him about the vision of a church descending from the sky above Newport Transporter Bridge, what might be happening inside the church, whether it is Saint-Nicholas's from the Pas de Calais, and whether it is prophetic. William answered none of these questions but referred to his admiration of the art in St Maurice's church in Lille and the paintings by Van Oost. Storm clouds do darken those biblical scenes, but there any similarity ends.

Orkney, 1996,
charcoal, 45 x 60 cm

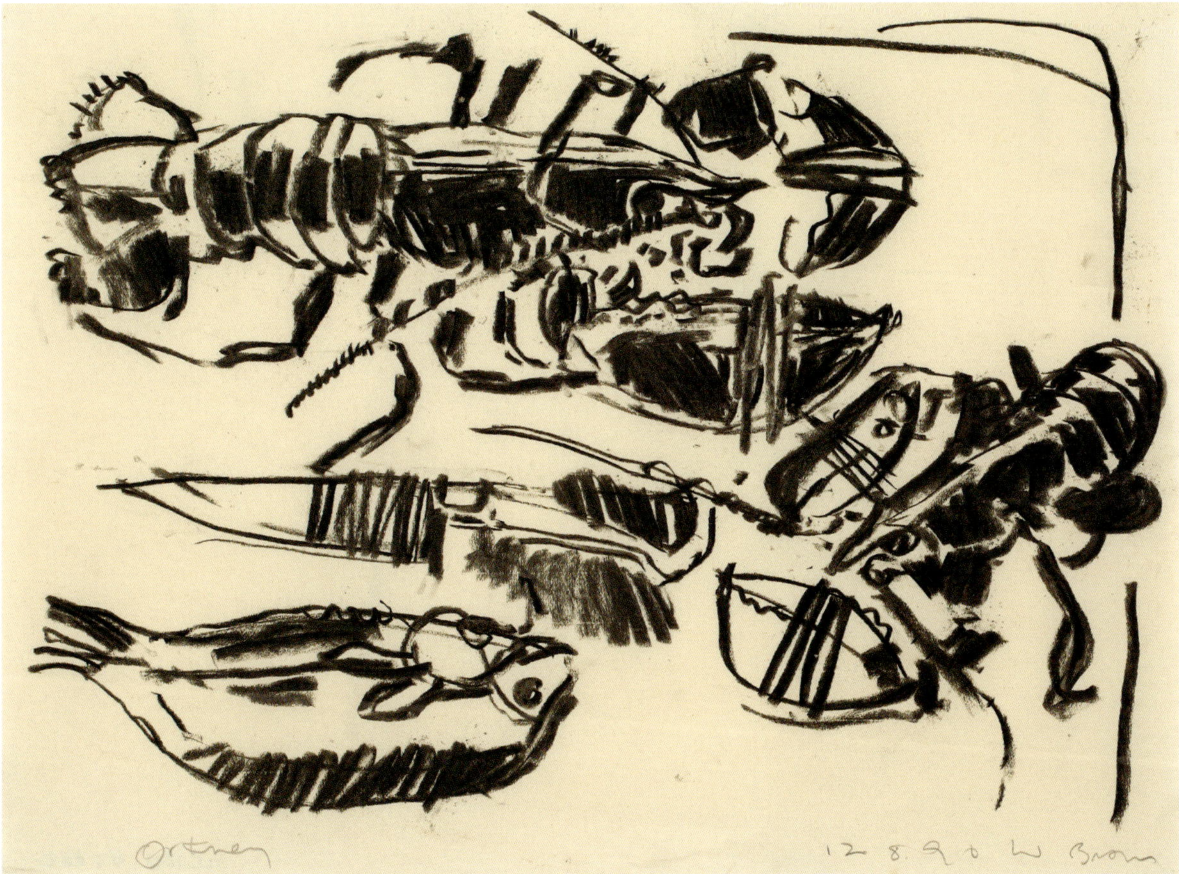

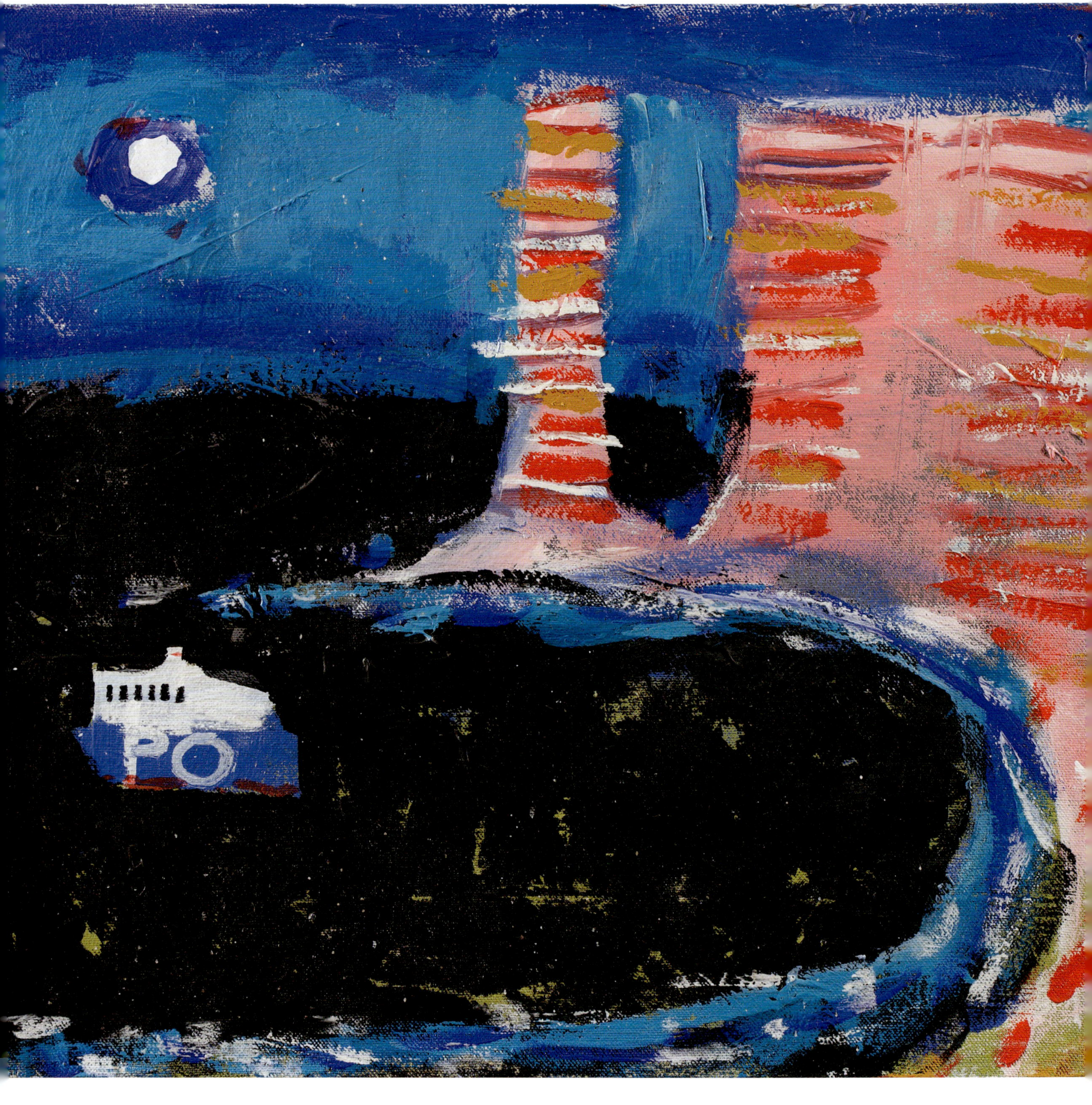
PO

William's paintings recognisably lift the church from Guarbecque to be poised in a bubble over Newport's bridge, as though, like Dorothy, picked up in Kansas and dropped in Oz. In another conversation with Suel, William revealed that he thought of the church as a 'New Jerusalem coming down from the sky.'[84] The paintings show a black cloud that enters from left like a ship's prow or a vast anvil. The cranes of Newport, the lace-like towers and gantry of the bridge and the chimneys of the power station are frail in the face of sublime power. He volunteered, 'there is an element of the Cataclysmic.' Suel wrote a poem of Apocalypse: 'this bridge, this church between life and death and every tear / on every face / was dried. / the storms were ended / and death was no more.'

Left:
Hoy Orkney, 1996,
acrylic on canvas,
42 x 46 cm

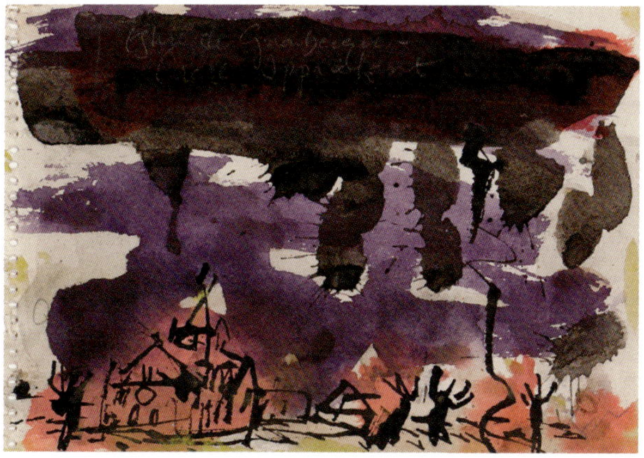

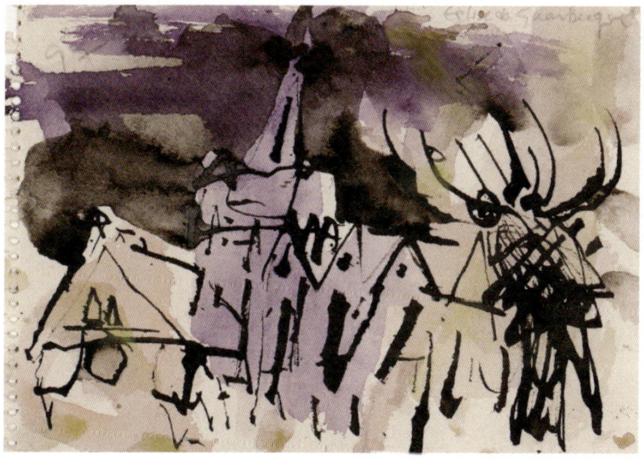

Eglise de Guarbeque,
both undated,
c. 1994, ink and
watercolour,
15 x 20 cm

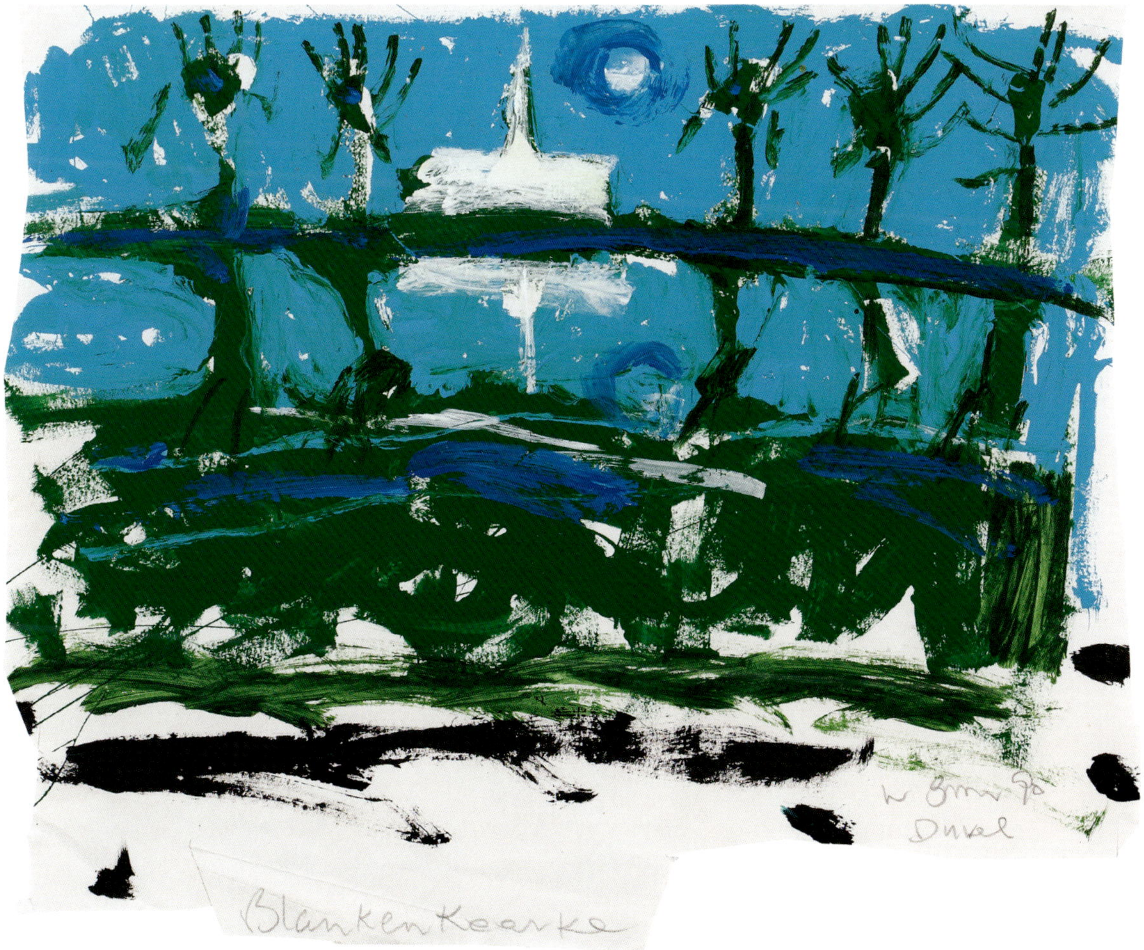

Blanken Kearke,
1990, acrylic on
paper, 45 x 50 cm

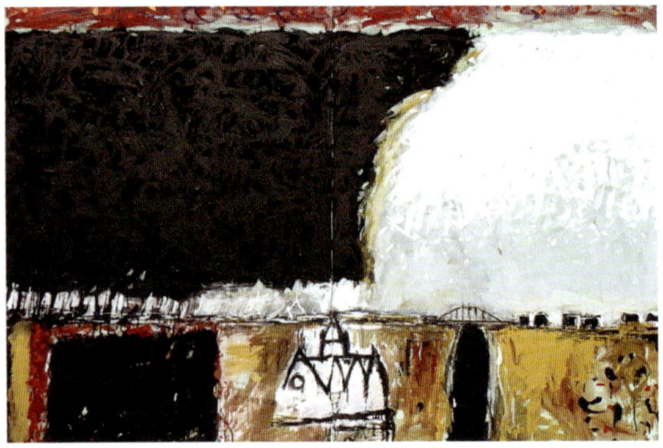

Approaching Storm, Berguette I (diptych), undated, *c.* 1995, oil on canvas, 152 x 228 cm

Untitled (approaching storm, Newport), 1997, oil on canvas, 115 x 193 cm

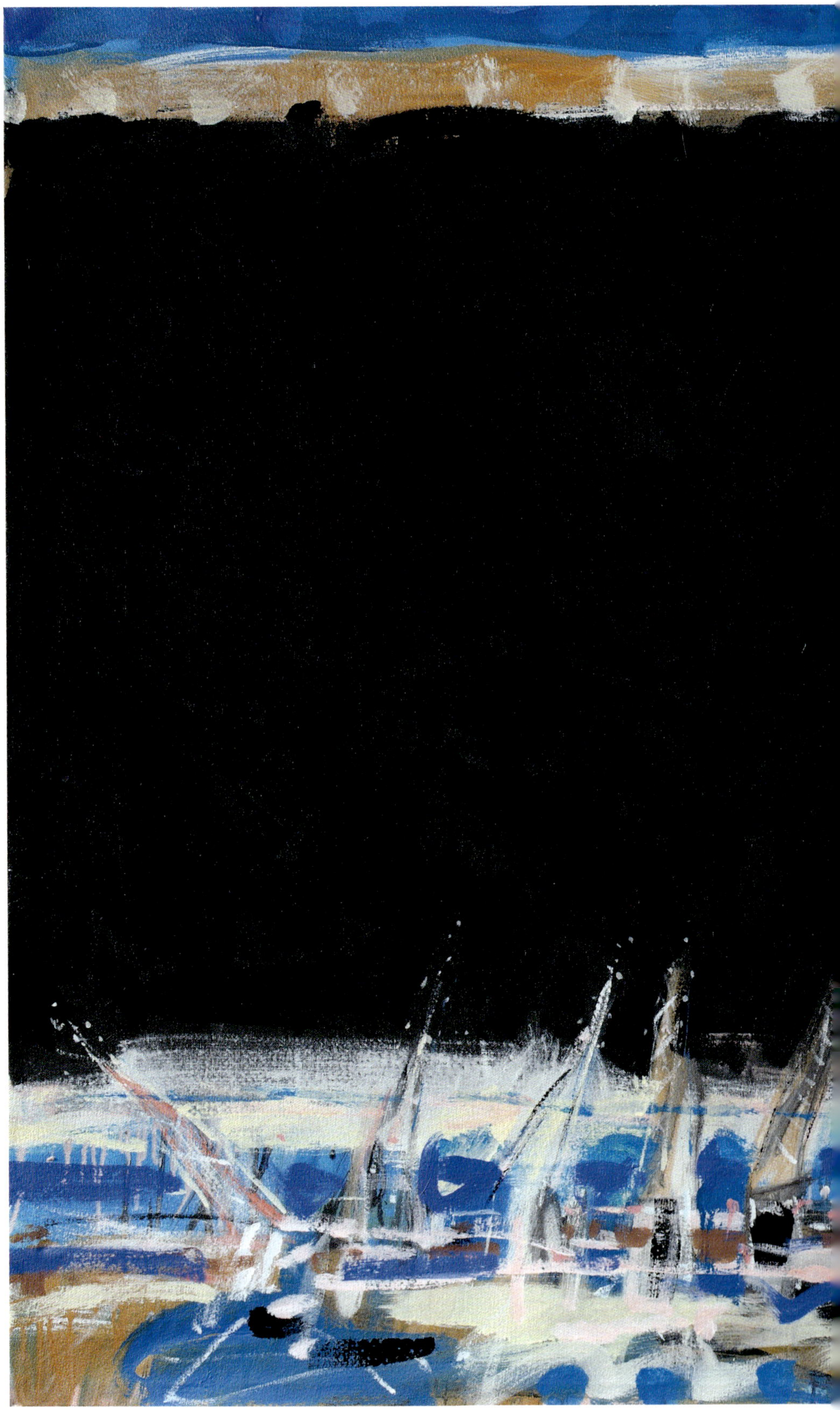

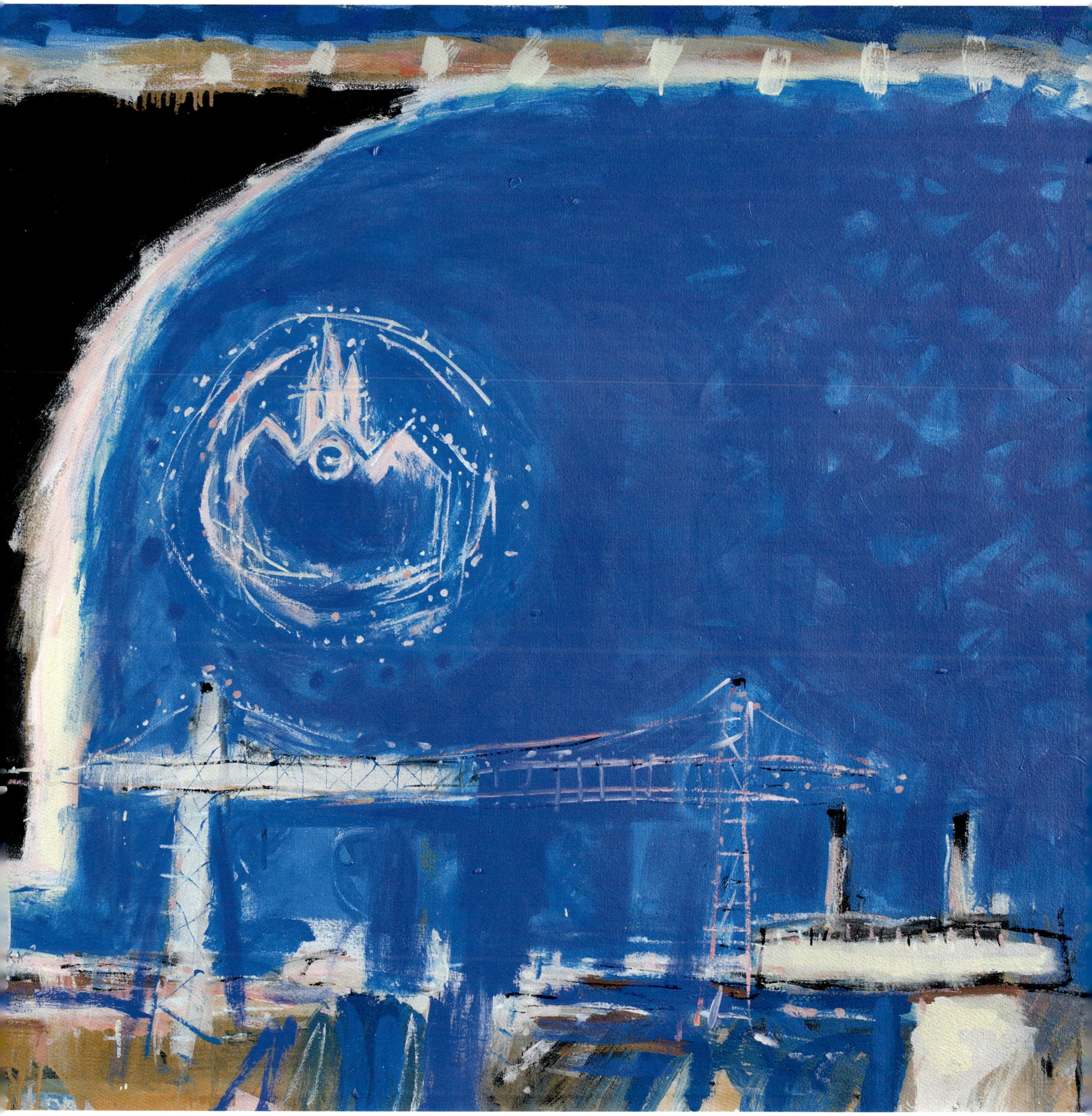

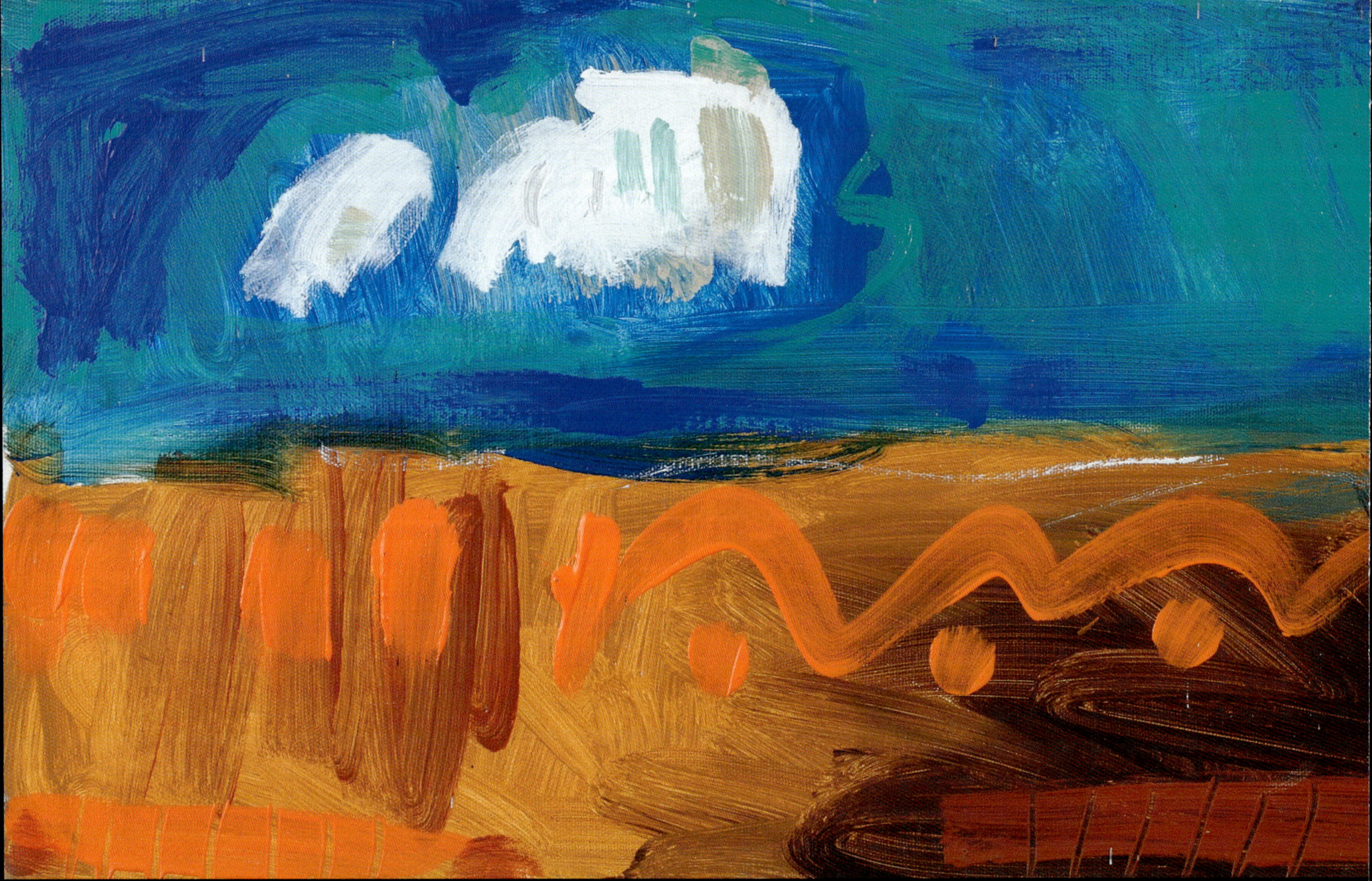

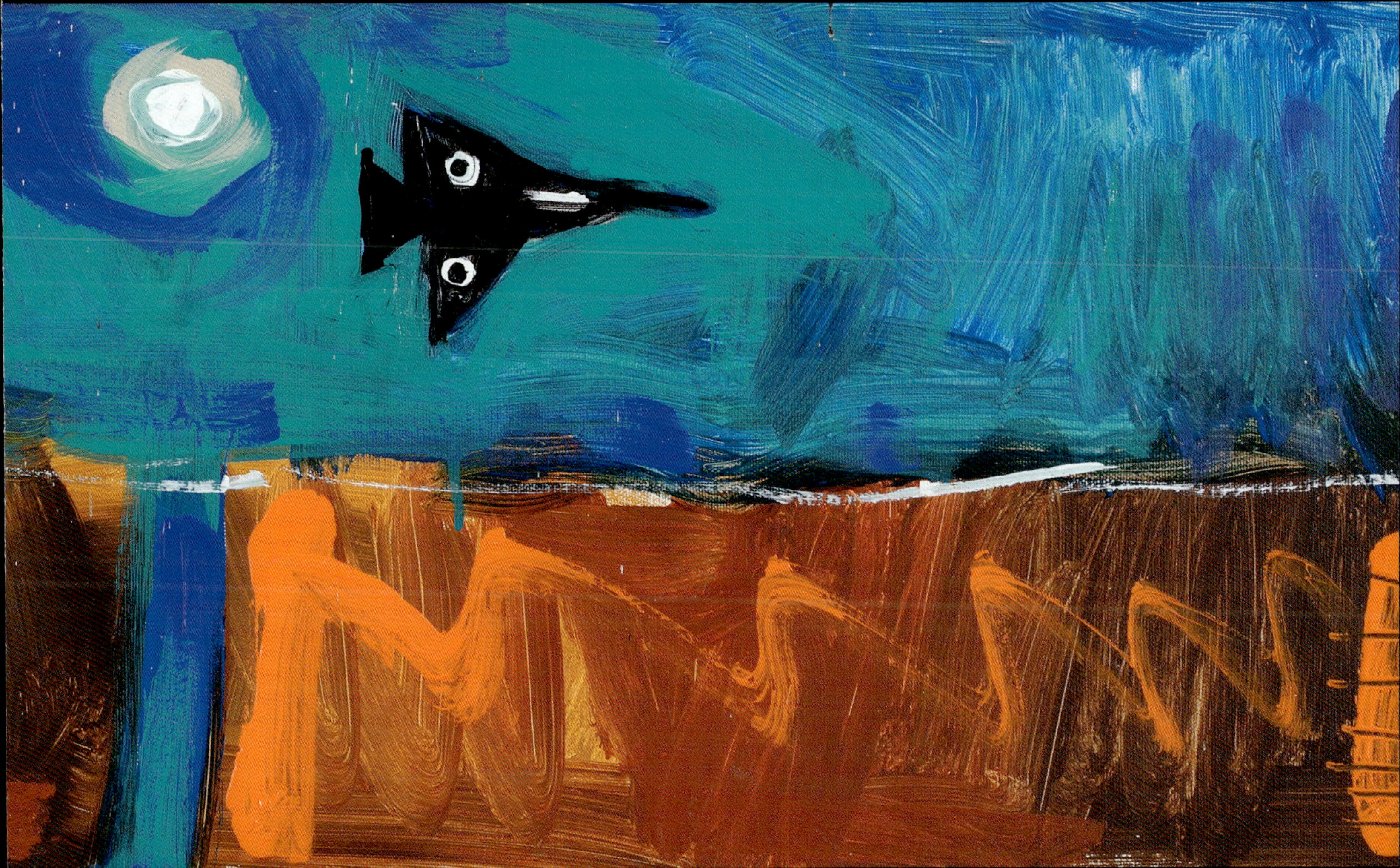

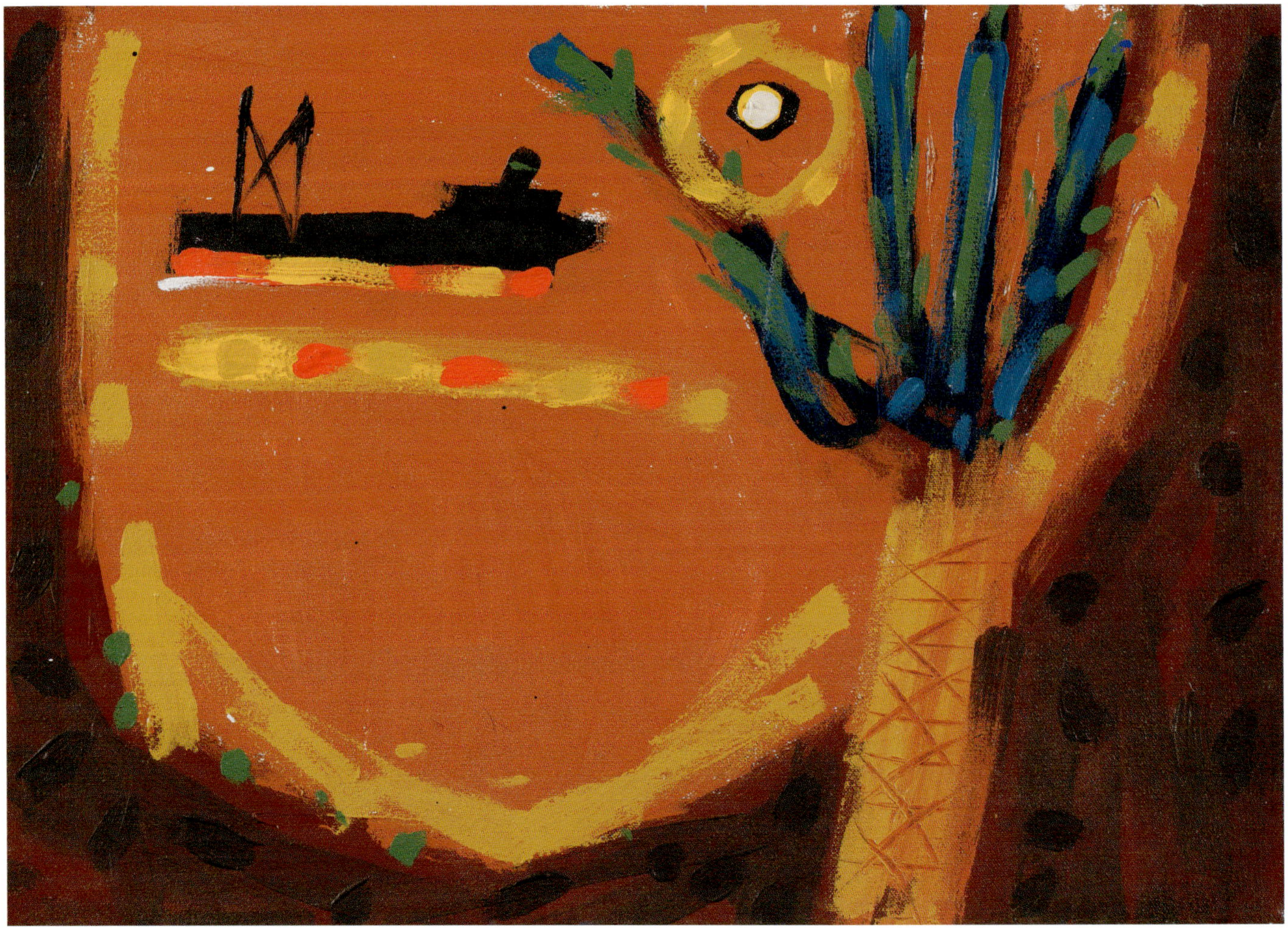

Phosphate Carrier,
2002, acrylic on
canvas, 38 x 54 cm

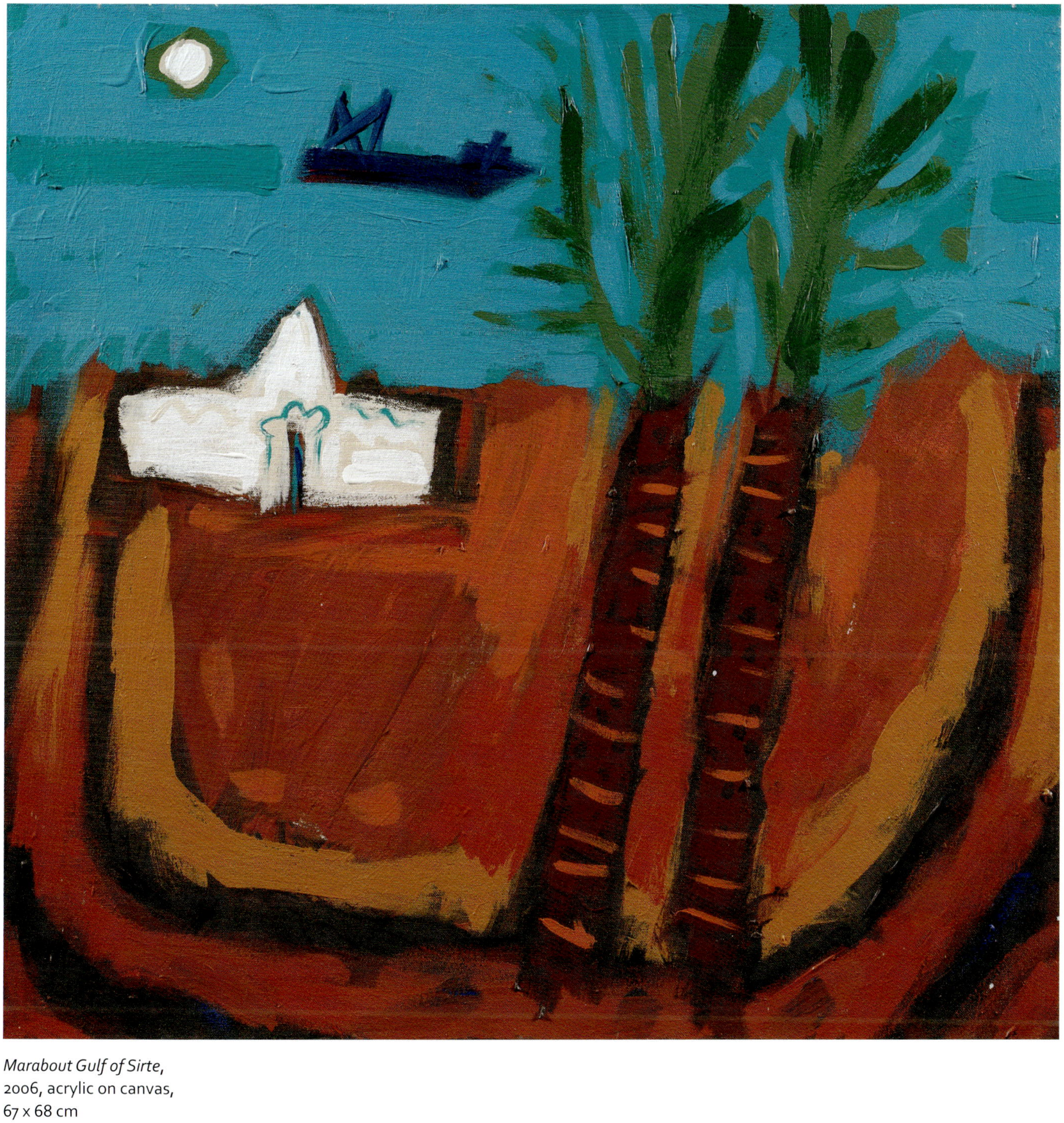

Marabout Gulf of Sirte,
2006, acrylic on canvas,
67 x 68 cm

All art is about recognition
– memory is the defining human trait.

Antiquities and histories

Like artists before him, William was moved and excited by the remains of past cultures, whether artefacts in museums or monuments in the landscape. Rather than a representational style or a romantic idiom, his approach was to extract symbols to be used in different contexts. An example was the Iron Age gold boat from the National Museum of Ireland, part of the Broighter Hoard found in a field in Northern Ireland. In a few lines he expressed, unmistakably, the tiny vessel with its mast and oars. He adopted it first in 1992 as a farewell to Carys's mother, Katie, when she died, interpreting it as a death boat or Charon's ferryboat across the Styx into the Underworld. He called a print in golden ink on cream

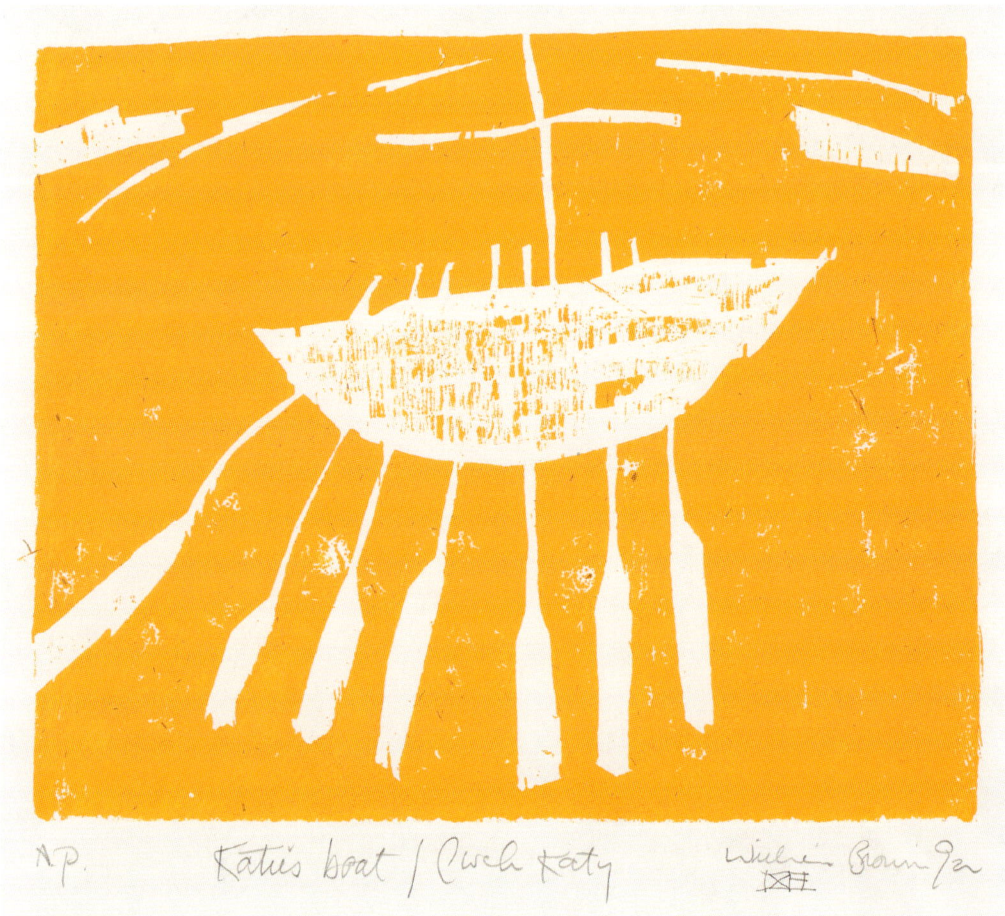

Katie's Boat / Cwch Katy, 1992, woodcut, 30 x 30 cm

Opposite: *Venus of Blaengwynfi*, 1999, oil on canvas, 68 x 41 cm

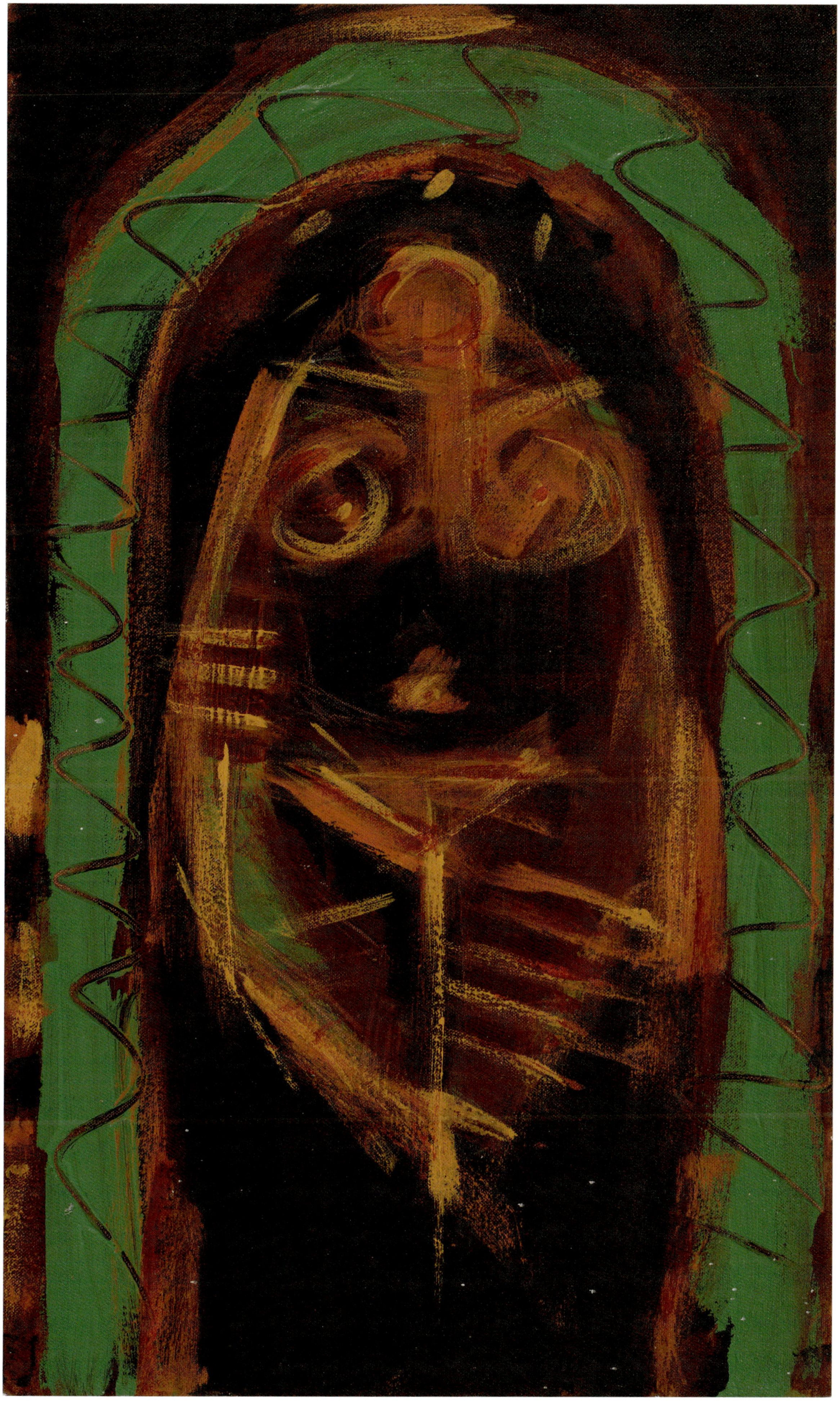

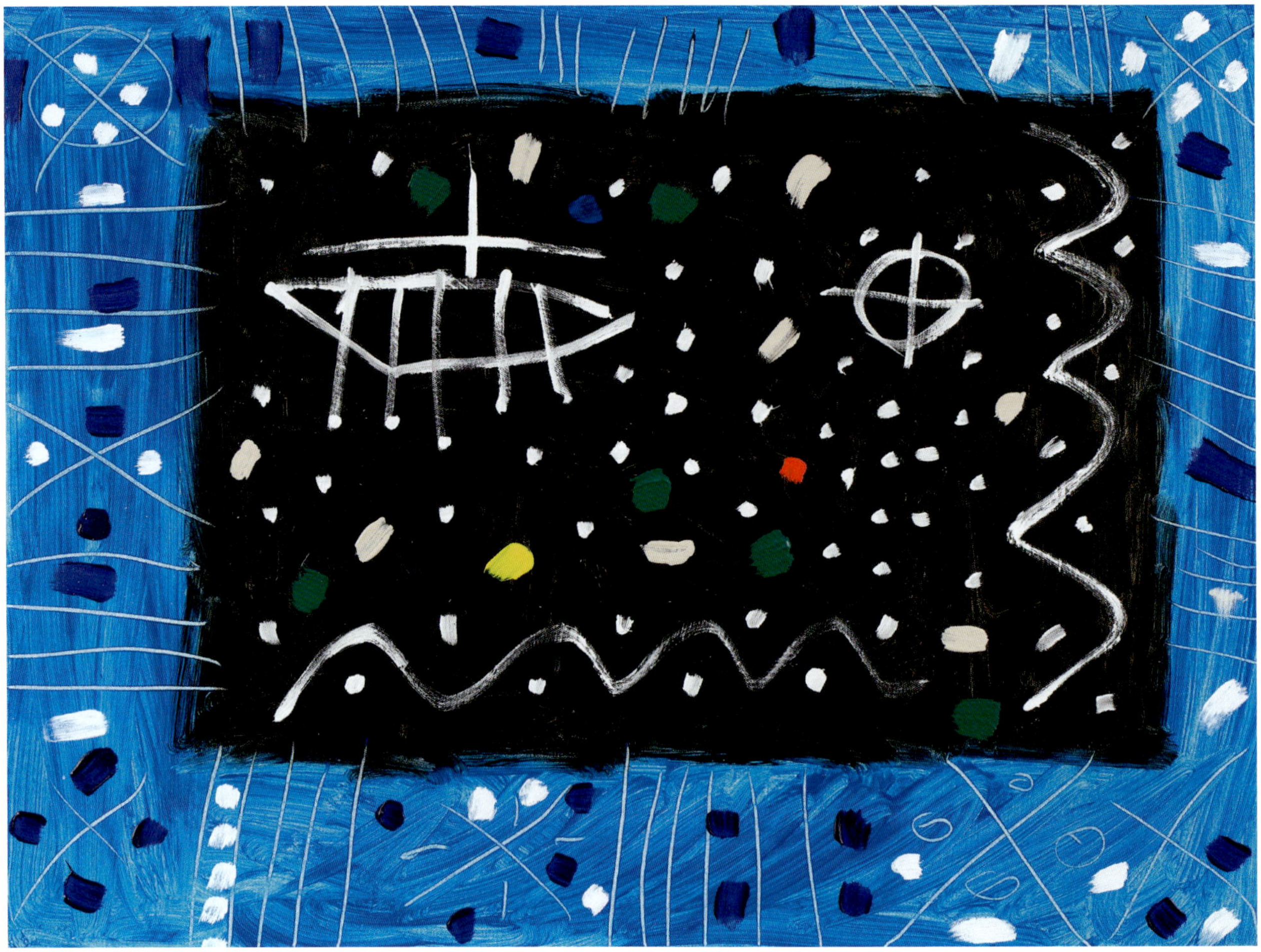

Untitled (boat and stars), undated, *c.* 2007, oil on canvas, 60cm x 80cm

paper *Katie's Boat / Cwch Katy*. He brought the same image into prints of the sky at night, his Drunken Boat paintings and other works. The ancient crosses of Devon and Cornwall stood sentinel among horses on the moors, and he was drawn to Welsh folk objects such as love spoons.

The Venus that appeared in so many paintings from 1997 onwards was inspired by the Palaeolithic figurine known as the Venus of Willendorf, in the Naturhistorisches Museum in Vienna – the most famous of many similar examples found of prehistoric female figure sculptures. William's paintings and drawings joyfully embraced the ovoid figure with emphatic breasts, hips and vulva but tiny arms and feet. Occasionally, his Venus had stags' horns. He named her Venus of Blaengwynfi after a former mining village far up in the Afan valley east of Port Talbot. William announced that he had seen the Venus there in a stain in the road – an instance of 'pareidolia', the phenomenon that results in seeing faces or figures in clouds or plates of food. He made transcultural associations in claiming her in a note written in 2008:

> So here she is, the Venus of Blaengwynfi, loosely plundered by the Celtic tribes – even the Romans had their goddesses. Mother, Sister, 'femail' – all these things if

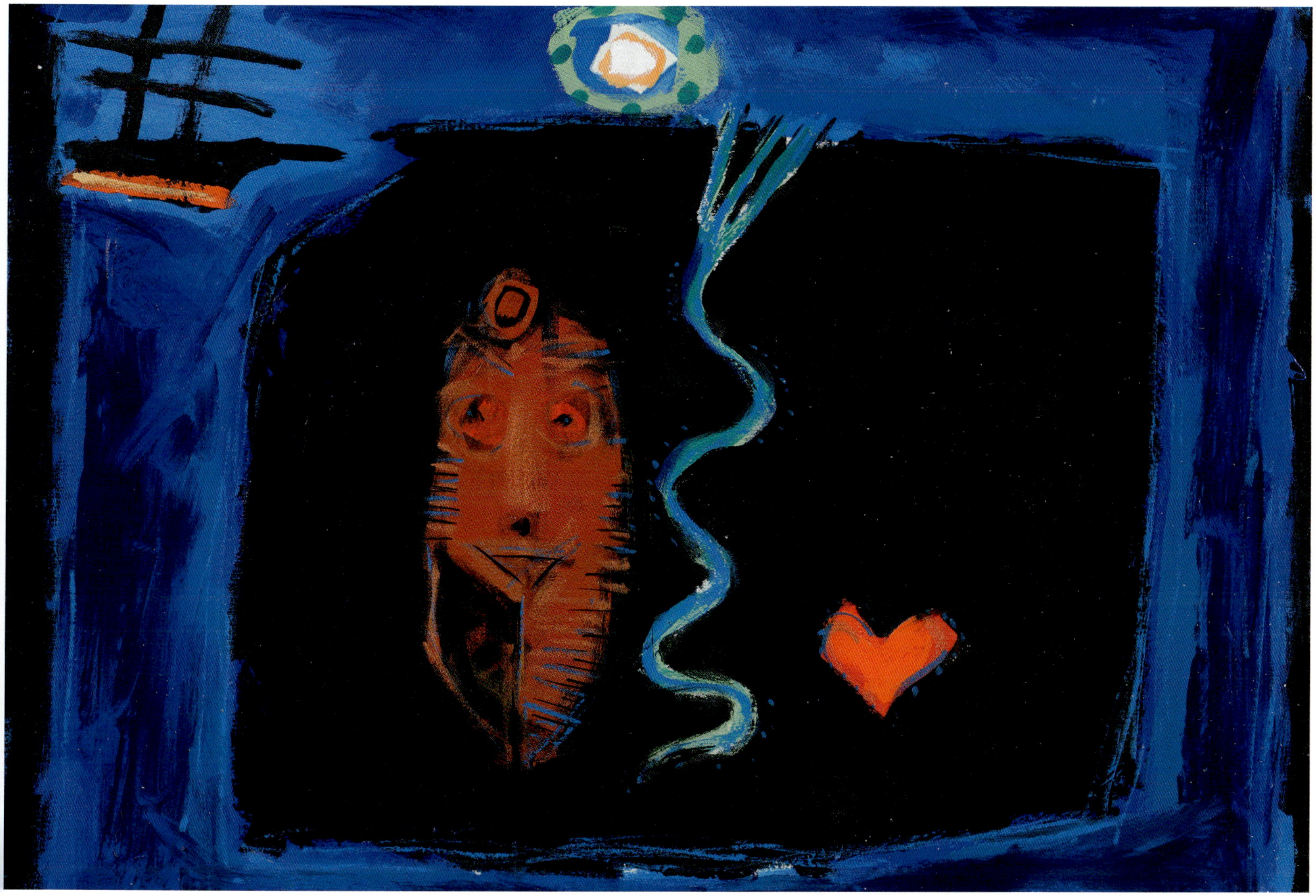

you know where to look. From Shelagh 'n Gigh to Rhiannon to Venus herself, the fetish exists. At once ugly and beautiful she remains a timeless emblem. Her greatest gift is the plough and furrow – Mary herself, all ears. A diet of worms or cockles but like the little effigy in Austria she crops up. Why shouldn't Wales have one as well! Hallowed, hollowed, holy, fecund, this is the original 'it' girl.

Island of the Dead, 1999, oil on canvas, 61 x 90 cm

The paintings often incorporated lines that recall scarification or ogham script, neither of which is associated with the original Venus figurines. Sometimes his figure was set inside an arch like the niches in the side walls of the Rhondda railway tunnel at Blaengwynfi, and William said that Carys's father Herbert was reminded by the drawings of coming through the tunnel as a boy on his way to school. Notions continued to coalesce. Simultaneously, William was exploring the Venus for a poetry chapbook with David Greenslade, *A Love Letter*. He wrote to David about how the imagery was evolving:

> David, Each evening – locked and frustrated into desire for tessellation / patternation (the Moroccan business could be precipitatory-ive). Happy as a pig in shite with my Altamira / Venus of Willendorf / Pilar musings. Colour becomes a distinct probability.

> The images are in my head and the Oriental Arabesque Boogie-Woogie. This problem is so easily solved that I'm suspicious and need to send all chambered contents: a 'bolus' (Med.) to the next neural stomach.

William's references were frequently cross-cultural. In 2000, he made drawings in a series of Celtic Heads based on the prehistoric stone bust found at Mšecké Žehrovice near Prague but placed in a context drawn from Canadian indigenous mythology. On the back of one drawing he wrote:

> Piper, Celtic Head, the Moon. Story from Canada, Ontario – Pointe au Baril [...] In the old time, when the Moon was a fish again ... Chipewyan / Ojibway myth. Each man dreams his dreams, no Drama! One man dreamed he was a snake, otter?, another man dreamt he was bear. That way, he could never, if he hunted, ever kill his dreaming.

His journey from Bilbao to Santiago de Compostela in January 1998 gave William the opportunity to see the Palaeolithic cave paintings of Altamira. First studied in 1879, they revolutionised understanding of the artistic capabilities of early people. He wrote in his journal of the tour:

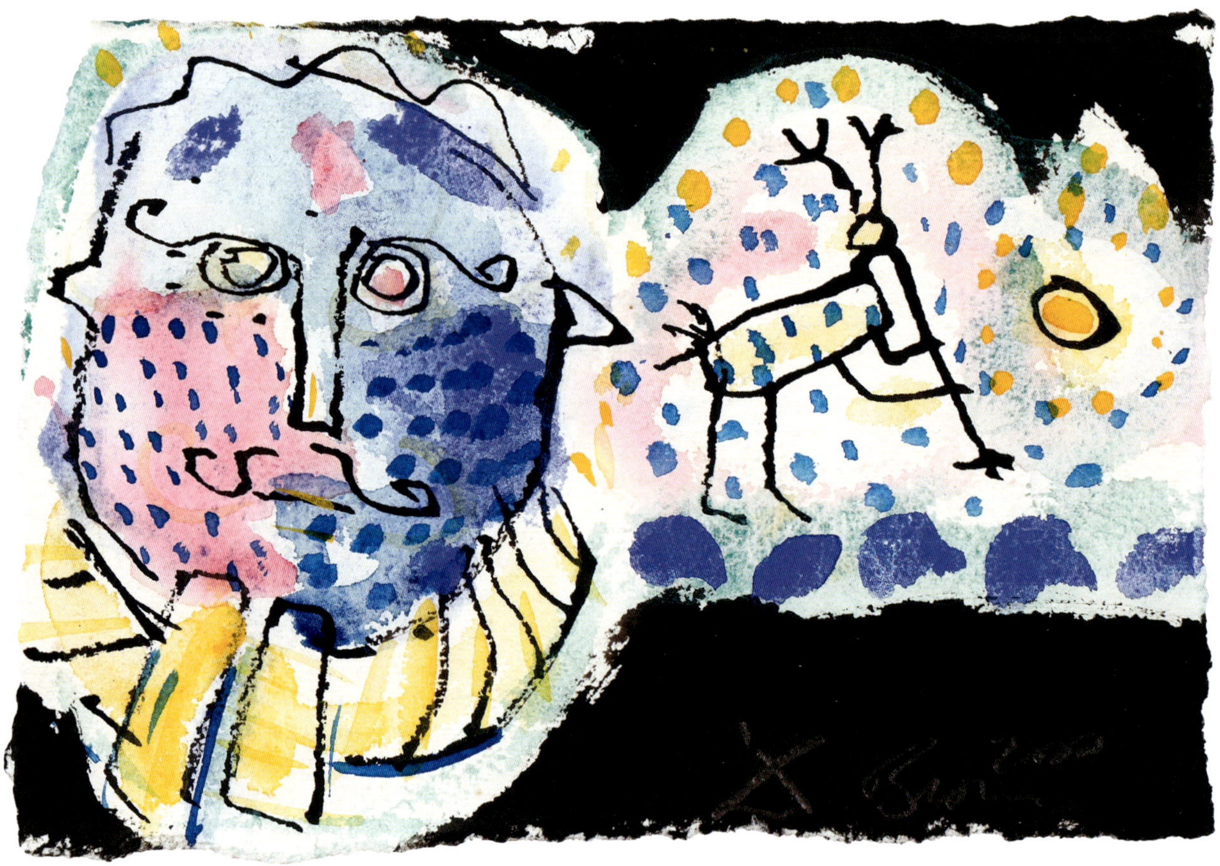

Celtic Head and Moon, 2000, acrylic and watercolour, 15 x 20 cm

Altamira: a little forward planning paid off and I had access to the Cueva dos Bisones in the mtns. Here was the fringe of the ice and a population of painters, hunters etc. etc. etc. We imagine this desire to decorate surfaces to be a modern conceit. Rather it remains a back of the cave activity to this day. I'll remember this at St. Stephens, my own studio at Llangynwyd, when I return.[85]

Like Picasso and other early Modernists, William was engrossed by the immediacy of the cave-artists' representations of bison, horses, deer and human hands. 'The pictures on the walls of the caves are as alive as any I've seen', he wrote, referring to them as a kind of cultural anthrax waiting to infect him.[86] He shared with the Palaeolithic cave painters a sympathetic appreciation of animals and an innate appreciation of connections between imagery and storytelling. His next exhibition at East West Gallery in London was titled 'The Moose Man Cometh – New Work from the Back of the Cave'. Some drawings captured running or swimming deer with an Altamira-like sense of purpose. The later sketch titled 'Farm near Altamira' [17] showed the wide connotations he perceived: spirals, handprints, dots and colour fields with notes to the Picos de Europa mountains, the solar orbit postulated by Copernicus and the second law of Keppler about planetary motion.

Sketches from Cave at Altamira, 1998, ink and wash, 35 x 23 cm

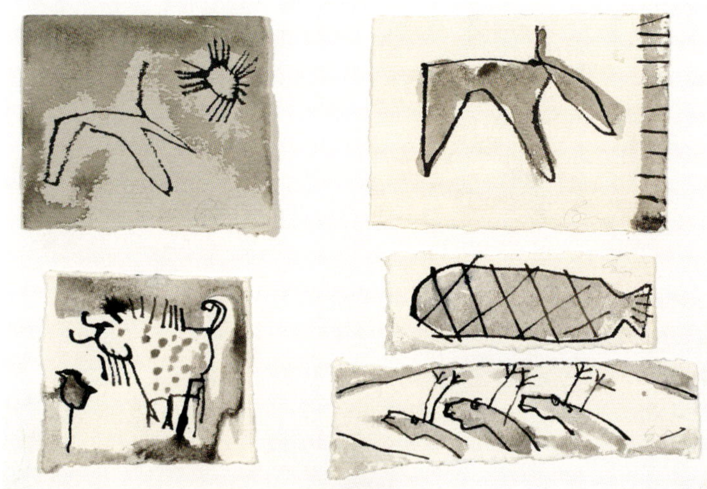

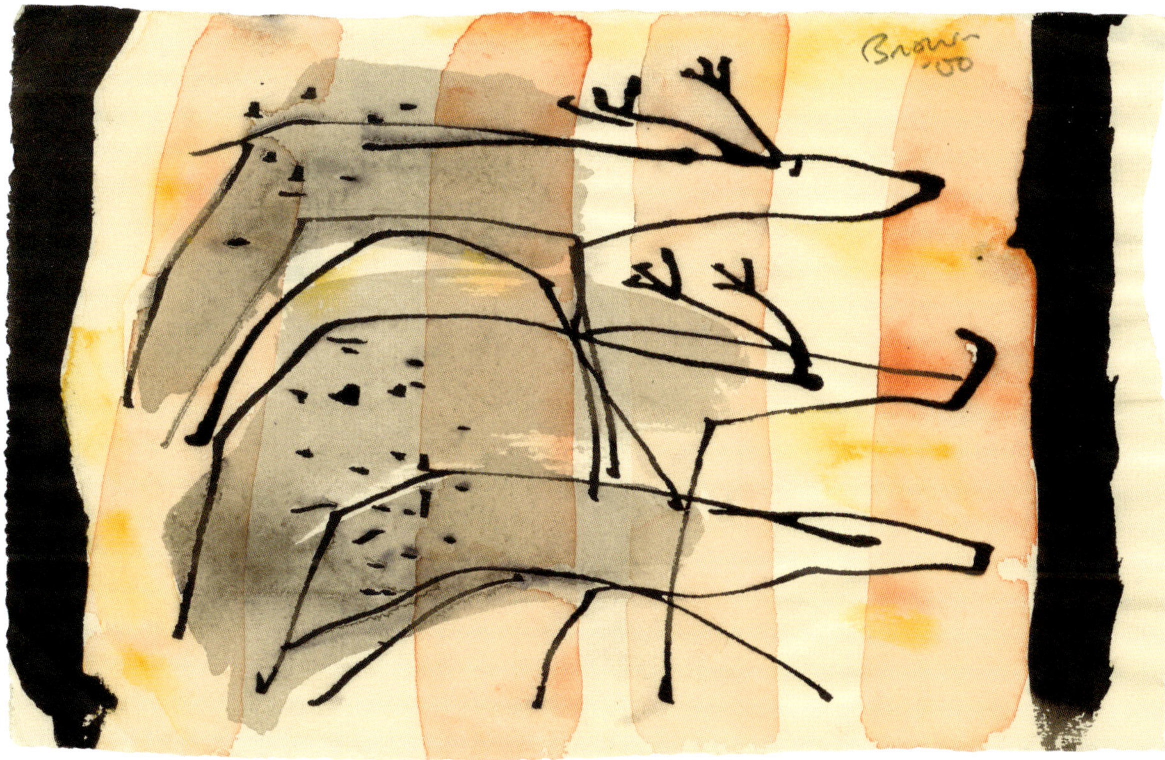

Untitled (Altamira), 2000, ink and watercolour, 15 x 24 cm

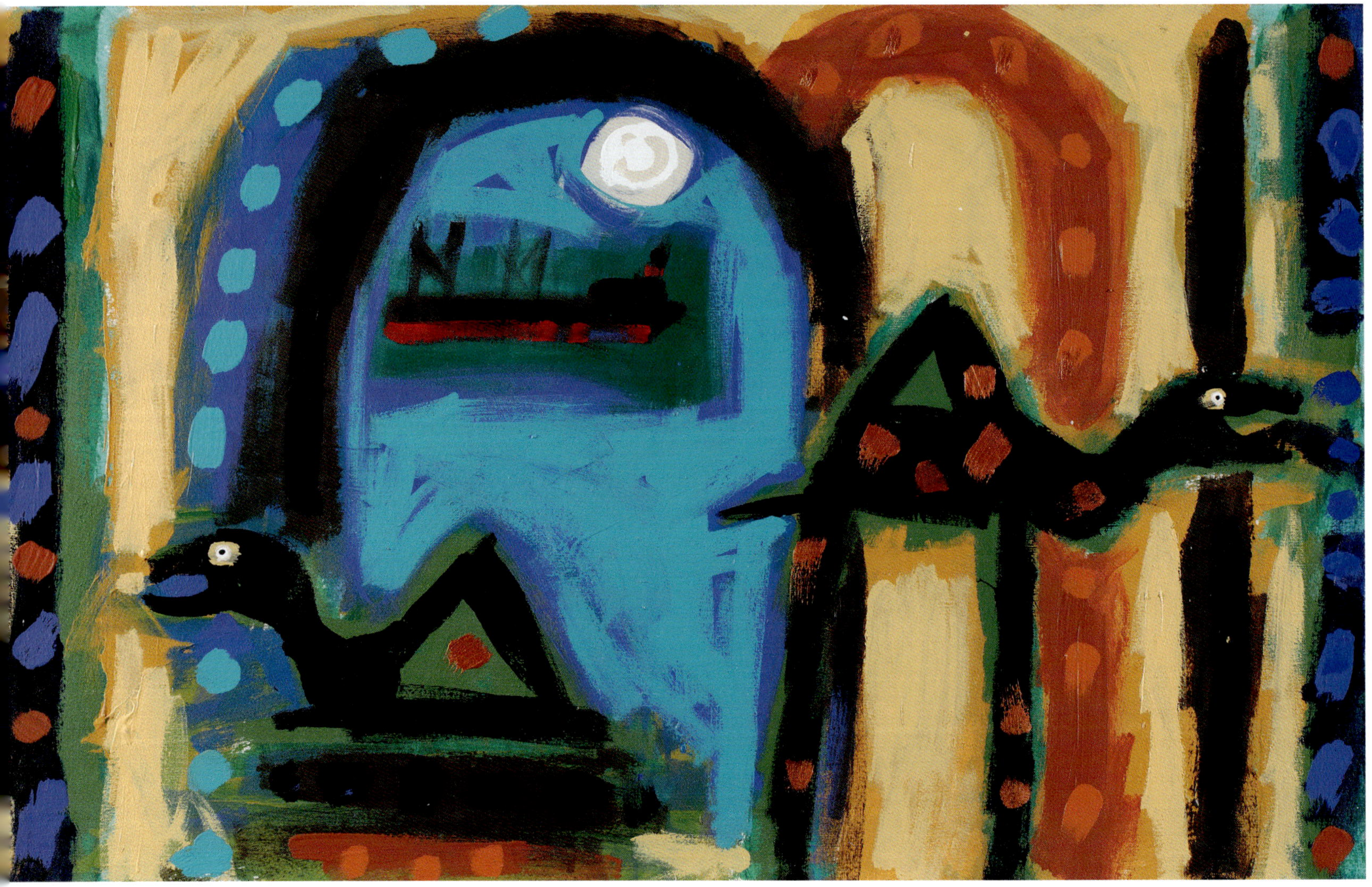

The Sea Gate Essaouira, undated, *c.* 2003, oil on canvas, 64 x 100 cm

Opposite: *Barakka Mishmewski Tariq 1,* 2003, oil on canvas, 86 x 65 cm

In the case of Berber rugs from Morocco, a visual language of geometric symbols existed already that expressed nature, survival, protection from evil, fertility and storytelling. William created compositions that combined rugs with other motifs or presented an image that was essentially his own version of a carpet but on stretched canvas. He used several marks superficially like those on the carpets but the symbol he painted most often was of a stylised sitting camel, said to represent endurance and prosperity.

Cacti were another motif seen in North Africa, but they moved closer to home when Colin Jones gave William one in a terracotta pot. William named the cactus Iolo, perhaps after the spiky bard and antiquarian of Glamorgan, Iolo Morganwg, and put it in numerous paintings from 2002 to 2005 on a kitchen table accompanied, variously, by kippers, a cat and the moon. This began a run of domestic interiors of subjects such as fruit on a table, often with interlopers such as a polar bear. The home William made with Carys in Newcastle Hill was the centre of his world, but his world was wide and many memories could come to visit.

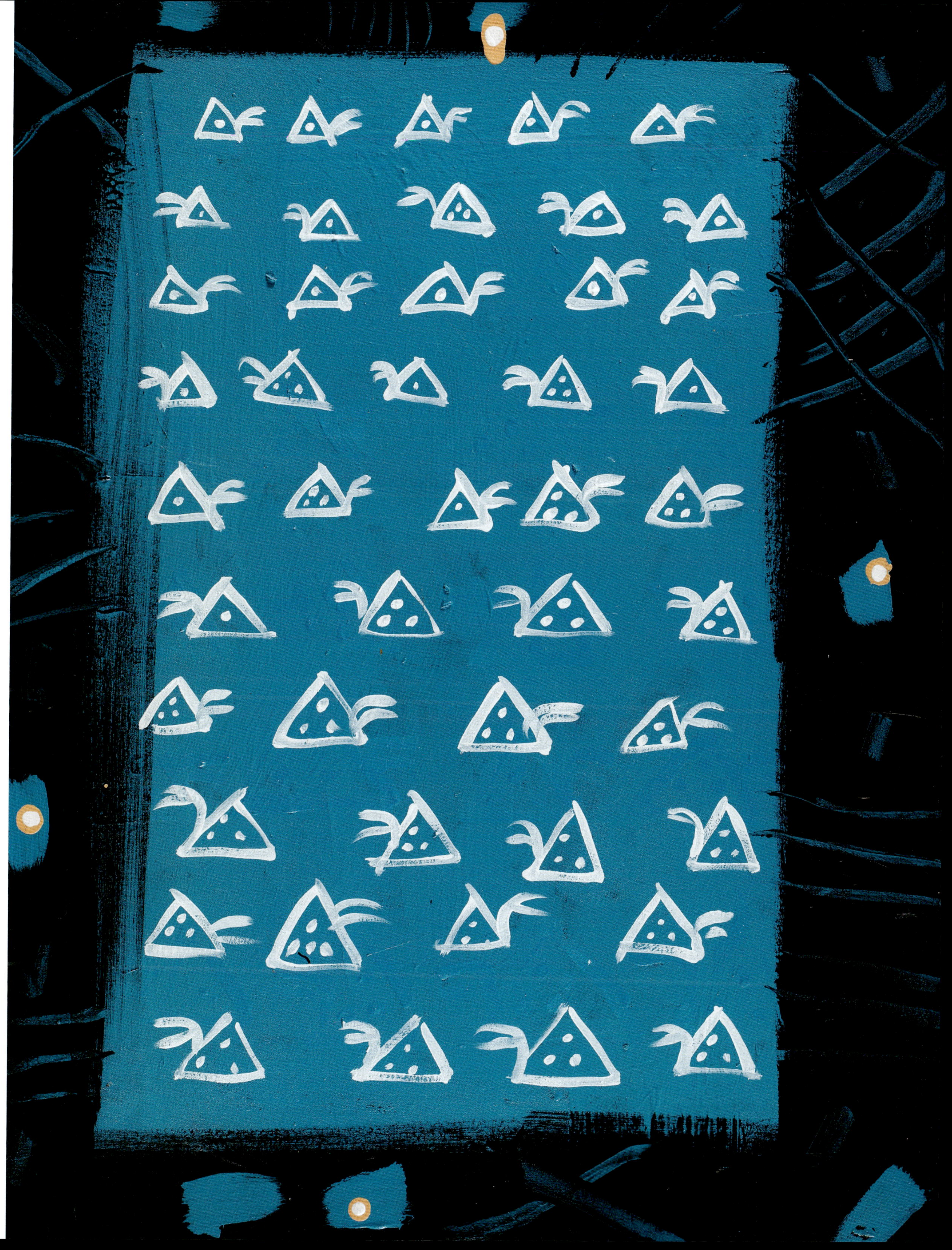

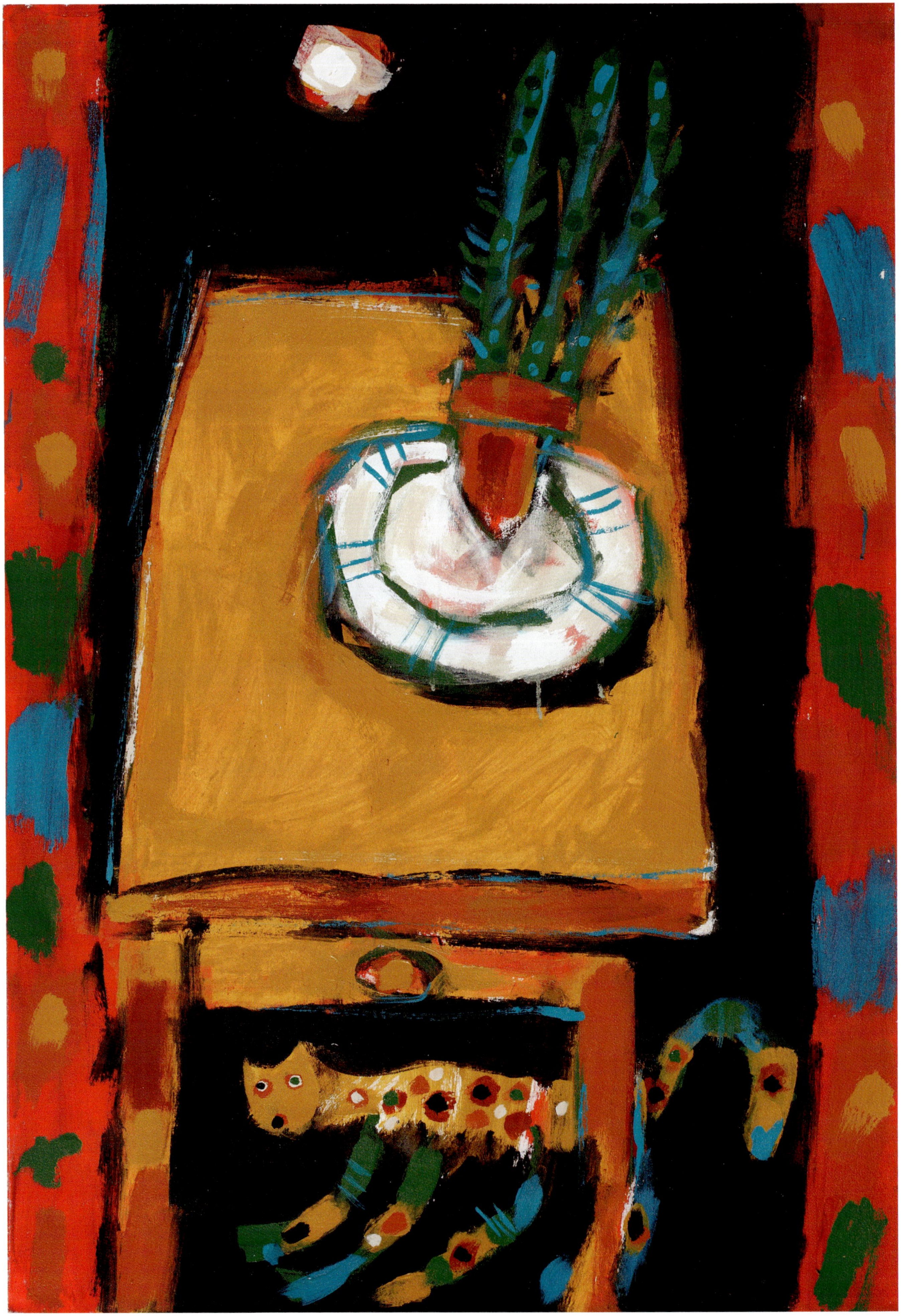

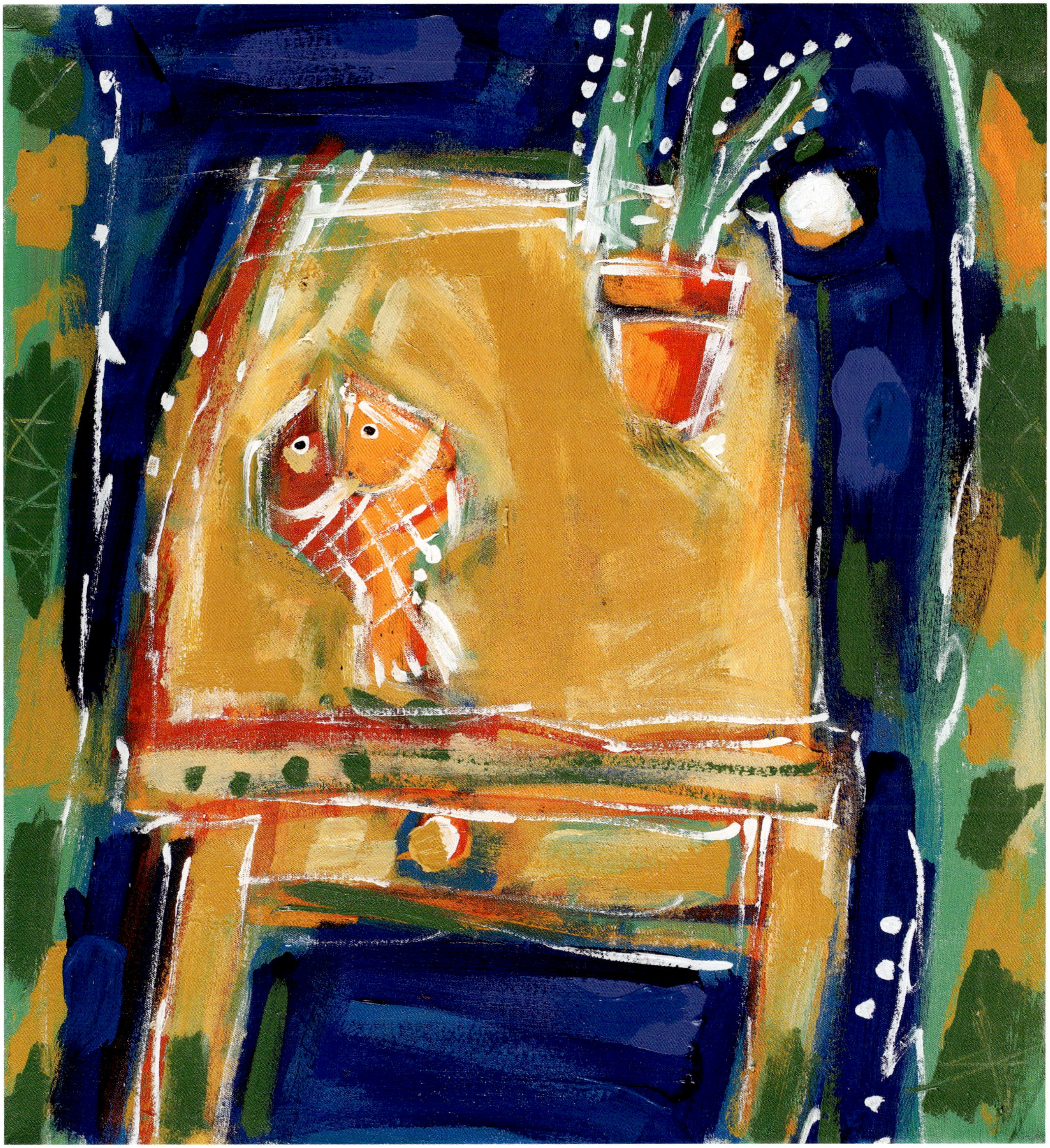

Nocturn / Kipper,
2007, acrylic on
canvas, 60 x 55 cm

Opposite:
Phebe's World II,
2004, acrylic on
canvas, 109 x 76 cm

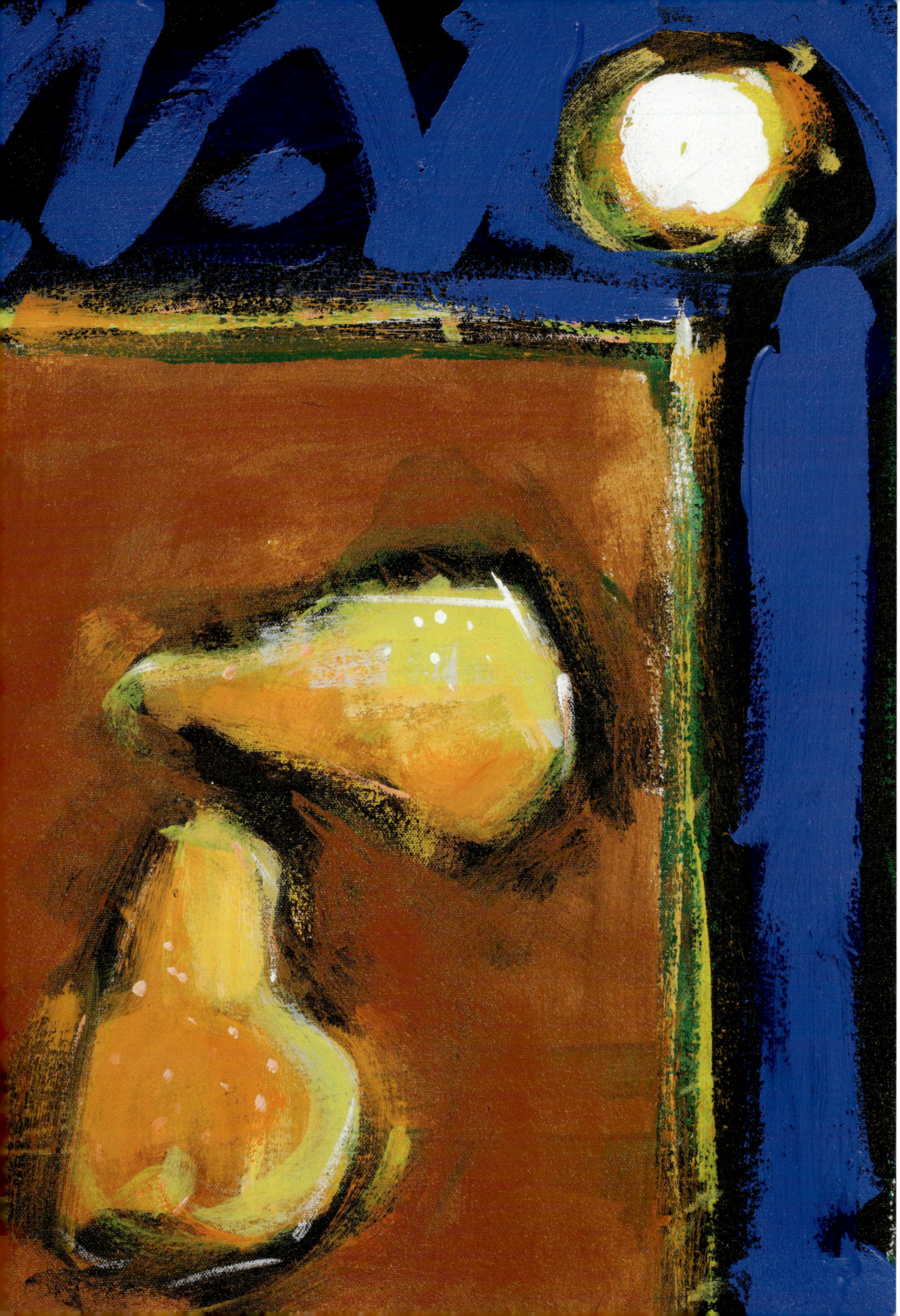

Opposite:
Pair of Pears,
undated, *c.* 2005,
acrylic on canvas,
40 x 30 cm

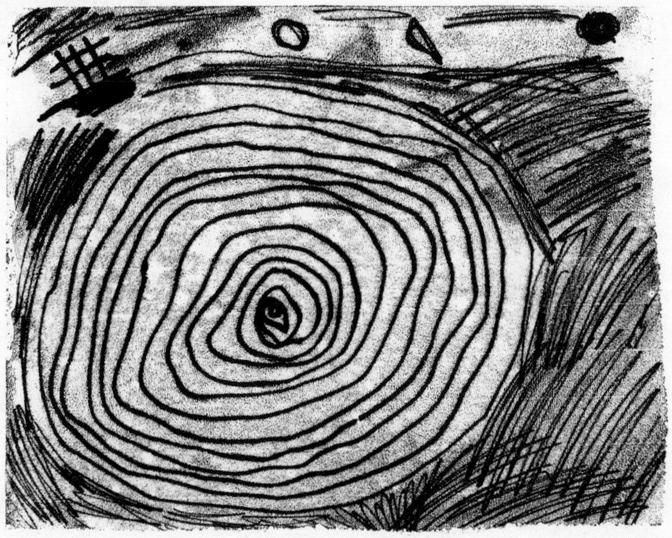

Untitled (drunken ship), undated, *c.* 2004, monoprint, 30 x 40 cm

Reading Arthur Rimbaud or learning of his travels in North Africa (or more likely both) led William to the great French poet as a subject of historical enquiry as well as stirring imagery. The phrase *enfant terrible* could have been invented for the teenage Rimbaud, who ran away from home and scandalised Paris through his passionate, drunken affair and wild travels with the older, married, Paul Verlaine, who at last shot him in the arm and went to prison for two years in 1873. In his astonishingly original work, which would influence the Surrealists decades later, Rimbaud sought visionary colour and meaning by writing in a self-induced state of hallucination. Among great visual artists for whom he was a formative influence was Sir Sidney Nolan, who was led by Rimbaud's illogical, intuitive associations to reject naturalism and access greater truths. They were a mirror to William's creative inclinations too. Rimbaud wrote, 'The poet becomes a seer through a long, immense, and reasoned derangement of all the senses. All shapes of love, suffering, madness. He searches himself, he exhausts all poisons in himself, to keep only the quintessences.'

Rimbaud's seminal poem 'Le Bateau ivre' ['The Drunken Boat'], written in 1871, when he was sixteen, became a lasting inspiration. William said, 'In the writing of Rimbaud, the images are so vivid they scald the imagination.'[87] The poem adopts the voice of a vessel that has lost its crew and describes itself filling up with seawater and drifting endlessly. The teeming imagery of wandering a wide world was translated into prints and paintings as a masted ship that spirals in a stupor, as a single image or as a motif among moons, whales, waves and walruses.

Et dès lors, je me suis baigné dans le Poème
De la Mer, infusé d'astres, et lactescent,
Dévorant les azurs verts ; où, flottaison blême
Et ravie, un noyé pensif parfois descend ;

[And from then on I bathed in the Poem
Of the Sea, infused with stars, lactescent,
Devouring the azure greens; where, flotsam-pale
And ravished, a pensive drowned man sometimes sinks;]

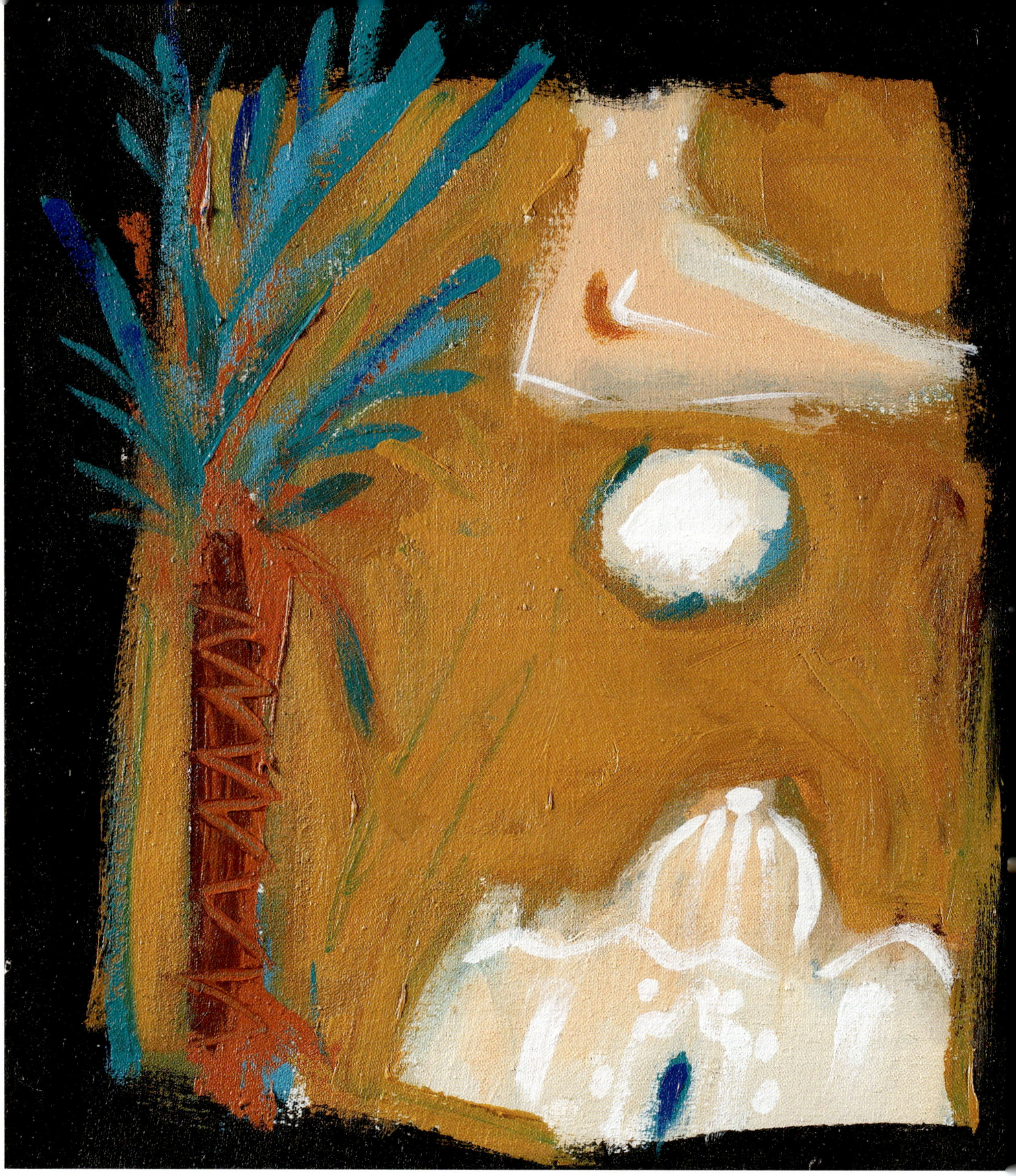

Kilim Marabout – Rimbaud's Leg, 2004, acrylic on canvas, 48 x 79 cm

Even more absorbing was the history of Rimbaud's later life, and specifically his right leg. Rimbaud had completed his reinvention of poetry by the age of nineteen and soon gave up writing for far-reaching travels, during which he worked as a street-vendor, soldier, French teacher, stevedore, quarryman and farm labourer. He became a trader at the tip of the Arabian Peninsula in Aden and then moved across the Red Sea, where he was the first European to explore the Ogaden. In 1888, he settled, for the first time in his life, trading in coffee and guns in the ancient city of Harar in Abyssinia (modern Ethiopia). After three years there he developed an infection in his right knee that gave him excruciating pain. He returned to Marseille where his leg was amputated. He died soon afterwards, aged thirty-seven.[88]

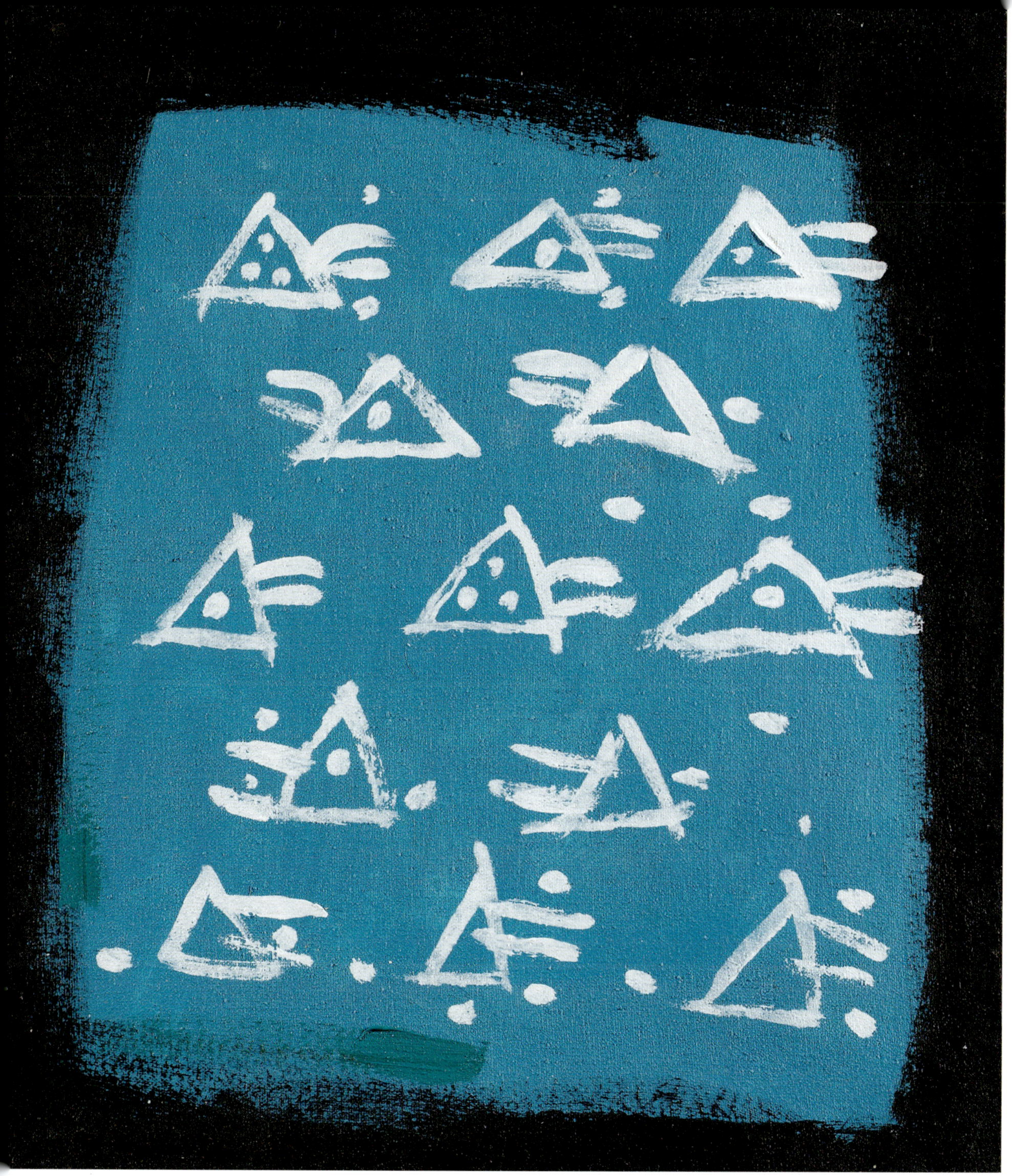

William was thinking in earnest about Rimbaud by 1991, when he approached the Musée Arthur Rimbaud at Charleville to suggest a project that would mark the centenary of the poet's death. Nothing came of that idea but William corresponded frequently about Rimbaud with Hervé Constant.[89] He returned to the theme in 2004 with a burst of paintings. Almost all took the leg as their motif, making it a kind of saintly relic. Sometimes it appeared on its own, flushed with life even though detached, or often with a kilim carpet, as in *Kilim Marabout – Rimbaud's Leg*, which showed a pale tomb of a marabout or holy man that rhymed in colour with a foot that hovered above the full moon.

The most elaborate work on the theme was a diptych, *Rimbaud at Harar / The Missing*

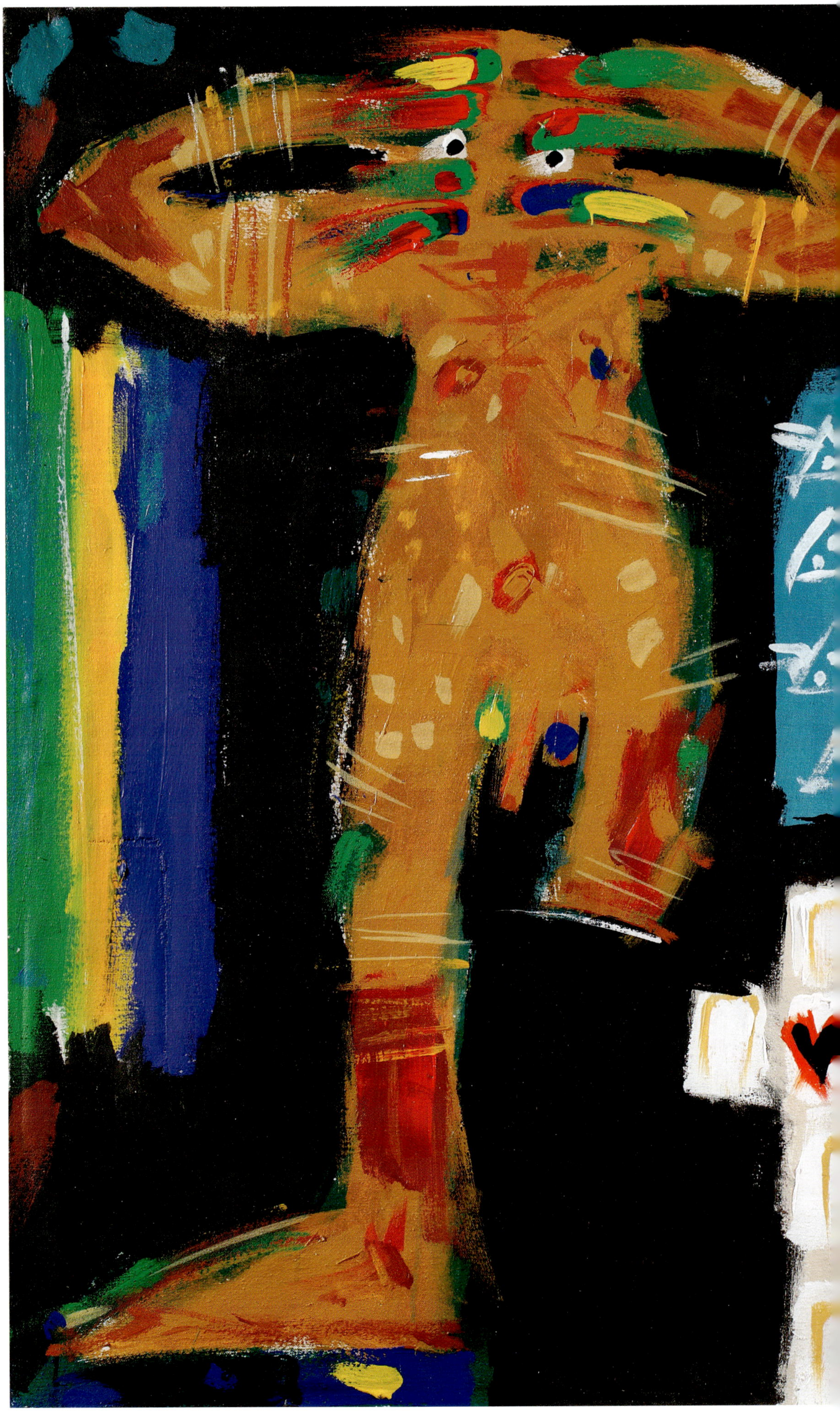

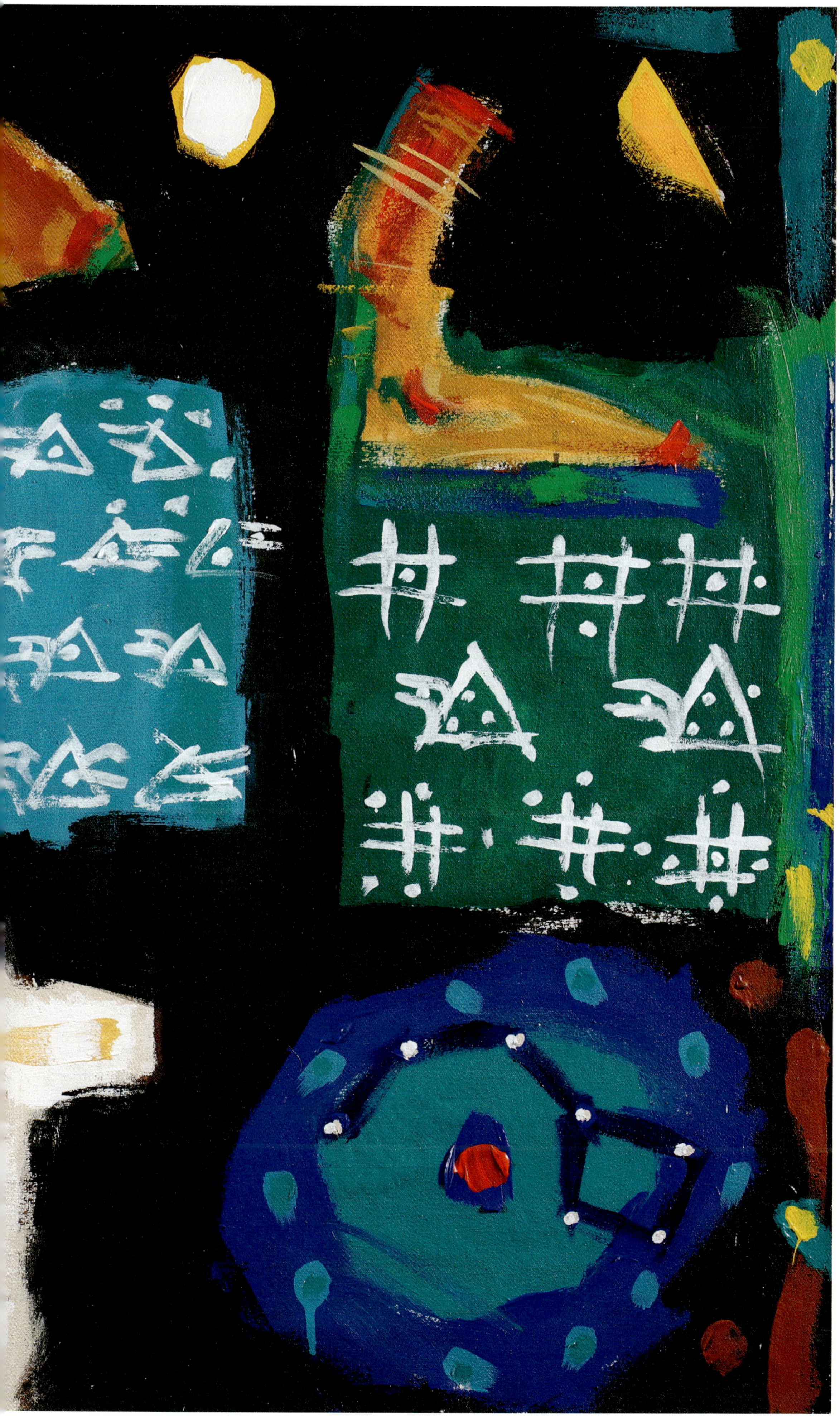

Rimbaud at Harar / The Missing Leg (diptych), 2004, acrylic on canvas, 93 x 144 cm

Leg [122–3]. This is dominated by the naked figure of Rimbaud covered in sores and cuts, with one leg missing (left rather than right). His hands are raised over his eyes as though peering fearfully into darkness. A sun and moon hang in the sky, the amputated leg stands on a carpet, stars reflect in a pool, and a white memorial cross bears the sign of a heart. David Greenslade asked William about the meaning of the heart. He evaded answering yet did not deny David's suggestion that it might be the Roman Catholic Sacred Heart, symbol of Christ's love for mankind, frequently expressed with queasy kitsch. Perhaps the implications were wider given how many of William's beasts are shown with visible, beating hearts, a representation of the life force in all creatures and the artist's empathy for them.

Contemporary disaster drew William's eye in the same way that the unfolding disaster of Rimbaud's death or the impending storm at Berguette affected him. He watched with half the world the awful, slow-motion demise of the Twin Towers in New York on 11 September 2001. In 2002 and 2003 he made several paintings of the familiar silhouette against a clear blue sky. The towers were black and marked with white lines, dotted, crossed and horizontal, suggesting runic writing or ogham. The first plane to hit the tower, taking a bite from its side, is not an

Reading the Runes 1, 2003, acrylic on canvas, 85 x 46 cm

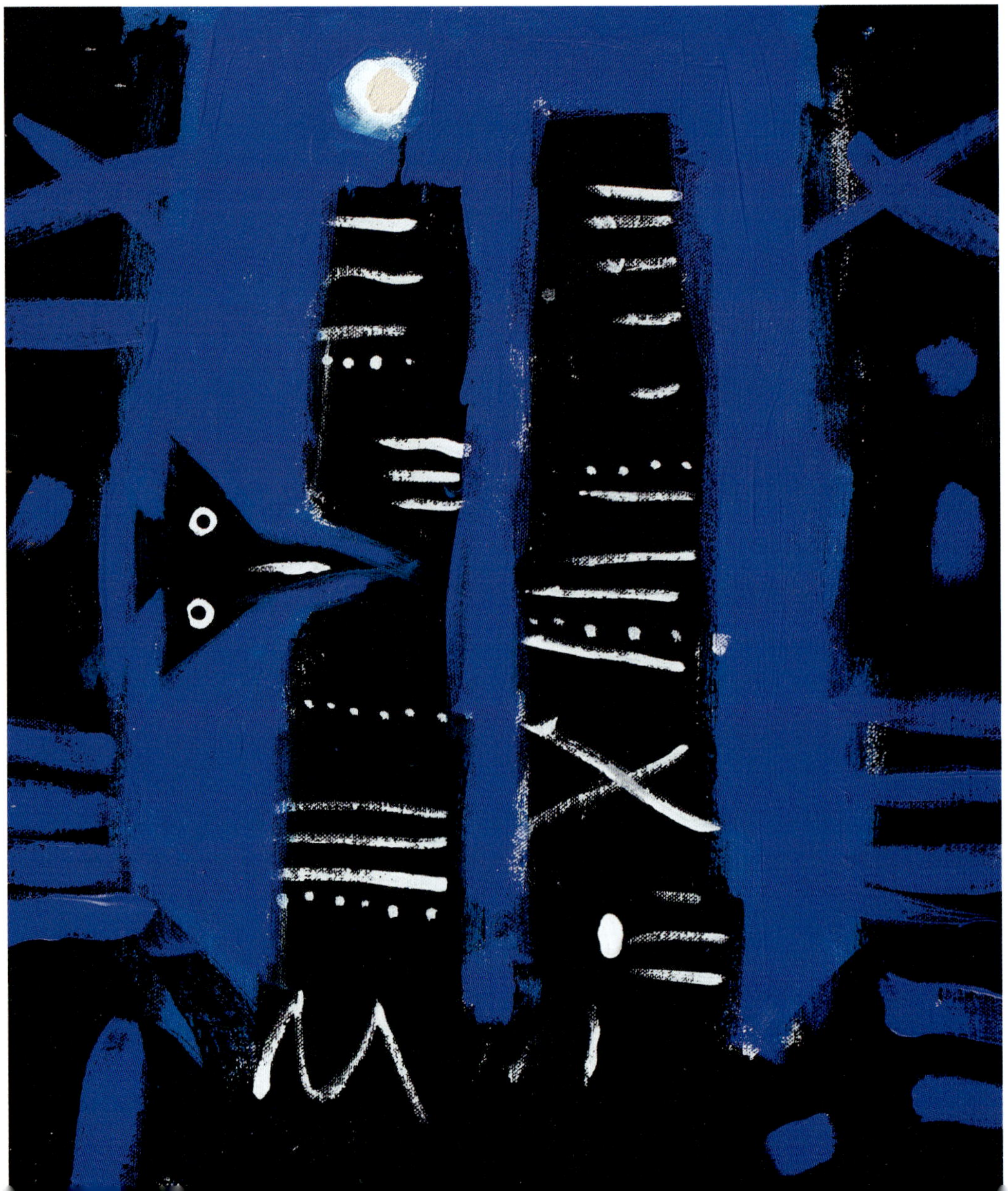

airliner but a banking Mirage. The title of the series, *Reading the Runes*, implies that causes and consequences might have been foreseen.

Another form of disaster story was represented by some of his last paintings, which he had begun in 1999 and returned to with vigour in 2007–8: a series inspired by Jules Verne's *L'Île mystérieuse*. In the novel, published in 1875, a group of prisoners escape the American Civil War in a hydrogen balloon. A storm carries them thousands of miles to an uninhabited volcanic island in the south Pacific. They succeed against the odds to begin new lives and repel pirates, aided by Captain Nemo of the Nautilus using a torpedo and an 'electric gun'. When the island is destroyed in a colossal eruption the settlers are rescued by ship. In all the paintings it was the eruption and the rescue that captured William's attention, not the balloon, nor the pirates, nor Nemo and his spectacular inventions. His theme was unlikely survival: in one painting, *Optimism*, the events are observed by a solitary dodo – perhaps the last surviving of its species [126–7]. The last of William's *Mysterious Island* paintings, dating from the year he died, is almost abstract – a glittering veil of coloured particles thrown into the sky above a mere dozen strokes that represent the island and the ship.

The Mysterious Island, 2008, acrylic on canvas, 24 x 30 cm

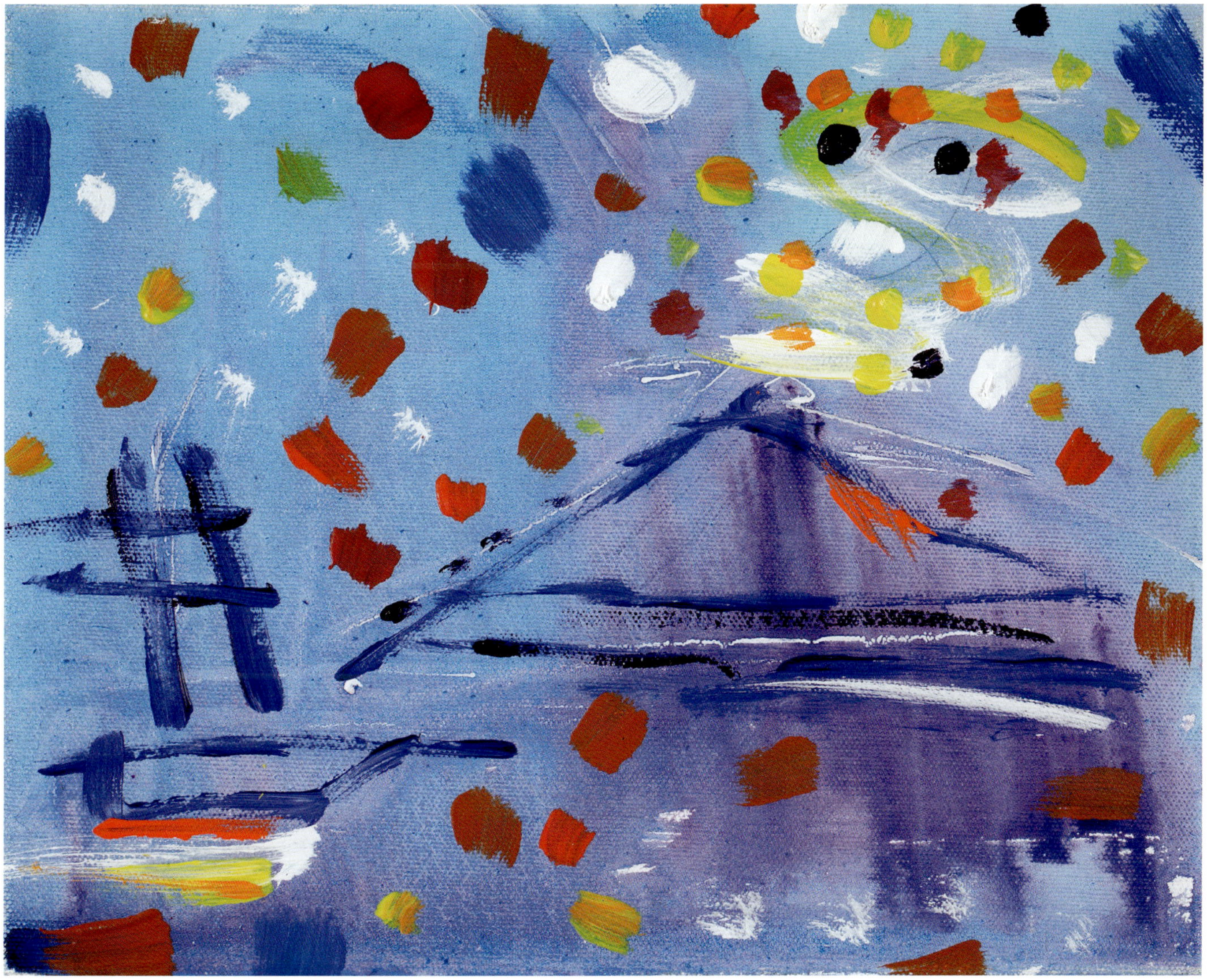

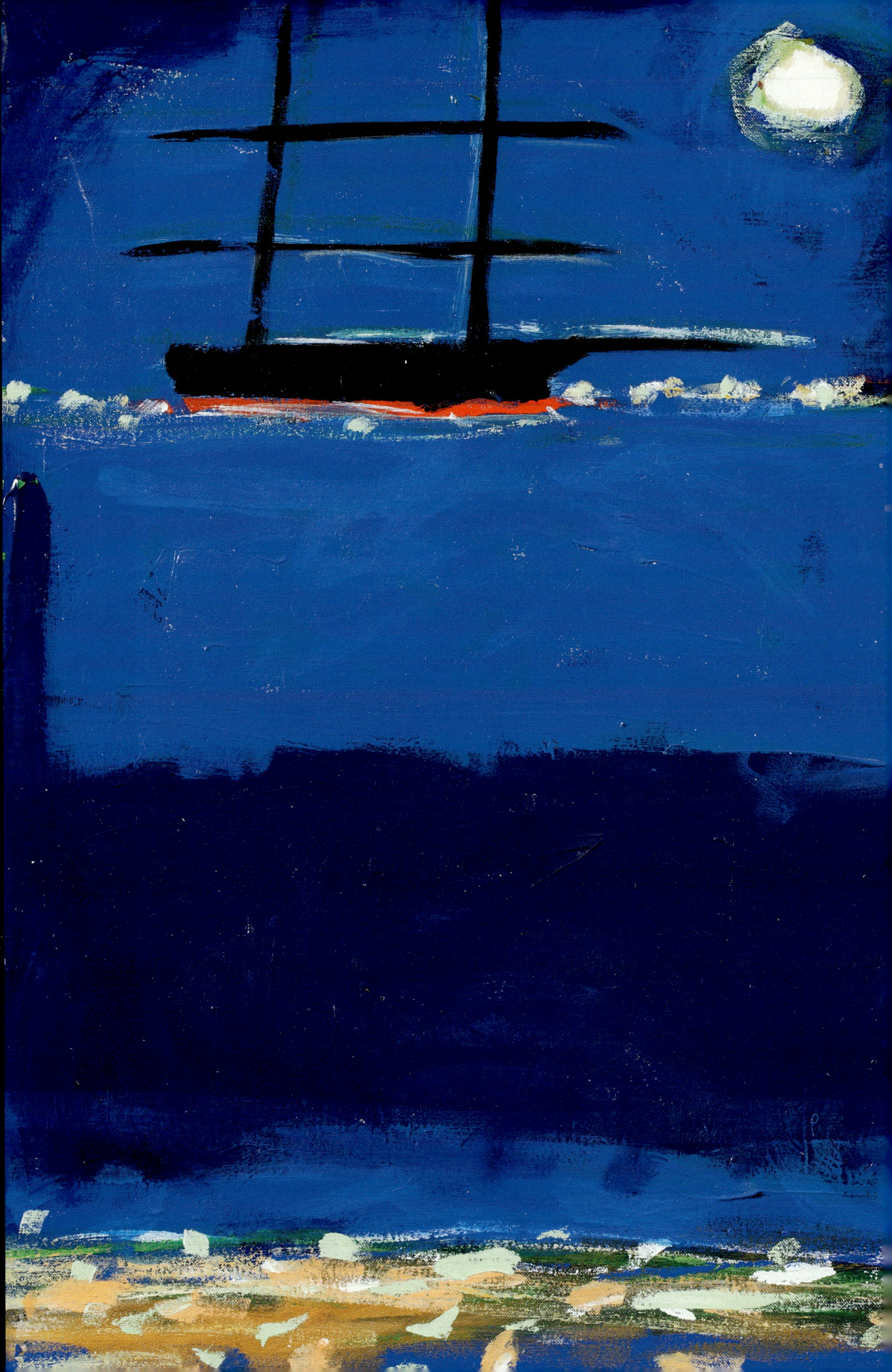

Optimism (Dodo), 1999, oil on canvas, 79 x 105 cm

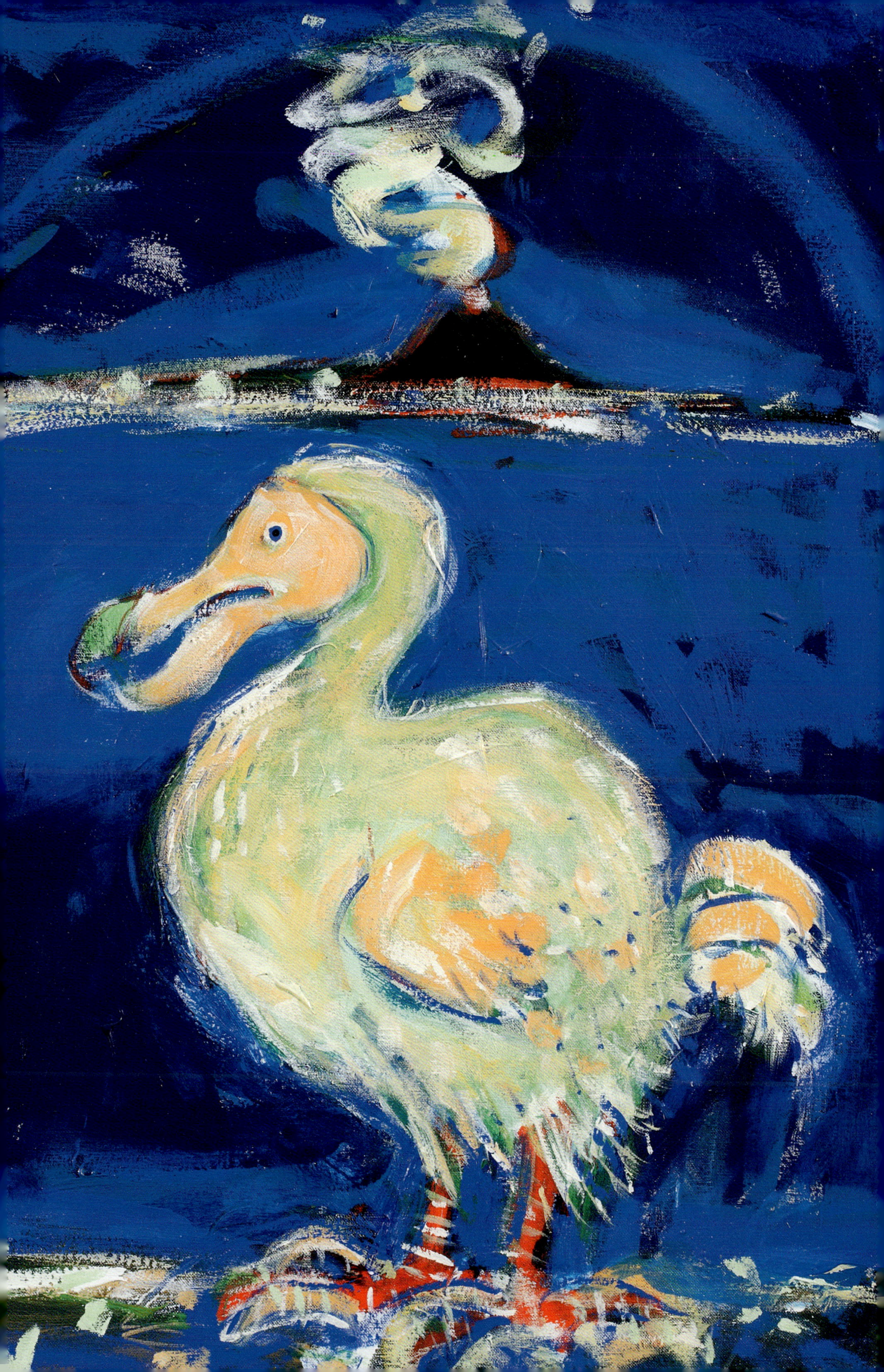

A defining trait of human nature is, I believe, the imagination – at once the alleviation of tedium, the bringing of a sense of fun and maybe, just maybe, illumination.

Afterlives
The myth of William Brown

William suffered periods of serious ill health beginning in his early thirties, when he was operated on for bowel cancer. Soon afterwards, in the mid-1980s, he was hospitalised in London when he began peeing blood after one of his visits to North Africa. Doctors considered it was caused by alcohol damage to his kidneys but it transpired he had been infected with bilharzia (schistosomiasis) while walking barefoot in infected water. In 2002, he presented with jaundice and was diagnosed with a heart murmur. He was offered heart surgery and told to stop drinking, but he said no to both. When he began organising exhibitions and events from home while unfit to travel he wrote to Dagma Štěpánková in Prague: 'I like / am suited it seems to working *en bousquet* = in the bunker. Perhaps, I am a bear. We seldom break cover.'[90]

Three years later he went to Tunisia again but was hospitalised at Bridgend on his return with liver and heart problems and severe back pain. In 2006, he was hospitalised with nausea and vomiting immediately after flying to Toronto. Admitted to St Joseph's, where he had been born, he was diagnosed with jaundice as well as atrial fibrillation. The doctor noted, 'He does drink a significant amount of alcohol.'[91]

Some months after his return to Wales he was taken into hospital at Bridgend once again. He died on 17 July 2008. He was fifty-four. Though the certificate cited decompensated alcoholic liver disease, after twenty years together Carys was convinced that the cirrhosis derived from his historical infection.[92]

His final painting was from the long-standing series *The Dark Fairground*, which had been developed alongside the idea of a book with David Greenslade to conjure an end-of-the-pier menagerie and freak show and echo Ensor's macabre carnivals populated by grotesques. William continued with it periodically but David sensed he didn't want to finish, perhaps because it required him to engage a darker side.[93] *All the Fun of the Fair* was among the loosest of William's works [130–1], flurries of colour mottling the canvas – a quality in common with his last *Mysterious Island* painting [125], *Owl and Pussycat* [22–3] and other works of 2008. As it transpired, these were exemplars of 'late Brown', evanescent and impressionist in the same way that 'late Turner' or 'late Monet' can be seen to be. In *All the Fun of the Fair*, a wolf, a polar bear and a Mari Lwyd appeared on a stage. Curtains of candy-colour red and white were sobered by dabs of blue, green, turquoise and ochre. Sgraffito squiggles bracketed the trio of performers: the Mari grounded and looking to stage front and the wolf and polar bear in profile, each with a vivid heart and levitated either side of a full moon.

William's funeral on 25 July was at Merthyr Mawr, two miles as the crow flies from his Welsh home and in the family parish of Laleston. It is a village of outstanding prettiness; a winding lane, thatched cottages, a delicate Victorian church on an ancient site, a collection of medieval crosses and grave slabs, and a system of great dunes down to the sea that conjures thoughts of the Sahara. Ivor Davies described 'a remote, shimmering scene in bright, warm air, a little church – full, with no more standing room, pressed together, overspilt in the green, wide-open graveyard.'[94] Friends, family and collaborators came from many countries. David Greenslade, Lucien Suel and Peter Meilleur read poems. Tributes were paid by William's brother-in-law Boston Hommel and by friends Malcolm Parr and Anthony Evans, who said, 'It seemed as if the images flew out of him, naturally, ceaselessly and effortlessly.'

A roughly shaped slab of slate was carved by Ieuan Rees. Within the outline of a bear – William's bear – were placed his name and dates below a maple leaf and the one word 'ARTIST'. Thirteen years later, Carys's name and dates were added.

William Brown's energy and vivacity in his short life gave him an extraordinary impact on those around him, especially in Wales, where it was hard to imagine he had lived for only eighteen years. Carys and David Greenslade published recollections by friends as *William Brown in Wales* – appreciations by poets, painters, printmakers, teachers, critics, curators. The contributions were heartfelt and many demonstrated that William and his work had in some way changed people's lives. Anthony Evans was an established artist when William moved into the studio next to him, and yet he credited William as a mentor: 'I had my first lesson in inventive, imaginative painting in his studio – I had my first lesson in how to use colour in his studio, I had my first lesson in "Art can be Fun" in his studio.' One of the children who attended his primary school workshops, Lara Davies, went on eventually to the Royal College of Art. As a child she was inspired by the exhibitions he brought to the school and liberated by his example, realising that

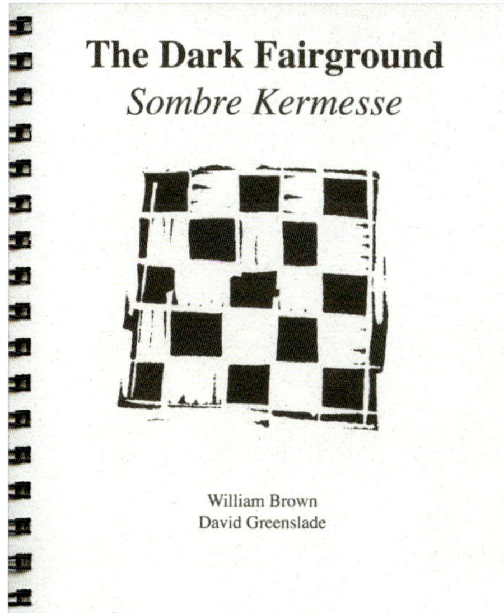

The Dark Fairground, 2009

Headstone at Merthyr Mawr

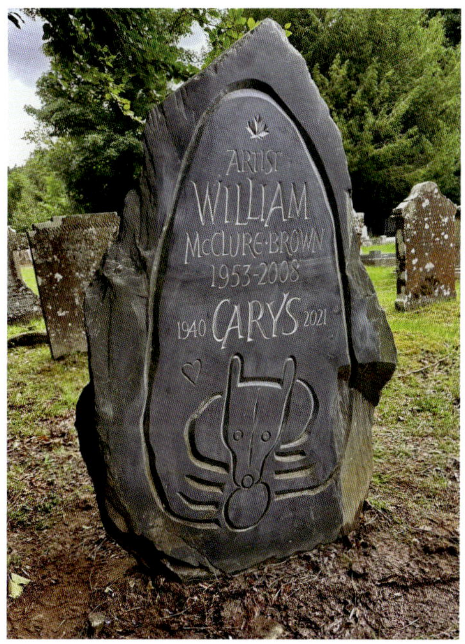

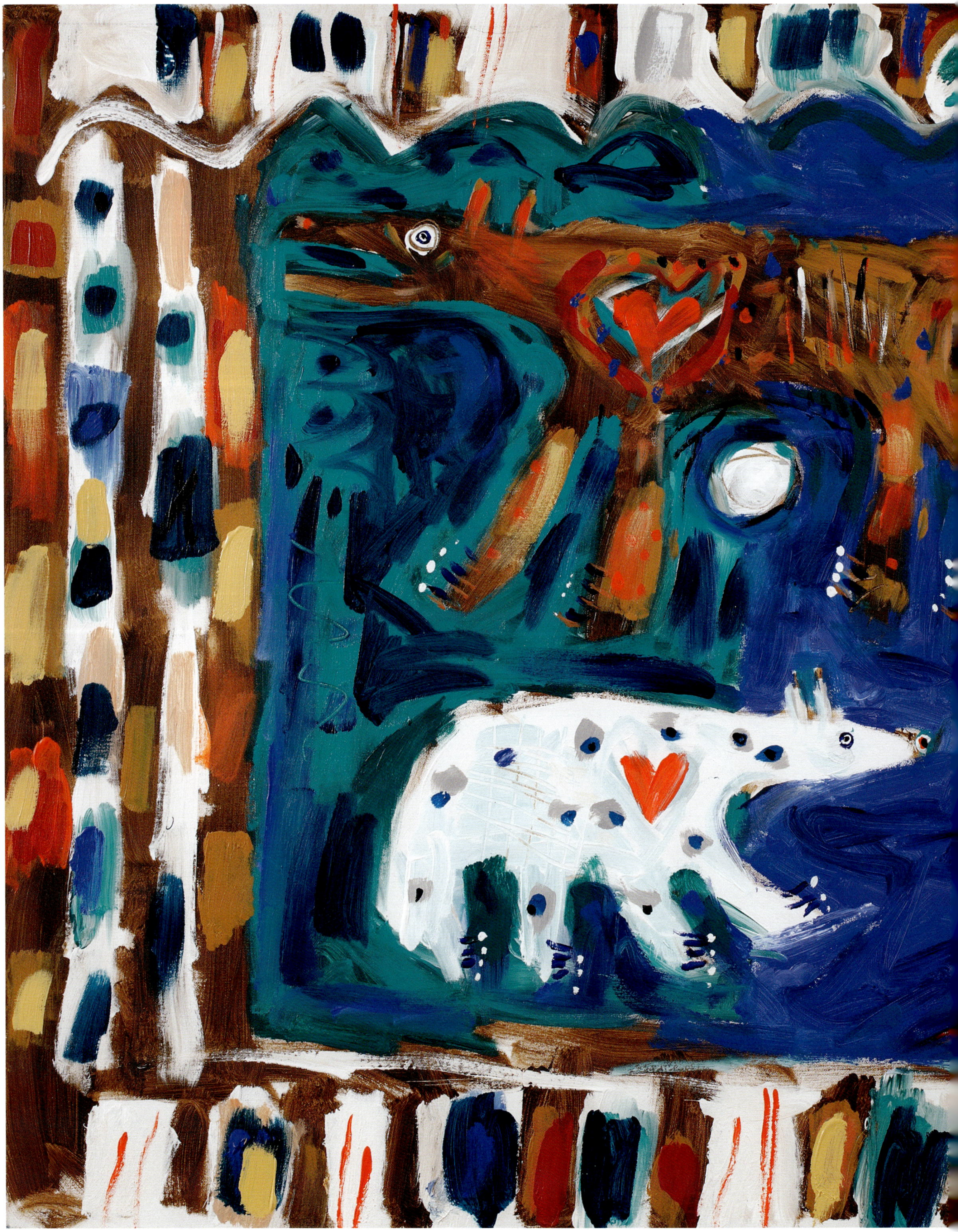

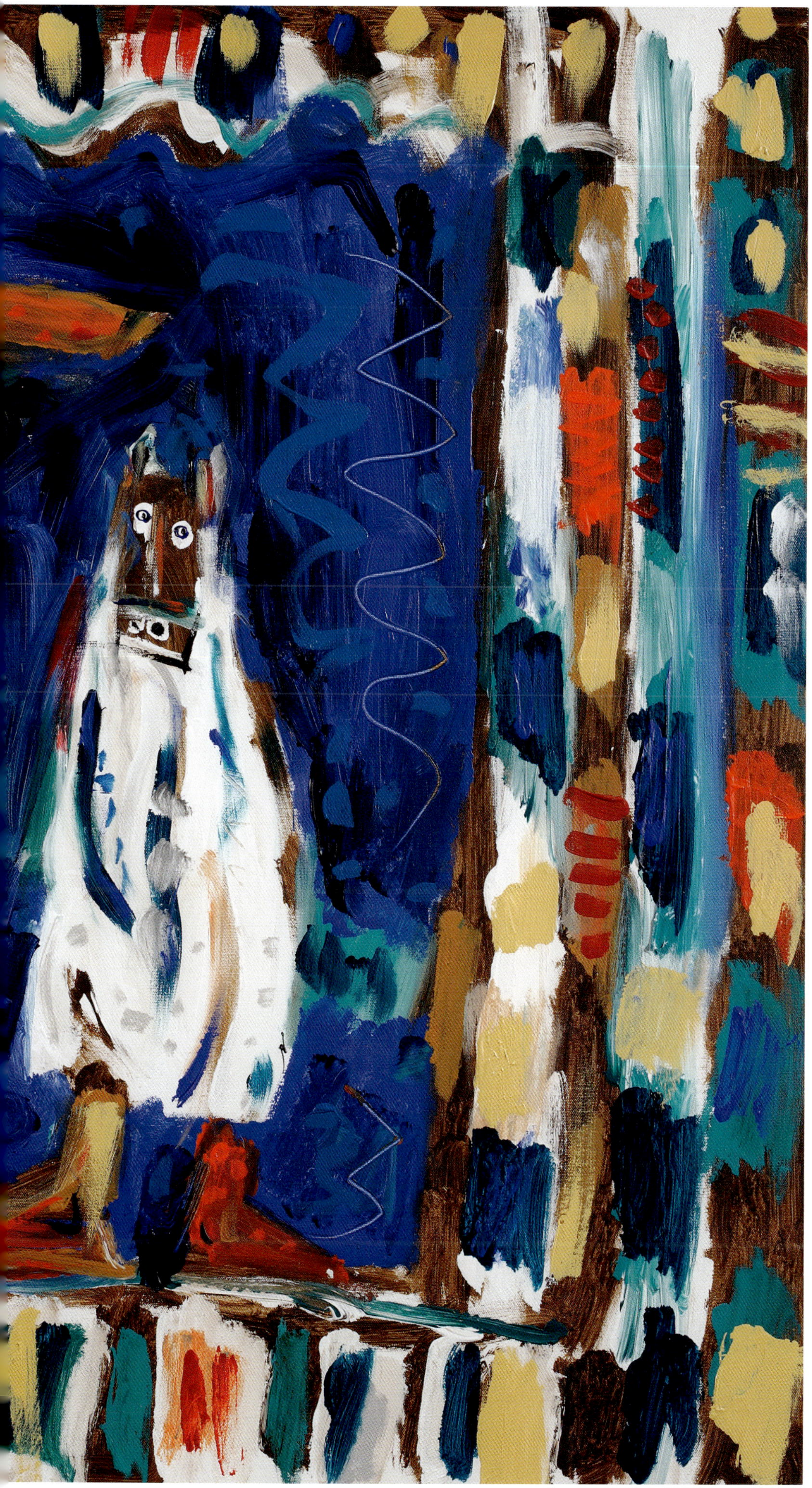

All the Fun of the Fair,
2008, acrylic on canvas,
135 x 95 cm

she could make art from life or from imagination, from observation or from stories. Carys and David received more contributions to the book than they could incorporate. David Woolley wrote a description of William that friends would recognise: 'warm, confusing, eccentric, joyous, peppered with those streams of crazy correspondence, endless project ideas, and drink fuelled escapades [...] in our minds, always, as a huge, enthusiastic, cryptic, loveable bundle of nonsense.' The sculptor Roger Moss wrote of William's impact:[95]

> Somehow he landed in Wales and immediately went viral, word flashed around – a great bear with a big personality had arrived, and look out because he never stops. He invigorated the landscape. There was never any obstacle for him when getting stuff done, not only for himself, but equally for his fellow artists, and not just of the visual persuasion. Not for him the solitary creative – sharing was always the game. [...] He didn't want safe, he sought fun, he defined his rules, followed them and didn't rely on fashion or opinion. He just kept going, kept making, he was an explosion without definition. He just wanted to take us all along. This way, through his single-minded wish to create, paint, draw, print, collaborate, converse, intrigue, tease, laugh, challenge, sup and share, was invigorating, exhausting and rewarding. No barriers, no hesitation, brilliant enthusiasm wrapped up in knowing winks, giggles and guffaws.

There were legacies in mainland Europe too. Lucien Suel wrote: 'He was an inspirational person for ideas and artistic projects. His kindness, his culture, his humour and the way he paid attention to everyone are still remembered by many people in north of France and Picardy. I am grateful for what he brought to me and generally speaking, for all that beauty he added to our world.'[96]

A permanent legacy is in the remarkable number of collections that hold William's works. Some were purchased; others he gave, in a spirit of gratitude and friendship and with a wish to share his imaginative world. While he was appreciated by some curators and collectors and many fellow artists, recognition was not widespread or established. The curator of his Glynn Vivian exhibition Alison Bevan wrote in an obituary: 'Despite a seemingly effortless, cornucopic talent, he rarely achieved the acclaim he deserved from the main contemporary art world, partly due to a failure to see that this irreverent, humorous and wonderfully eccentric man was actually unerringly serious about his art.'[97]

The exhibitions didn't stop when William died. East West Gallery held a memorial exhibition in 2008. Pauline Griffiths began exhibiting William's work at The Art Shop in Abergavenny the year before he died and continued to do so regularly afterwards. William's parents came to visit. In 2009 St David's Hall in Cardiff showed 81 works under the title *Just William*. Kevin Sinnott held an exhibition for William in his gallery in Pontycymer in 2020, which opened as the Covid-19 pandemic began, closed, and reopened that summer. Sinnott wrote: 'I sometimes wonder why on earth have I gone to such a massive single handed effort to create Gallery STUDIO18 and then the opportunity to display this stunning body of work with

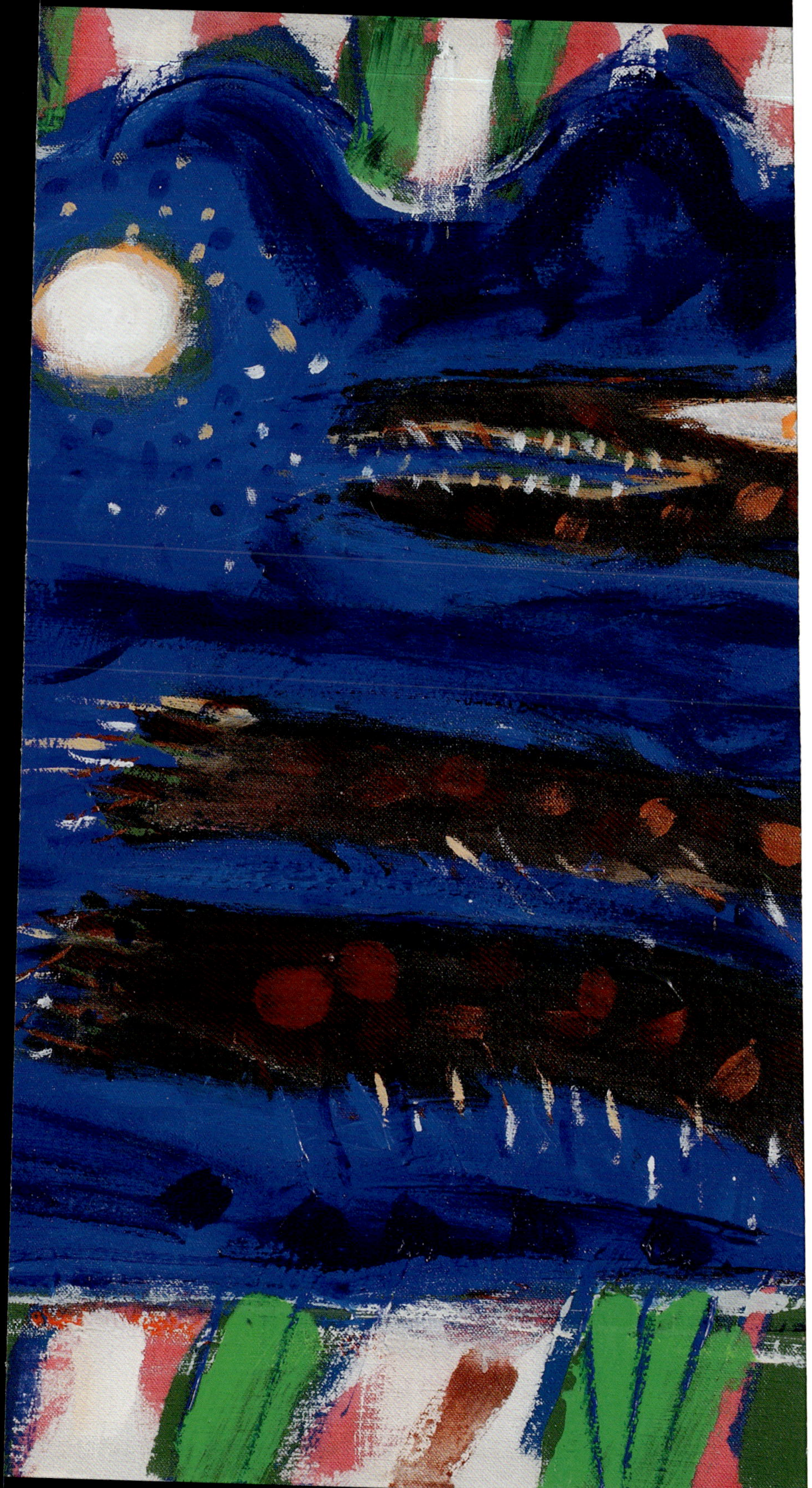

Carys, the artist's widow and her strong family roots in the town of Pontycymer, comes along and I am rewarded by knowing that I have had a hand in something truly memorable.'[98]

In apt contradiction of the natural order, collaborations continued even after William's death. In 2019, Keith Bayliss and Roger Moss created an exhibition in dialogue with William titled 'Venus'. They wrote: 'Although the story changed with each telling, William Brown insisted that a Welsh Venus, to rival the Venus of Willendorf, had been unearthed in the hills above Blaengwynfi. Following William's death ten years ago,' they explained that they hoped 'to make an exhibition in which the three artists could at last explore the idea of "Venus" and come together again to share their discoveries.'[99] That same year a book appeared in French in the names of Lucien Suel and William Brown, drawing together their joint works in one volume of ninety pages, *Ourson les Neiges D'Antan? Poèmes illustrés.* It was a pun on a picture title William had used as long ago as 1983, *Ou Sont les Neiges D'Antan?* (Where are the snows of yesteryear?), but with the words for 'where are' replaced with 'teddy bear'.

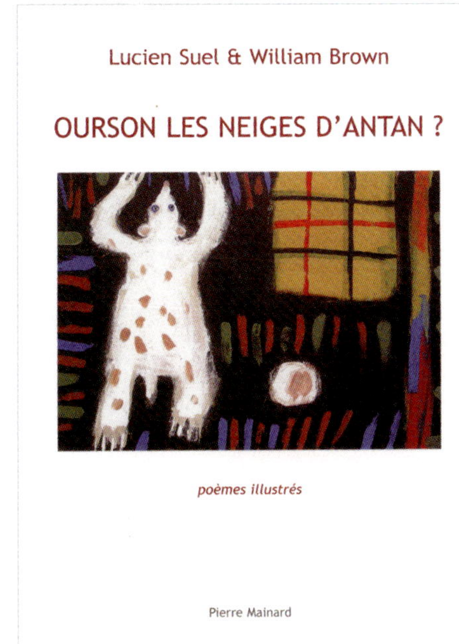

Ourson les Neiges D'Antan?, 2019

William wrote in 1996, 'I am unable to reconcile my wish to wreak havoc and my desire to put things together'.[100] In truth, his whole career could be described as exactly such a reconciliation, a triumphant combination of order with disorder.

Underneath the brightness and bravado was an artist who tackled big themes such as the clash of cultures or the climate crisis, sometimes with provocative irony, who used electric colour and fluid form and who invested his work with a profound understanding of art and literature. He made work that a five-year-old child could respond to instantly or that any viewer could consider in depth. Paint, ink, lines and shapes were melted in the crucible of his lifetime's experience to cast dreams, memories and thoughts. He said in 2001: 'The palette, the colour, is as strong a theme as the narrative in the work. I honestly do believe if you can't make work to your satisfaction, what's the point? How can you prove, or satisfy or say anything with conviction to another?'[101]

Like the acutely observant image-makers who drew mammoths and bison onto the walls of caves 30,000 years ago, William McClure Brown demonstrated an economy of mark making, a passion for symbols, and a belief in the vitality of painting as a way of sharing ideas. He made paintings profligately all his life, as though he had a thousand miles of cave to fill.

Next page:
The Dark Fairground, 2008, acrylic on canvas, 61 x 120 cm

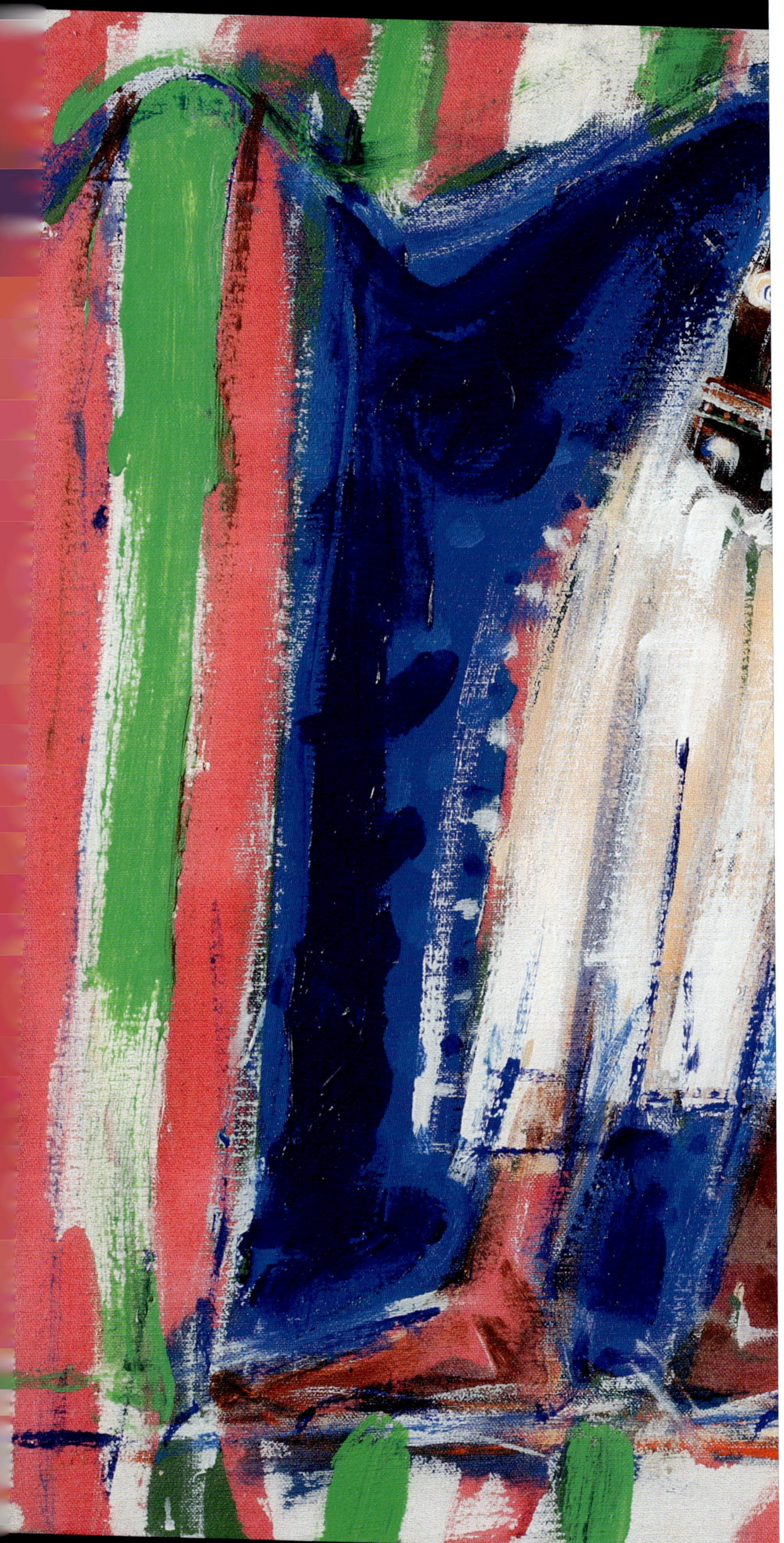

Notes

1 Raymond Williams in the manuscript of his novel *The Grasshopper* (1955), quoted in Dai Smith, 2008. *Raymond Williams: A Warrior's Tale*, p.11.

2 Interview with Lucien Suel in Newport Museum and Art Gallery, 1998, p.5.

3 Interviewed in HTV Wales, *High Performance*, 2001.

4 Letter to David Greenslade attached to email to William Brown from M. Stemp of saint-exupery.org 18 March 2005. Greenslade collection.

5 Robert Harding, personal communication 6 December 2025, attested to William's knowledge of casting; William interviewed by Laura Gill, 1989; Jenny White, 2004.

6 Invitation, Plymouth Arts Centre, 1986.

7 Furse, in City and County of Swansea, 1996, p.6.

8 Iwan Bala, in David Greenslade and Carys Brown, *William Brown in Wales*, p.55 (hereafter abbreviated WBIW).

9 Robert Harding personal communication 6 December 2025.

10 Undated letter to David Greenslade, Greenslade collection.

11 Anthony Evans, WBIW, p.8; Robert Harding personal communication, 6 December 2025.

12 Brown, 1998.

13 David Greenslade collection: recollection by David Greenslade in unpublished essay; undated letter to David Greenslade.

14 Carys's father, Herbert Davies, was the headmaster who appointed Marks as head boy and helped with his successful application to Balliol College, Oxford. Herbert supplied a character reference for Marks's trial in the US; personal communication, Huw Griffiths, 27 June 2026. Undated letter to David Greenslade, Greenslade collection.

15 Interview in HTV Wales, 2001. *High Performance*; Quoted in Laura Gascoigne, 1998, p. 19; Gareth Davies, WBIW, p.12.

16 Laura Gascoigne, invitation card, The Art Shop, Abergavenny, 2009; quoted in Laura Gascoigne, 1998, p.19.

17 Personal communication Richard and Branwen Dawson, 2026.

18 Recollection by David Greenslade in unpublished essay, David Greenslade archive.

19 Furse, 1986b.

20 Carys Brown, quoted in *Wales Online*, 2008a; personal communication, Lucienne Evans, April 2024; quoted in Laura Gascoigne, 1998, p.19.

21 Comment in Image and Word, 1993; interview with David Greenslade, 10 November 2023.

22 Iwan Bala, WBIW, p.55.

23 Artist's statement, January 2007.

24 Interview with Lucien Suel in Newport Museum and Art Gallery, 1998, p.6.

25 Interview with Joady Brennan, 21 April 2026.

26 Interview with Lucien Suel in Newport Museum and Art Gallery, 1998, p.6.

27 Personal communication from Kathleen Hommel, 15 May 2026; statement in Welsh Group, 2000, p.10; interview in HTV Wales, 2001.

28 Personal communications from Sharon Berg, 11 April 2026 and 8 April 2026.

29 Personal communication from Sharon Berg, 26 May 2026. The child, Mark Ratusznic, sought to contact his birth-father as an adult and met Carys soon after William had died. Of William's creative flatmates, Philip became a commercial artist but died young and Sharon and Brian both became published writers. Sharon's autobiographical novel of her period with William, *Tell That to Picasso*, has been published in excerpts including 'Jigsaw Puzzle' in Sharon Berg, 2016, *Naming the Shadows* and Sharon Berg, 2025. '1970: the Portrait that Wasn't' in *Ultramarine Literary Review*. https://www.ultramarinereview.com/post/1970-the-portrait-that-wasn-t

30 Personal communication from David Greenslade based on conversations with William.

31 Personal communication from Sharon Berg, 9 April 2026; Joe Rosenblatt comment to David Greenslade, David Greenslade archive.

32 Personal communication from Sharon Berg, 26 May 2026; email from Sharon Berg to David Greenslade, 8 April 2016; personal communication from Sharon Berg, 9 April 2026; letter and emails to William from Ila Berg 2005–6.

33 Joady Brennan email to the author, 23 April 2026.

34 Joady Brennan email to the author, 23 April 2026.

35 William Brown statement in Welsh Group, 2000, p.10.

36 Ihor Holubizky, 'Gershon Iskowitz Life and Works', Art Institute of Canada: https://www.aci-iac.ca/art-books/gershon-iskowitz/biography/; interview with Joady Brennan, 21 April, 2026.

37 Jeff Aaron memoir for David Greenslade, David Greenslade papers.

38 Personal communication Joady Brennan; Jeff Aaron memoir for David Greenslade, David Greenslade papers.

39 Gary Plastow recollection, David Greenslade archive; Malcolm Plastow recollection, David Greenslade archive.

40 Jonathan Futtrell, 2018. 'Mick Owens, the artful life of a generous man'. https://jonathanfutrell.com/2018/03/13/mick-owens-an-artful-life-of-all-sorts/

41 Leo Tolstoy, 2010. *War and Peace*, translated by Louise and Aylmer Maud and Amy Mandelker, book 2, part 3, chapter 7, pp.464–5; file on masonic membership, William Brown's papers.

42 Clare Henry, 1981. 'West Country Artists', *Glasgow Herald*, 31 August 1981.

43 Clement Sarah, 2016. 'Robert Clement Obituary', *The Guardian*, 8 November 2016.

44 Robert Clement, letter to David Greenslade, 18 September 2015; published in WBIW, p.46.

45 Robert Clement, letter to David Greenslade, 18 September 2015; published in WBIW, p.46.

46 Decree nisi, Bow County Court, 6 April 1988; story recounted to David Greenslade; personal communication 29 May 2026.

47 Signed lease dated 6 July, 1987, William Brown papers; this and successive paragraphs are primarily based on the author's interview with Carys Brown, 27 July 2021.

48 Quoted by David Greenslade in WBIW, p.4; Alison Bevan personal communication 4 July 2026.

49 Terry L. Williams, WBIW, p.20.

50 Personal communication from Kathleen Hommel, 3 June 2026.

51 William Brown statement in Welsh Group, 2000, p. 10; Dorothee and Johannes Glaw, WBIW, pp.85–8; Robert Harding, personal communication 6 December 2025.

52 Keith Bayliss, WBIW, p.70; exhibition invitation, 1990.

53 Adrian Paul Metcalf, WBIW, p.52; undated letter William Brown to David Greenslade, Greenslade collection.

54 Claire Curneen, personal communication, 31 May 2026.

55 Letter from David Solomon to William Brown, 2 May 1997, William Brown papers; David Solomon, interviewed by the author 11 May 2026.

56 Hannah Jones, 2001; Carys Brown in interview with the author, 12 August 2021; Abbey Abbas, WBIW, p.10.

57 Quoted by Carys Brown in interview with the author, 12 August 2021; letter to Dagmar Štěpánková, undated, c.2006.

58 Keith Bayliss, gallery text for *Just William 1953–2008*, St David's Hall, Cardiff, 2009.

59 David Greenslade unpublished essay, 'The Chicken or the Egg', David Greenslade archive.

60 David Greenslade unpublished essay, 'Meeting Mr Brown', David Greenslade archive; Peter Finch, WBIW, pp.18–19.

61 Interview with David Greenslade 10 November 2023.

62 David Greenslade, personal communication, 30 May 2026.

63 Bernard Mitchell, WBIW, p.9; personal communication from Alison Bevan, 3 July 2006.

64 Quoted in John C. P. King, 2008.

65 Greenslade, 2005, pp. 59; William Brown quoted in Laura Gascoigne, 1998, p.19.

66 Welsh Group, 1994; quoted in Cen Williams, 1999, back cover.

67 Translation: 'One day I saw myself. On the street, a dog, in the rain. It was me.' Alison Lloyd (ed.), 1995. *Intimate Portraits*, p.34. The Scottish Register of Tartans identifies three McClure tartans: one red with stripes of black, blue, green and white; one green with stripes of red, black, white and blue; and one green with stripes of white, blue and pink. No yellow is to be seen. A yellow tartan with black line is the MacLeods'. Another William Brown myth?

68 William Brown letter to Dagmar Štěpánková, December 1998, published in WBIW, p.77; Lucien Suel, WBIW, pp.7, 57.

69 Interview with David Greenslade 10 November 2023.

70 Personal communication from Keith Bayliss, 3 July 2026.

71 Quoted by Lucien Suel, WBIW, p.7.

72 Welsh Group, 2000, p.10.

73 Greenslade, 2005, p.61; Laura Gascoigne, 2009. p.57.

74 Told by Boston Hommel in his eulogy at William's funeral, 2008.

75 Pete Williams, WBIW, p.16.

76 John Furse, text for exhibition, 2002.

77 West Country Artists, 1981.

78 24 February, 1990. Courtesy of The Box, Plymouth.

79 *Matthew* was John Cabot's ship in which he crossed the Atlantic in 1497, 500 years earlier; interview with Lucien Suel in Newport Museum and Art Gallery, 1998, p.10.

80 Malcolm Parr, undated, 'Wales and William Brown' p.30.

81 New Art at the Old Library, artist's statement, undated, c. 1992.

82 Anon, 1992.

83 C. D., 1995.

84 Lucien Suel, WBIW, p.7.

85 Brown, 1998.

86 Interview with Lucien Suel in Newport Museum and Art Gallery, 1998, p.7.

87 Interview with Lucien Suel in Newport Museum and Art Gallery, 1998, p.10.

88 Rimbaud in Harar, https://tezetaethiopia.wordpress.com/2005/05/31/rimbaud-in-harar/

89 Hervé Constant, WBIW, p.42.

90 Published in WBIW, p.79.

91 Discharge report by Dr G. Sue-a-Quan, St Joseph's Health Centre, 21 April 2006.

92 Personal communication, Sue Alder, 9 June 2026.

93 Interview with David Greenslade, 10 November 2023.

94 Quoted in Greenslade and Brown, p.84.

95 Anthony Evans, WBIW, p.8; Lara Davies, WBIW, p.21; David Woolley in David Greenslade archive; Roger Moss, WBIW, p.74.

96 Lucien Suel, WBIW, p.57.

97 Alison Bevan, 2008.

98 Interview with Pauline Griffiths 18 October 2021; https://studio18.wales/2020/03/12/william-brown-exhibition/

99 Llantarnam Grange exhibition card, February 2019.

100 Quoted in City and County of Swansea, 1996, p.11.

101 Interviewed in HTV Wales, 2001.

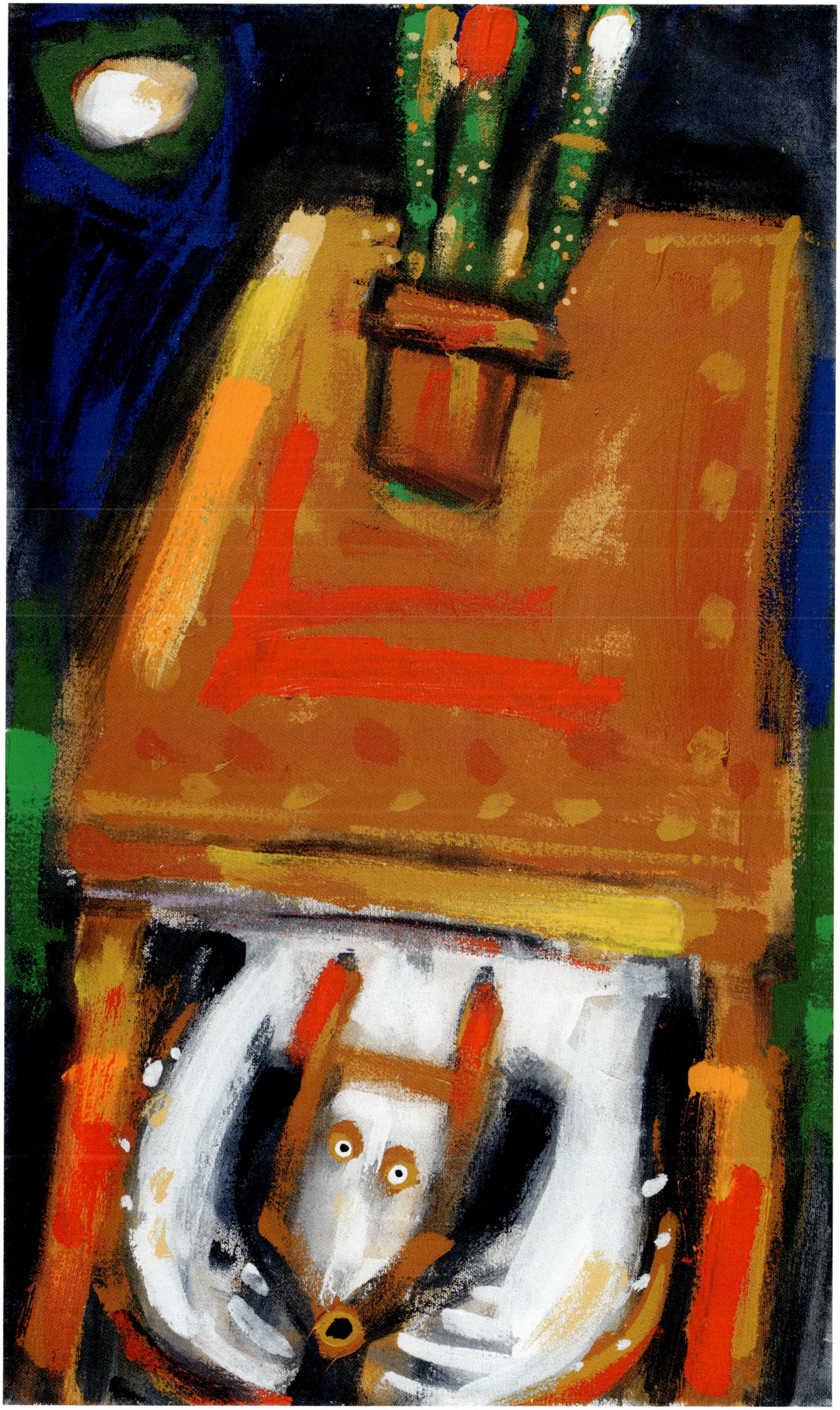

Still life with Snowball – Polar Bear, 2005, acrylic on canvas, 66 x 40 cm

Chronology

1953 William McClure Brown born, Toronto, 11 December, to Alex and Cathy Brown of 65 Belmont Drive, Bramalea, Ontario

1962 Aged eight, family tour to Thunder Bay

Operations on his feet

1969 Quit Bramalea Secondary School aged fifteen, periodically ran away from home

1970 Lived with Philip York, Brian Purdy and Sharon Berg, Brampton

1973 Son with Sharon Berg given for adoption, Mark Ratusznic

Moved with Sharon to Downtown Toronto

Worked at Grossman's Tavern and Gwartzman's art supplies store

Met Gershon Iskowitz

1975 Relationship with Sharon ended, second child born, Ila Berg

Moved in with Joady Brennan, Toronto

1976 Married to Joady Brennan, Toronto

1977 Moved to Somerset with Joady and lived near Taunton, at Ash Priors and later Buddle Oak, Halse

1978 Began working part-time as technician at Somerset College of Arts and Technology, Taunton

Encouraged in printmaking by artist Mick Owens; first travels to North Africa with him

1979 Last abstract paintings

1981 Organised group exhibition, *West Country Artists*, Edinburgh Festival

1983 Divorced from Joady Brennan

Commissioned by Tony Foster and Bob Clement to give printmaking workshops in Devon schools

First solo exhibition, Spacex, Exeter

Married to Ruth but separated soon afterwards; moved to New Cross and Brockley, London; worked as painter and decorator

1984 Operation for bowel cancer, London

1985 South West Arts Project Award £1,000 for travel to Tunisia and Algeria

1986 Hospitalised in London with schistosomiasis / bilharzia; possible liver damage

1987 Leased ground floor of 23 Leonard Street, London EC2 and given a place to stay in Devon by Bernard Samuels of Plymouth Arts Centre

Met Carys Griffiths during residency at Woodford Junior School, Plympton, Devon

Carys and William visited William's family; trips to Hudson Bay and Moose Factory Island; met Cree and Inuit artists

1988 Divorced from Ruth

Moved full-time to Devon

Married to Carys, 30 July

1989 Visited Canada for most of August

Mail Art project, Gütersloh, Germany, met Johannes and Dorothee Glaw, Josef Janda

Began print series of Canadian history and polar exploration

1990 British Council Award for exhibition in Gütersloh, Germany

Moved to Newcastle Hill, Bridgend, after Carys was appointed Head at Plasnewydd Primary School, Maesteg

Quickly absorbed into Welsh artistic community

1991 Solo exhibition in Canada: Art Gallery of Peel, Brampton

Community project in Swansea valley with Keith Bayliss

Successive return trips to Morocco and Tunisia

1992 Welsh Arts Council travel award to Orkney with Adrian Paul Metcalfe

Germany with Johannes and Dorothee Glaw

Joined community of artists in studios at the Old Library, Cardiff

1993 Organised touring exhibition Contemporary Printmaking in Wales

1994 Organised touring exhibition 6″ x 6″ with Peter Wills

1995 Commissioned by Brecon Jazz

Exhibition at Isbergues, France, aided by Lucien Suel

First loup-garou images

1996 Artists evicted from studios at Old Library in Cardiff

Rented a studio and then purchased St Stephen's Church, Llangynwyd

Pivotal solo exhibition, Glynn Vivian Art Gallery, Swansea

First Mari Lwyd images

1997 Began regular exhibitions with East West Gallery, London

Introduced by Ivor Davies to David Greenslade

Le Nouveau Bestiaire, with Lucien Suel

First Venus of Blaengwynfi paintings

1998 Journey with Malcolm Parr from Bilbao to Santiago de Compostela funded by Arts Council of Wales; caves of Altamira

1998 Installation and events with David Greenslade at National Eisteddfod of Wales

1999 Animated video for Gorky's Zygotic Mwnci, *Spanish Dance Troupe*

2000 North American Festival of Wales, Ottawa, with David Greenslade

2001 Visits Tangier, Prague, Ireland, Brittany

2002 Heart murmur diagnosed; suffered from jaundice

Marseille, London, France, Canada

Fire in Llangynwyd studio

2003 Canada, France, Devon

2004 Canada, Tunisia, Iona

2005 Greece, Tunisia, Canada

2005 Made honorary member of Orbus Pictus Europa, Czech Republic

Hospitalised at Bridgend with liver and heart problems and back pain

2006 Canada, Greece, Scotland, France, Tunisia

In hospital in Toronto with jaundice and atrial fibrillation

2008 Died Princess of Wales hospital, Bridgend, 17 July, aged fifty-four

Exhibitions

Exhibitions by William Brown were so numerous that keeping a full record was almost impossible. The first two sections of this list comprise solo and mixed exhibitions documented by invitations, posters, reviews or catalogues. A further list shows exhibitions that were claimed in artist's biographies or notes but are as yet unverified. Exhibitions were in the UK unless stated otherwise.

Solo and two-person exhibitions

1983 *Hot & Cold Running*, Spacex, Exeter

1984 *William Brown and Peter Bartlett*, Brewhouse Theatre, Taunton

1986 *William Brown: Paintings, Drawings, Prints*, Plymouth Arts Centre

William Brown: Woodcuts, Plymouth City Museum and Art Gallery

1988 *William Brown: New Work*, New Street Gallery, Plymouth

Winterreise / A Winter's Journey: paintings, drawings and prints, Greenwich Theatre Gallery, London

A Winter's Journey, Hexagon Gallery, Reading

1989 *William Brown – New Work*, Barbican Theatre, Plymouth

Wintereist / A Winter's Journey, Brewhouse Theatre and Arts Centre, Taunton

Woodcuts by William Brown, City Museum and Art Gallery, Plymouth

1990 *Arbeiten auf Papier*, Mediothek, Gütersloh, Germany

William Brown: Paintings and Print, Llantarnam Grange Arts Centre, Cwmbran and Swansea Arts Workshop

Pitminster Studio, Taunton

1991 Cross Gallery, Pontardawe, Swansea

William Brown: Recent Work, Polytechnic of Wales, Pontypridd

Recent Paintings and Prints by Keith Bayliss and William Brown, Café Praxis Gallery, Bristol

William Brown: Paintings and Prints, Art Gallery of Peel, Brampton, Ontario, Canada

1992 *William Brown: New Paintings*, Midlands Arts Centre, Birmingham

Cythera? New Paintings by William Brown, Llanover Hall, Cardiff

William Brown, Tricycle Gallery, London

1993 *William Brown*, Tamworth Arts Centre

1995 *Roar!*, Art Furniture and Interiors, Cardiff

Impressions: William Brown, Salle des Expositions, Isbergues, France

1996 *Voyages: works on paper*, with Keith Bayliss, Gallerie Vyšehrad, Prague, Czech

What's Behind the Blanket?, Glynn Vivian Art Gallery and tour

1997 East West Gallery, London

1998 National Eisteddfod, Bridgend

Beyond Loup-Garou: Au-delà du Loup-Garou, Newport Museum and Art Gallery

1999 *The Moose Man Cometh – New Work from the Back of the Cave*, East West Gallery, London

New Work by William Brown, Oriel Canfas, Cardiff

2000 North American Festival of Wales, Ottawa, Canada

2001 *Sombre Ducasse*, Theatre Biplan, Lille, France

Recent Prints by William Brown, an Artist from Wales, Esther Allen Greer Museum, University of Rio Grande, Ohio, USA

Muskoka Land of Ghosts, East West Gallery, Notting Hill, London

2002 Ripples Ice Cream Parlour, Swansea

2003 *Still Life with a Snowball*, East West Gallery, London

2004 *William Brown*, Grand Theatre, Swansea

Let's Get Away from it All, Café Brava, Cardiff

Approaching Storm, Oriel Canfas, Cardiff

2005 *Uh-oh!*, Oriel Ceri Richards, Swansea

Raspberry Ripple, East West Gallery, London

Newport-Guarbecque que Révélation, Gallerie le Bailliage, Aire sur la Lys, France

2006 *The Haunted House: Keith Bayliss and William Brown*, Dylan Thomas Centre, Swansea

Palmyra: Works on Paper by Abbi Abbas and William Brown, Nizwa College, Oman

2007 *William Brown: New Work*, The Art Shop, Abergavenny

Oh ... No! New Paintings, East West Gallery, London

Canada exhibition, St Donat's Arts Centre

2008 *Paintings and Prints by William Brown*, Chalk Hill Gallery, Guildford

William Brown 1953–2008: A Celebration of his Life, East West Gallery, London

2009 *Canadian Shield*, University of Wales Institute Cardiff

Just William 1953–2008, St David's Hall, Cardiff

From under the Bed, The Art Shop, Abergavenny

Visitor from Nefta, Dylan Thomas Centre, Swansea

2010 *The Dark Fairground*, Porthcawl Pavilion, South Wales

From the End of the Pier, Oriel Ceri Richards Gallery, Taliesin Arts Centre, Swansea

2012 *William Brown: Some Newly Discovered Work*, The Art Shop, Abergavenny

2013 *William Brown: from here and there*, Kooywood Gallery, Cardiff

2014 *William Brown 1953–2008: a collection of unseen drawings and works on paper*, The Art Shop, Abergavenny

2016 *Dreaming Awake*, The Art Shop and Chapel, Abergavenny

2018 *Bogeyman – The Man of Myth*, The Art Shop and Chapel, Abergavenny

2020 *William Brown at Studio 18*, Studio 18 Pontycymer, South Wales

2026 *Pursued by a Bear*, The Art Shop and Chapel, Abergavenny

Group Exhibitions

1981 *Brewhouse Open*, Brewhouse Theatre, Taunton

Eight West Country Artists, Falmouth Arts Centre

West Country Artists: Edinburgh Festival, Edinburgh College of Art

1982 *Brewhouse Open*, Brewhouse Theatre, Taunton

1983 *William Brown, Mick Owens, Malcolm Plastow*, Chalcot Gallery, Primrose Hill, London

Christmas Presence: Paintings and Drawings by William Brown, Bruce Bond, Nick Gray, Mick Owens, Seven Turner, Malcolm Plastow, Showroom Gallery, Bonner Road, London

Brewhouse Open, Brewhouse Theatre, Taunton

1985 *Visitors' Exhibition 85*, Penwith Galleries, St Ives

Brewhouse Open, Brewhouse Theatre, Taunton

Ontario Open, Toronto, Canada

Contrasts: William Brown, Geoffrey Franklin, Malcolm Plastow, Bridgwater Arts Centre, Somerset

1986 *The Artist's Eye: William Brown, Christopher Deakin, Steve Joy, Ken Sprague*, South West Arts, touring to 10 schools and colleges in Devon

1987 *William Brown and Malcolm Plastow, recent paintings, prints and drawings*, Wood Wharf Studios, Greenwich, London

Lewisham Festival, Studio Exhibition, 85 Upper Brockley Road, London

1988 *Brewhouse Open Art 1988*, Brewhouse Theatre and Arts Centre, Taunton

Bridging the Gap: an exhibition of proposed designs for repainting Oxford Road railway bridge, Reading, three civic locations

EE-I-EE-I-O, Delahaye Gallery, Cirencester

Open British Printmaking Exhibition 1988, Royal West of England Academy, Bristol

1989 *Brewhouse Open Art 1989*, Brewhouse Theatre and Arts Centre, Taunton

Dartmoor – Ten Views, Red House Arts Centre, Crediton

Out of the Wood: The Tree as Image and Symbol, Crafts Council Galleries, London and nine other venues to 1991

Mail Art 1989, Isbergues, France

Millfield Open Art Exhibition, Millfield School, Somerset

Laing Collection Exhibition, Croft Gallery, Bristol

1990 *Print.News*, Oriel, Cardiff

Printmaking 1990, The Small Mansion Arts Centre, London

Old Macdonald Had a Farm, The Old School, Bleddfa

Exposition d'Art Postal: 100 Pierres Pour Jean Tousseul, Chateau de Seilles, Andenne and Gallerie 9A, Liege, Belgium

1991 *Keith Bayliss, Richard Bowers, William Brown, Jeremy Cole, Peter Wills*, International Mail Art Archive, Pisa, Italy,

The Sea, The Sea, Devon Guild of Craftsmen, Bovey Tracey

Three artists at the Tricycle: Esther Bramble, William Brown, Bette Spektorov, Tricycle Gallery, London

Wild Creatures, Old Library, Cardiff

1992 *Contemporary Printmaking in Wales*, Glynn Vivian Art Gallery, Swansea; Tour until 1995 to St Donats Arts Centre, South Wales; Small Mansion Arts Centre, London; Libramont Expo, Belgium

Fingerprints, Newport Museum and Art Gallery

William Brown, Albert Duplock, Daphne McClure, Graham Rich, Gordon Hepworth Gallery, Newton St Cyres, Devon

Mostyn Open, Oriel Mostyn, Llandudno

Prints by Invitation, Brewhouse Theatre and Arts Centre, Taunton

Anthony Evans, Gareth Davies, Keith Bayliss, William Brown, Cardiff Central Library

Mail Art Exhibition: L'Arte e un' Esperienza Verificale – Art is a Verifiable Experience, Centro Documentazione Arte e Letteratura, Sacile, Italy

1993 *Junge Kunst in Gütersloh*, Schalterhalle der Volksbank Gütersloh, Galerie Friedemann and Galerie Grabenheinrich, Gütersloh, Germany

Hay-on-Wye Festival of Literature

Image and Word: The Five Schools Project, Swansea Arts Workshop Gallery

City of Dreams, Contact Gallery, Norwich

Ars Celtica, Oriel Ceri Richards, Swansea

Someday my Prints: An Exhibition by South Wales Printmakers, Old Library, Cardiff and tour to Plymouth City Museum, Royal Exchange Manchester, Seoul

Xylon International Prints, Winterthur, Switzerland

1994 *Sources and Origins: An International Exhibition of Prints*, Oriel Ceri Richards, Swansea

Artists' Original Prints, Hill Court Gallery, Abergavenny

Woodblock Printing: William Brown, Steve Thorpe, John Hunt, Rod Nelson, Bridgwater Arts Centre, Somerset

Welsh Group: Changing Views, Old Library, Cardiff

Three Wheelers: Works by William Brown, Sue Lovell, Angela Torrington, Tricycle Gallery, Kilburn High Road, London

6″ x 6″ International Exhibition of Small Artworks, Peter Wills Gallery, Bridgend and tour to Midland Art Centre, Tamworth Art Gallery, Wyeside Arts Centre, Glynn Vivian Art Gallery and other venues

Contemporary Art from Wales, De Leeuwenhorst, Netherlands

1995 *Open Boxes*, Old Library Cardiff and tour to Brighton, Builth Wells, Pontypridd, Llanover Hall to 1997

Intimate Portraits, Glynn Vivian Art Gallery, Swansea

The Visual Word: An exhibition of Responses, Old Library Cardiff; Swansea Arts Workshop; Mostyn, Llandudno

1996 *Visions of Redemption*, Bezalel Arts Trust, Catholic Chaplaincy, Oxford

The Bridgend Folio, Bridgend Civic Offices, Bridgend

1997 *Euotpia – Mail-Art from the West*, Gouvernement, Limburglaan 10, Maastricht, Netherlands

New Art at the Old Library, Old Library, Cardiff

1998 *La Bise: The North Winds*, Model House, Llantrisant

1999 *56 Group Wales*, Howard Gardens Gallery, UWIC, Cardiff

Creating an Art Community: 50 Years of the Welsh Group, National Museum of Wales, Cardiff

2001 *Dreaming Awake: Eight Artists from Wales*, Terezin Memorial and tour to Horice, Pisek and Olomouc, Czech

Five Artists from Wales, Bruges, Belgium

Looking Out: The Welsh Group, Paintings and Drawings, Newport Museum and Art Gallery

Looking at Lovespoons, Brecon Museum

2003 *Summer Exhibition*, Albany Gallery, Cardiff

Icons: Snow in August, Oriel Canfas, Cardiff

2004 *Gross Innovations, The Welsh Group*, Cynon Valley Museum, Aberdare, St David's Hall, Cardiff and other venues

NYU in London: A Season of Rimbaud, The Corsica Studios, London

Homage to the Horse, Pontardawe Arts Centre

Maghrebe – Responses to North African Textiles by Invited Artists, Oriel Canfas, Cardiff

Epona, St Donats Arts Centre

Y Fari Lwyd, MoMA Machynlleth

Artists of the East West Gallery, Royal Over-Seas League, London

2005 *Mineraux/Minerals – Roger Moss, Keith Bayliss, William Brown*, Le Bailliage, Aire-sur-la-lys, France; Centre Historique Minier de Lewarde, Douai, France

Yr Wyddor, Oriel Canfas, Cardiff

Animal Vegetable and Mineral: Keith Bayliss, William Brown, Anthony Evans and Roger Moss, Rhondda Heritage Park

National Eisteddfod of Wales

Shelter Cymru Art Auction, Welsh School of Architecture, Cardiff

2006 *Islands*, Oriel Canfas Gallery, Cardiff

Orbis Pictus: Europa, VOJNA Memorial Pribram, Czech

Welsh Artist of the Year, St David's Hall, Cardiff

The Painted Pot, Newport Museum and Art Gallery

SLK: Scents, Locks, Kisses, Olfactorisch Mail-Art Project, Hasselt, Belgium

2007 *Welsh Artist of the Year*, St David's Hall, Cardiff

2010 *Art for Children*, MoMA Machynlleth

2019 *Venus: Keith Bayliss, William Brown and Roger Moss*, Llantarnam Grange, Cwmbran; Oriel Q Gallery, Narberth

Claimed but unverified exhibitions

1971	Brampton Public Library, Canada
1978	Green Lane Gallery, Derby
1984	Mowhawk College, Hamilton, Ontario, Canada
	York University, Toronto, Canada
1988	Brittany, France
1991	Plymouth Arts Centre
1992	St David's Hall, Cardiff
1995	Centre Gallery, London
1996	Carcassonne, France
1997	Aberystwyth Arts Centre
1999	St Donat's Arts Centre, South Wales

Still Life in the Haunted House (It's a Still Life), 2006, acrylic on canvas, 46 x 94 cm

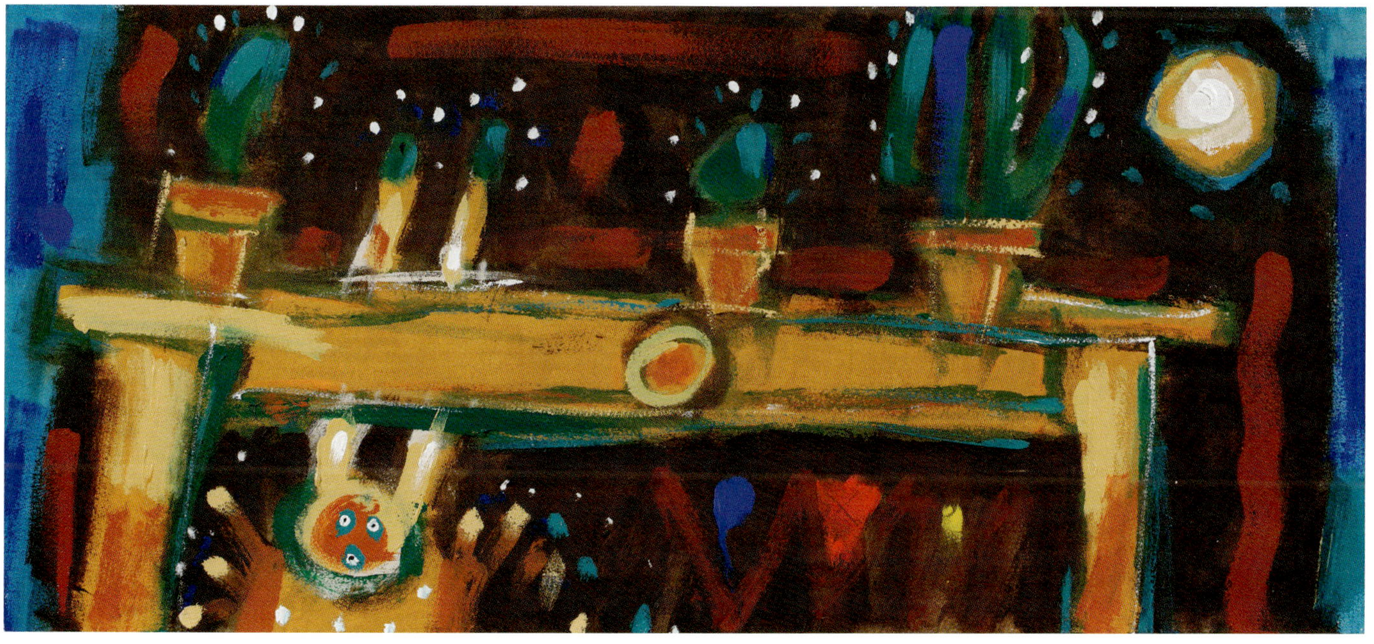

Works in public collections

Aberystwyth University School of Art Museum and Galleries

Mari Lwyd Chat, 1999, linocut, 48 x 55, gift of Contemporary Art Society for Wales

The Box, Plymouth City Council

Moose factory /Asleep by a Frozen Sea, 1989, woodcut
Captain Henry Hudson in the Long Night, 1989, woodcut
Scrimshaw, 1990, woodcut
The Dream of the Walrus, 1990, woodcut
Call me Ishmail, 1990, woodcut
The Fateful Voyage of the Nonsuch in Search of the North West Passage, 1990, woodcut
Jonah, 1990, woodcut

Glynn Vivian Art Gallery

Moose Chat, 1989, print
Cwmafon, 1992, print
Cold Front, undated, print
Near Briton Ferry, undated, print
Calf at Hendrecaradog, Rhos, undated, print
Obelisk at El Djem, Tunisia, undated, print
Scottish Dairying, 1989, print
At the Dump, 1989, print
Cemetery Gates, Ebenezer Chapel, Rhos, charcoal on paper
Animal Studies, Rhos, undated, print
A Very Particular Hill, undated, monoprint
Llandarcy, undated, monoprint
Llandarcy 6.6.90, 1990, monoprint
Scrimshaw, 1990, print
At Ewenny Priory, undated, print
The Arrival of the Orcadians at Hudson Bay, undated, print
Moose Factory / Asleep by a Frozen Sea, 1990, print
The Arrival of Diesel at Ouarzazate, undated, print
Mirage, undated, print
Call me Ishmael, undated, print
Latitudes, undated, print
Dancer, undated, print
Eccleiastes 12 1–7, undated, print
The Well and the Obelisk, undated, print
Mynydd Drumau nr. Bryncoch, undated, print
Above Pontardawe, undated, monoprint
Cemetery Gates Rhos and Ebenezer Chapel, undated, monoprint
Chapel, Bryncoch and Llandarcy, undated, monoprint

Mynydd Drumau nr. Bridgend, undated, print
Kos (design for mugs), undated, print

Llangynwyd Village Hall
Yr Ymwelydd (The Visitor), 2004, oil on canvas, 71 x 56

Llantarnam Grange Art Gallery, Cwmbran
Blue Maraabout, undated, oil on canvas, 24 x 30 cm
Untitled, undated, oil on canvas, 24 x 30 cm
And the Wolf, undated, oil on canvas, 24 x 30 cm
Untitled, undated, oil on canvas, 24 x 30 cm

MoMA Machynlleth
Hannibal's Luck, undated, acrylic on canvas, 32 x 50

National Library of Wales, Aberystwyth, Dr H. E. and Mrs C. Roese Art Collection
The Walking Dog, undated, watercolour, 20 x 15
The Visitor, undated, watercolour, 20 x 15
Pastoral, 1998, print, 53 x 76
The Venus of Blaengwynfi, 2005, print, 19 x 15
Mari Lwyd (ar y Bryn Coch), 1999, oil on canvas, 97 x 73

Newport Museum and Art Gallery
Transporter Bridge, 1998, oil on canvas, 71 x 32
Transporter Bridge, 1999, watercolour, 55 x 102
Mari Lwyd, 1998, acrylic on canvas , 85 x 107
Electra, 1997, felt-tip pen and wash
Ponte Vecchio, 1998, crayon and wash
Tree and Wolves, undated, print
Tartan Bear, undated, print
Human and Two Bears, undated, print
Abstract Horse, undated, print

Peel Art Gallery Museum and Archives, Brampton, Ontario, Canada
One painting and eight prints

Royal Museums Greenwich
Henry Hudson in the Long Night, 1990, print
McClure Searches for the Ghost of Franklin, 1990, print
Scrimshaw, 1990, print
Winter Quarters Resolute Bay, 1990, print
The Fateful Voyage of the 'Erebus' in Search of the North West Passage, 1845, 1990, print
Moose Factory /Asleep by a Frozen Sea, 1990, print

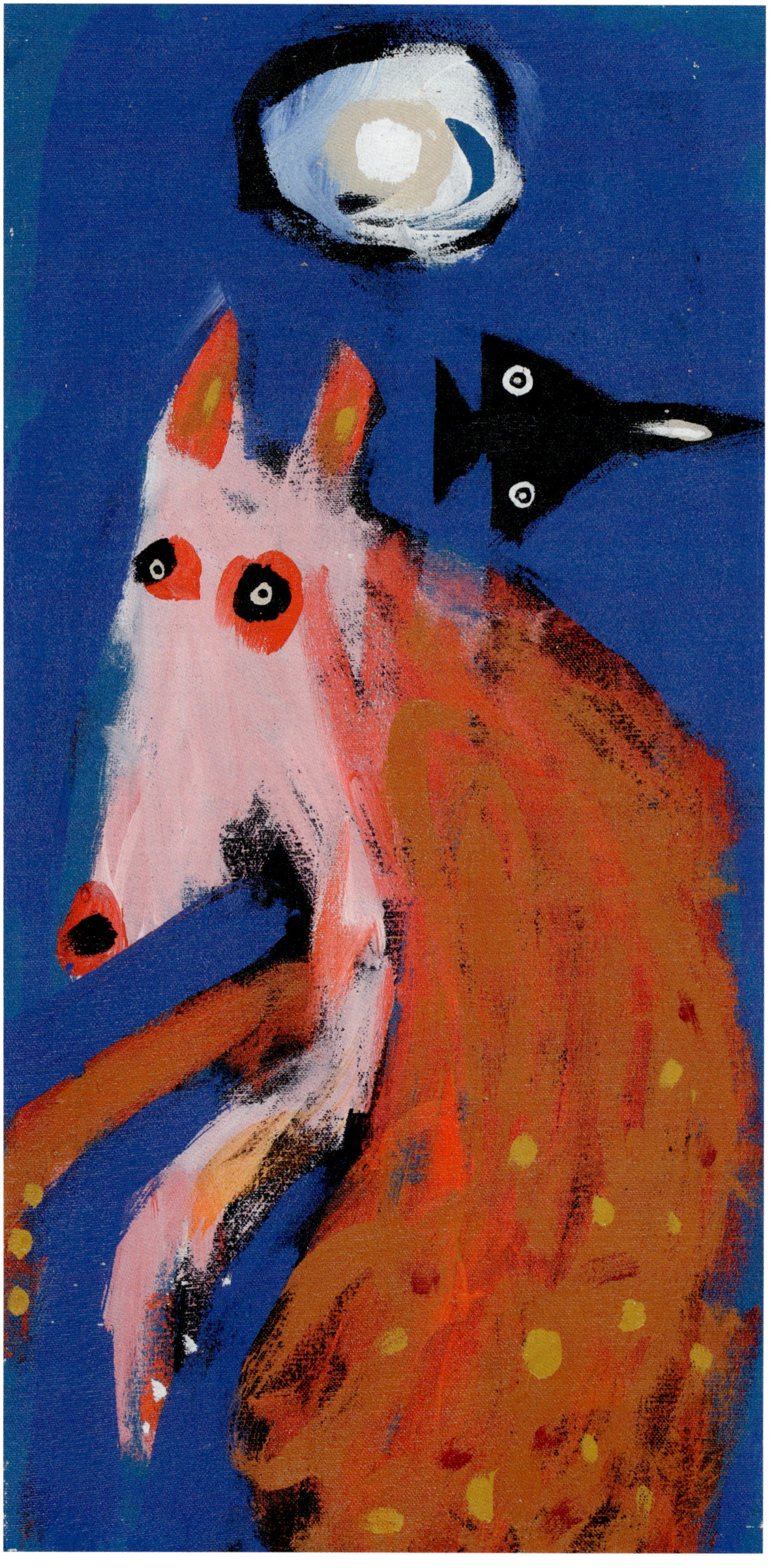

Lou Garou, 2006,
acrylic on canvas,
61 x 30 cm

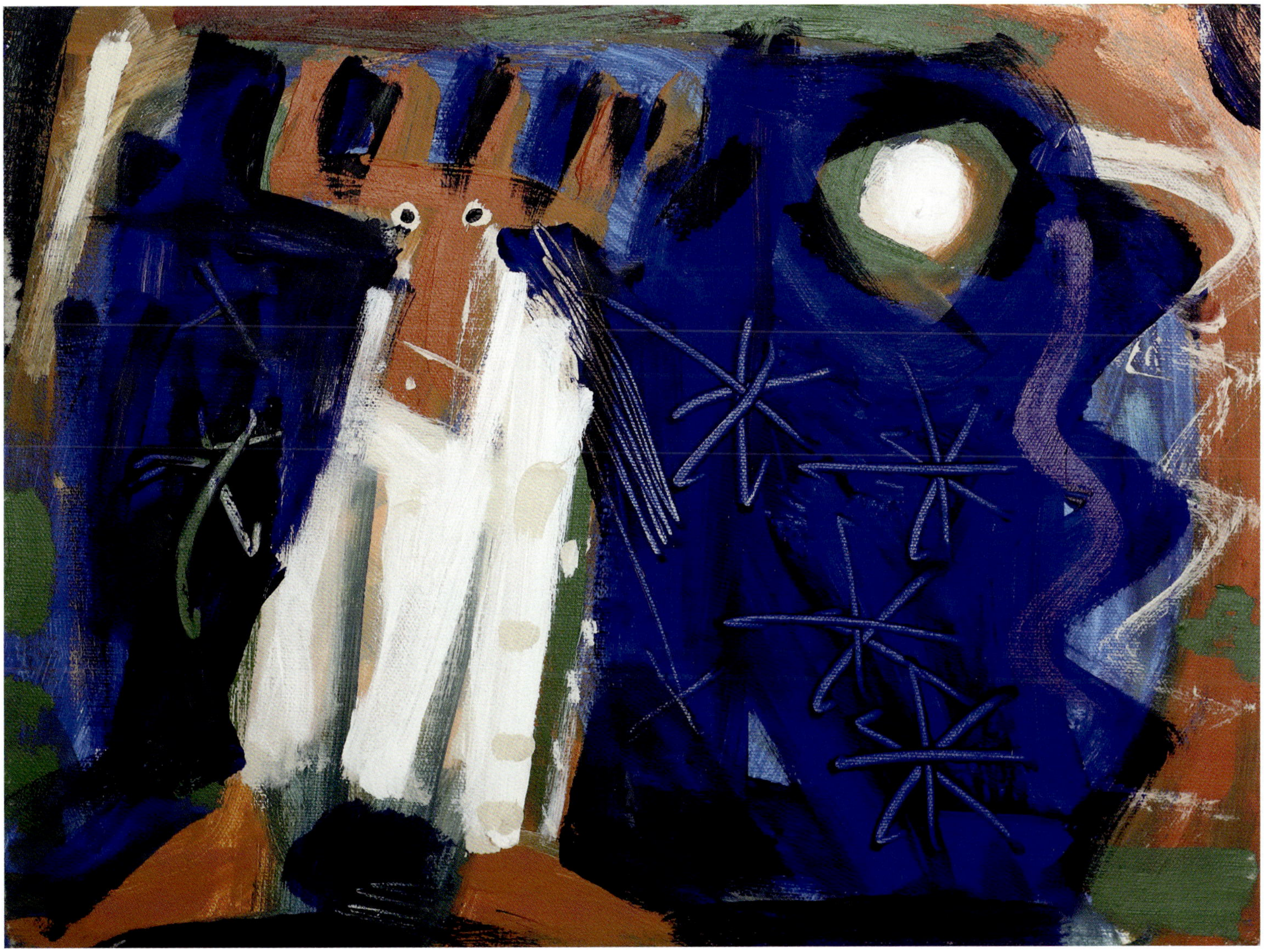

Mid Winter + The Moose Man Cometh, 2007,
acrylic on canvas,
30 x 40cm

Bibliography

Catalogues

Art Services, 1993. *Image & Word: The Five Schools Project.*

City and County of Swansea, 1996. *What's Behind the Blanket? Paintings by William Brown.* (Essay by John Furse.)

Contemporary Printmaking in Wales, 1992.

Lloyd, Alison (ed.), 1995. *Intimate Portraits.*

Newport Museum and Art Gallery, 1998. *Beyond Loup-Garou: Au-delà du Loup Garou: an exhibition of painting, drawing and prints by William Brown.* (Interview by Lucien Suel.)

Newport Museum and Art Gallery, 2001. *Looking Out: The Welsh Group, Paintings and Drawings.*

St David's Hall Exhibition Space, 2009. Just William: an exhibition by William Brown, 1953–2008. (Essay by Keith Bayliss.)

Welsh Group, 1994. *Changing Views.*

Welsh Group, 2000. *Revelations: Processes of Making Art.*

West Country Artists: Painters and Sculptors Living in Devon and Somerset, undated 1981.

Books and articles about William Brown

Anon, 1992. 'Cliffhanger drama', review in *Hampstead and Highgate Express*, 17 May 1992.

Anon, 1995. 'Le peintre brittanique William Brown expose à Isbergues', unidentified French newspaper, 26/7 Feburary 1995, p.8.

Anon, 2008. 'Death of local artist who made Wales his home'. *The Gem*, 24 July 2008.

Bevan, Alison, 2008. 'William Brown, 1953–2008'. *Western Morning News.*

'William Brown', *Barn*, July/August 1998, pp.92. 50–5.

Birkholz, von Rolf. 'Reizvolle Vielfalt an Technik und Schöpferischem Ausdruk, *Neue Westfälische*, 6 October 1992.

Bodinger, Katie, 2008. 'Canadian-born artist flourished in Welsh valleys'. *South Wales Echo*, 5 August 2008.

Bower, Michelle, 1996. 'William's idea is a real work of art!', *Glamorgan Gazette*, 31 October 1996, p.15.

Buckman, David, 1998. *The Dictionary of Artists in Britain since 1945.*

C. D.. 1995. 'Aciéries, granges et charcuterie', *L'Echo de la Lys*, 24 February, 1995, pp.1, 16.

Dalton, John, 1989. 'William Brown/John Crossley', *The Guardian*, October 1989.

Furse, John, 1986a. 'William Brown: Woodcuts, Plymouth City Museum and Art Gallery', *Arts Review*, 23 May 1986, p.236.

Furse, John, 1986b. 'Indra Khanna, William Brown, Plymouth Arts Centre', *Arts Review*, 23 May, 1986.

Furse, John, 2003. 'Still Life with a Snowball: Paintings by William Brown, East West Gallery', *BrUNIMA Bulletin* 112.

Furse, John, 2005. 'Review: Just William and the Raspberry Ripple', *BrUNIMA Bulletin*, May 2005.

Gascoigne, Laura, 1998. 'Serious Fun', *Artists and Illustrators* 144, September 1998, pp.18–21.

Gascoigne, Laura, 2003. 'William Brown: Still Life with a Snowball', *What's on in London*, 22–9 January 2003, p.25.

Gascoigne, Laura, 2008. 'Obituary: William Brown, painter and printmaker.' *The Independent*, 26 July 2008.

Gascoigne, Laura, 2009. 'William Brown From Under the Bed'. *Cambria*, October/November 2009, pp.55–7.

Gill, Jennifer, 1989. 'Primitive life and colour', *Western Morning News*, 14 November 1989.

Greenslade, David and Brown, Carys (eds), 2018. *William Brown in Wales, Through the eyes of those who knew him.*

Greenslade, David, 2005. 'Performing in the Llan: David Greenslade on the art of William Brown'. *Planet*, 169, pp.59–62.

Greenslade, David, 2008. 'William Brown 1953–2008'. *Planet*, 191, p.92.

Greenslade, David, 2015. 'A Lunar Sensibility: David Greenslade on a wonderful "waking dream" of ongoing collaboration between Czech and Welsh artists and writers associated with late Surrealism'. *Planet*, 217, pp.102–111.

Hitchman, Isobel and Jones, Peter, 2015. *Post-War to Post Modern: A Dictionary of Artists in Wales.*

Hoellering, Andrew, 1991. 'The Sea, The Sea', review, *The Guardian*, 18 July 1991.

Janda, Josef, 1996. 'Výstavea velšských výtvarníků na Vyšehradě' [exhibition of Welsh artists at Vyšehrad], *DaníTelegraf*, 16 October, 1996.

Jones, Hannah, 2001. 'Arist uses colours from beyond the curtain', *Western Mail*, 2 January 2001.

Jones, Lisa, 2008. 'Artist had a love of Valleys and his home country'. *South Wales Echo*, 22 July 2008.

King, John C. P., 2008. 'William McClure Brown: Painter and Printmaker'. *Toronto Star*, 4 August 2008.

Majewska, Sylvia, 1995. 'Celf a chrefft Cymru', *Ninnau*, 1 December 1995, p.5.

McLean, Pauline, 1996. 'Surprising brush with fear', *Western Mail*, 23 August 1996

Moore, David, 2008. 'Obituary: William Brown'. *The Guardian*, 30 July 2008, p.32.

Moore, David, 2012. *A Taste of the Avant-Garde: 56 Group Wales 56 Years.*

Moore, David, 2018. *The Welsh Group at 70.*

Parker, Simon, 1989. 'The cut and thrust of a wood-carver', *Western Morning News*, 14 March 1989.

Parnell, Laurence, 1984. 'Artists in different worlds', *Somerset County Gazette*, 3 February 1984.

Parr, Malcolm, c.1995. 'Wales and William Brown', *SwagMag* 5 (Swansea Writers and Artists Group), p.30.

Thomas, Ceri, 2008. *Mapping the Welsh Group at 60.*

Trowbridge-Matthews, Alexandra, 2008. 'William Brown', *Roundyhouse*, 25, p.12.

Wakelin, Peter, 1998. 'Colourful painter in wolf's clothing', review in *Western Mail*, 16 July 1998.

Wakelin, Peter, 1999. *Creating an Art Community: 50 Years of the Welsh Group.*

Wales Online, 2008a. 'Tributes are paid to artist, 54', *Wales Online*, 22 July 2008.

Wales Online, 2008b. 'Wanderer put down strong roots in Wales', *Wales Online*, 5 August 2008.

White, Jenny, 2004. 'A Tale of Two Artists', *South Wales Evening Post*, 2 April 2004, p.8.

Williams, Cen, 1999. *Let's Look at Loup-Garou: The Work of William Brown.*

Audio and video

BBC Wales, *Company*, 10 August 1992, interview by Maureen Staffer.

HTV Wales, *High Performance*, 2001, arts magazine with Nicola Heywood-Thomas.

Relay Publications / ACCAC, 1999. *Let's Look at Loup-Garou*, educational audio tape.

Publications by William Brown

Brown, William and David Greenslade, 1998. *March.*

Brown, William and David Greenslade, 1999. *A Love Letter to the Venus of Willendorf.*

Brown, William and David Greenslade, 2004. *On the Go.*

Brown, William and David Greenslade, 2009. *The Dark Fairground / Sombre Kermesse.*

Brown, William and Jones, Col, 2002, *Elastic Black Dog.*

Brown, William and Majewska, Sylvia Marie, 1995. *To Gedder Ap Art: A Portfolio of Prints.*

Brown, William and Suel, Lucien, 1995. *Ten Poems by Lucien Suel and Ten Ink Drawings by William Brown.*

Brown, William and Suel, Lucien, 1997, *The new bestiary / Le nouveau bestiaire.*

Greenslade, David and Brown, William, 2000. *Old Emulsion Customs.*

Jones, Colin and Brown, William, 2001. *Tair Arth / Three Bears.*

Jones, Colin and Brown, William, 2002. *Tales from the The Wild Chair / Chwedlau o'r Gadair Wyllt.*

Jones, Colin and Brown, William, 2002. *The Mari Lwyd: Wales's Strangest Folk Custom.*

Suel, Lucien and Brown, William, 2006. *Haikus d'Hannibal / Hannibal Haikus.*

Suel, Lucien and Brown, William, 2019. *Ourson les Neiges D'Antan? Poèmes illustrés.*

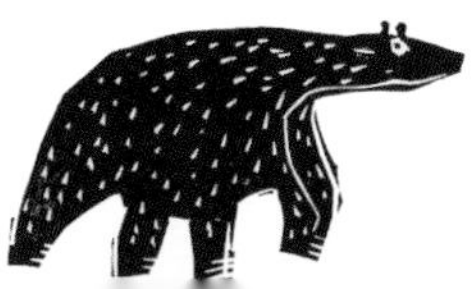

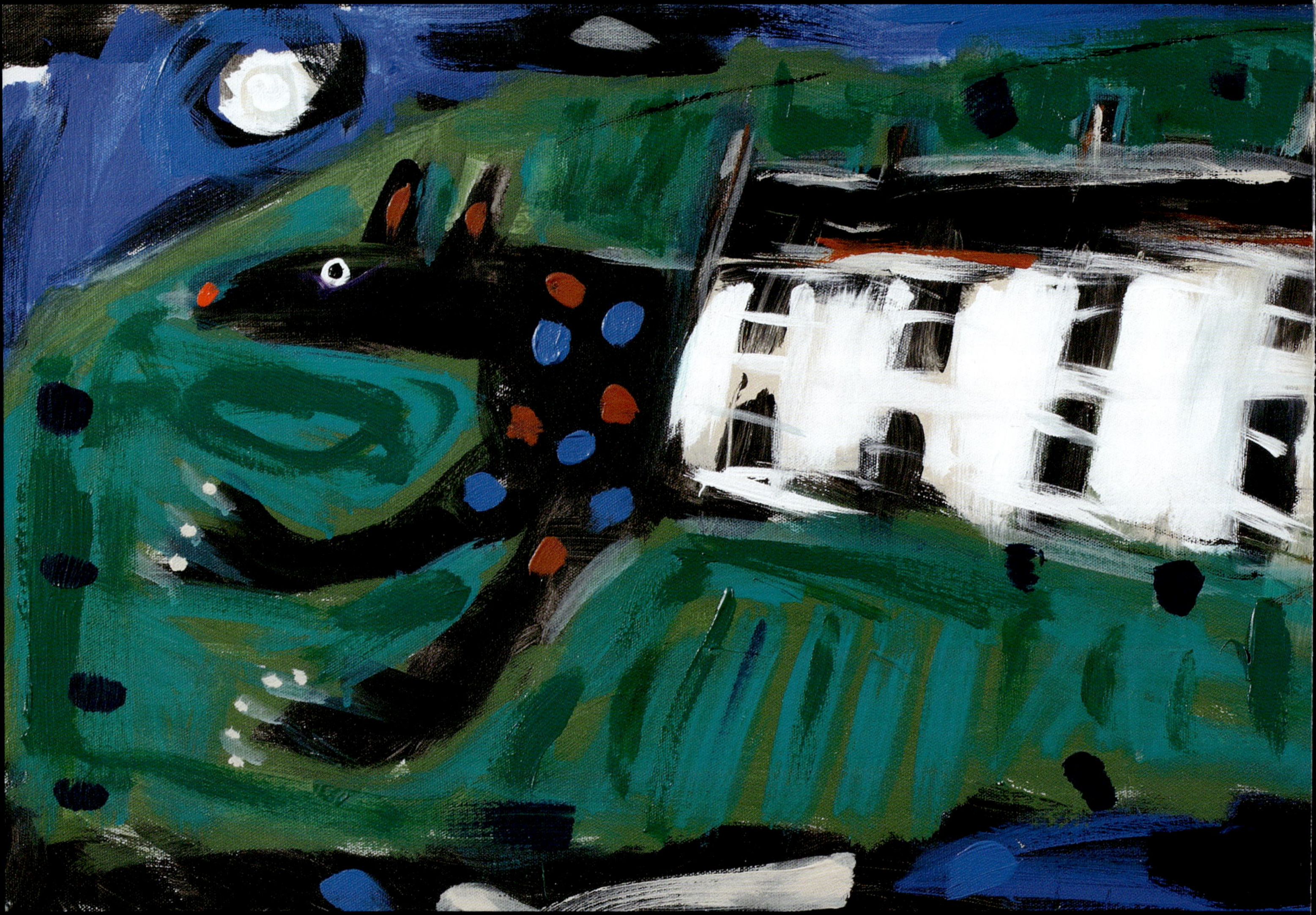

Boo, Too, 2007,
acrylic on canvas,
40 x 120 cm

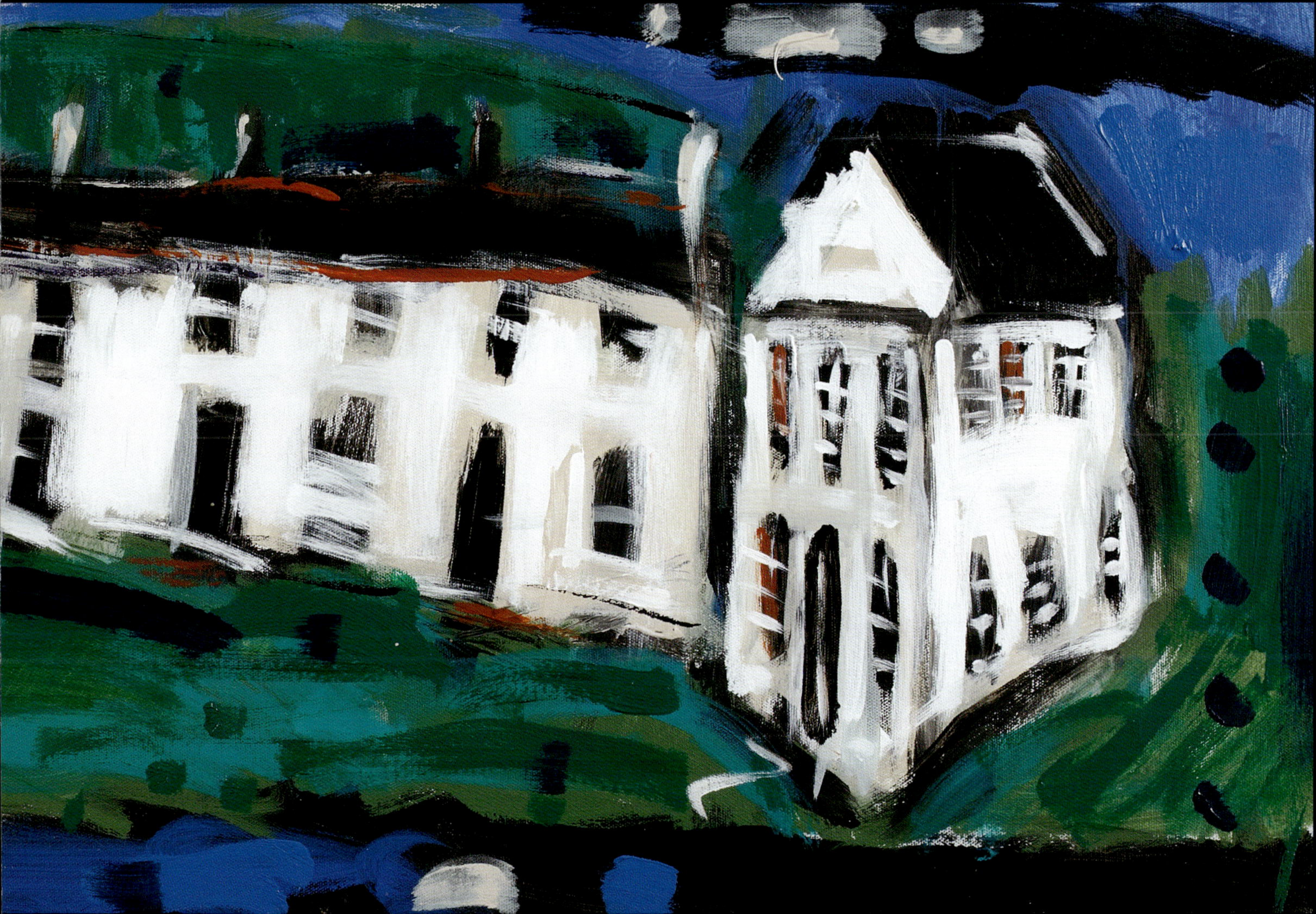

Index

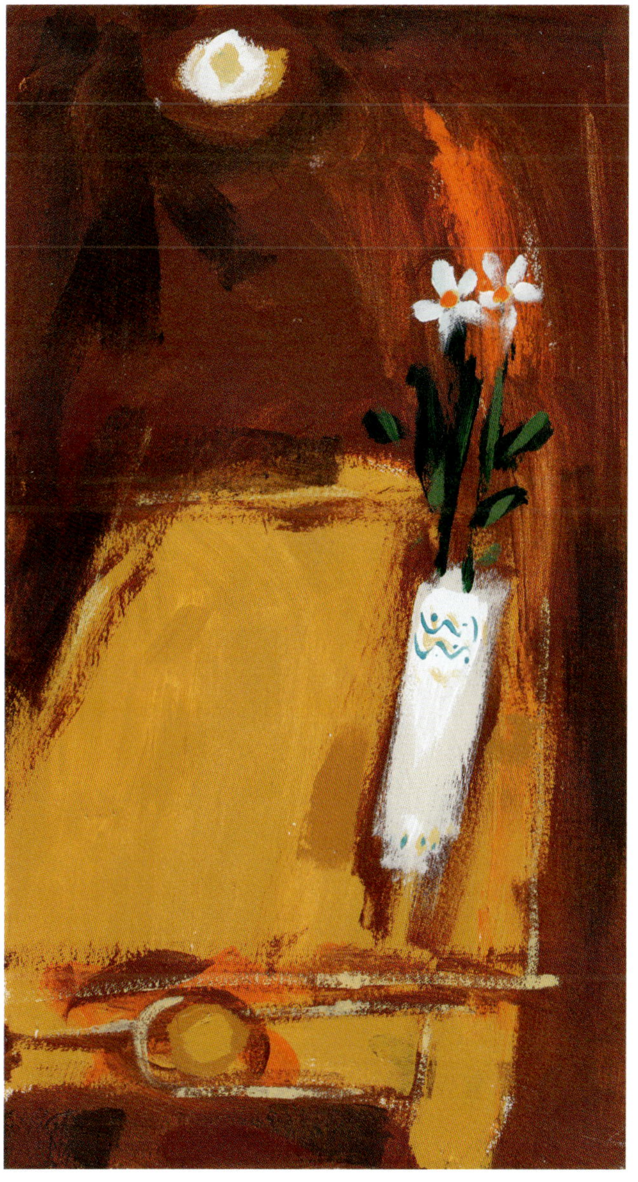

Flowers on Table, undated, acrylic on canvas, 30 x 60 cm

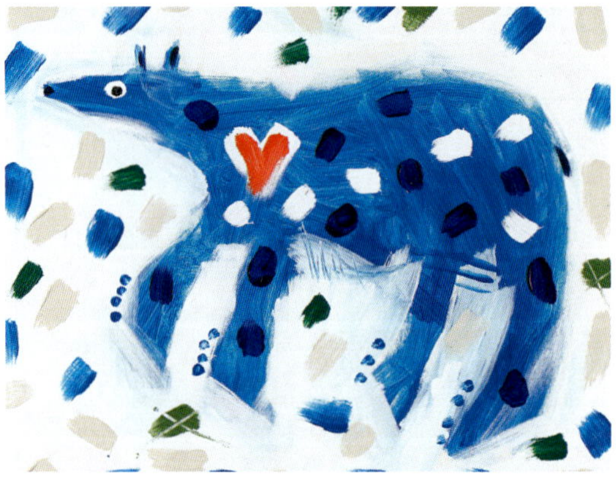

Untitled (bear), undated,
c. 2007, acrylic on canvas,
60 x 80 cm